Surveying the Canadian Pacific

Surveying the Canadian Pacific

Memoir of a Railroad Pioneer

R. M. Rylatt

Foreword by William Kittredge

University of Utah Press
Copublished with the
Tanner Trust Fund
Salt Lake City

∞ The paper in this book meets the standards for permanence and durability established by the Committee on Production Guidelines for Book Longevity of the Council on Library Resources

University of Utah Publications in the American West, Volume 26

Library of Congress Cataloging-in-Publication Data

Rylatt, R. M.
    Surveying the Canadian Pacific : memoir of a railroad pioneer /
R.M. Rylatt ; foreword by William Kittredge.
        p.   cm. — (University of Utah publications in the American
West ; v. 26)
    Includes index.
    ISBN 0-87480-361-6 (alk. paper)
    1. Canada, Western—Description and travel.   2. Canada—Exploring
expeditions.   3. Frontier and pioneer life—Canada, Western.
4. Canadian Pacific Railway Company—History—19th century.
5. Rylatt, R. M.   I. Title.   II. Series.
F1060.9R985   1991
971.2—dc20   90-53554
                                                                  CIP

Contents

Foreword

In 1871 a resolute Englishman named R. M. Rylatt was hired to serve as an on-the-scene agent in charge of supplies and equipment for a party connected to the Canadian Pacific Railroad Survey through the largely unexplored Rocky Mountain borderland between Alberta and British Columbia. This is his recounting from those times, written from recollection and notes.

The threat of territorial take-over by the United States was a driving force in mid-nineteenth-century Canadian political thinking. It was very real. In 1847 the Americans had absorbed Texas and California. The Fraser and Cariboo gold rushes of the 1850s might have served as an excuse to absorb British Columbia. Just south of the Métis colony that had grown up along the Red River, Minnesota was a state and making no secret of annexation plans. In the early 1860s expansionist energies in the United States were overwhelmed by the Civil War, but in 1867, the war over, the United States government paid the Russians $7.2 million dollars and absorbed Alaska. Where would they look next?

A transcontinental nation, from tideland to tideland, that was the Canadian dream. The political maneuverings through this period were complex and intense, but there was one constant: if there was to be such a Canada, a great international nation, confederation was imperative. In 1868 the Canadian government bought Rupert's Land (the great northwest) from Hudson's Bay Company for $1.5 million.

The Canadian government immediately began planning to bind the expanse of their territories, so huge and predominantly uninhabited, into a nation. British Columbia was impoverished and looking to be annexed by either the United States or Canada. The Canadian government promised them a transcontinental railway within a decade. In 1871 British Columbia became a Canadian province. The great nation-making enterprise was on. Three thousand miles of rail-line were to be built across largely unmapped country, from Montreal to the Pacific.

On March 31, 1871, the Canadian Minister of Public Works recommended organization of the Canadian Pacific Survey. In April a man named Sandford Flemming was appointed Engineer-in-Chief. Flemming was robust and bearded, forty-five years old, half his life still before him, an outdoorsman who went on to devise a workable system of standard time, plan the Pacific cable, and act as Canadian Ambassador to Hawaii and Chancellor of Queens University. He was also a veteran traveler who was to cross Canada by foot, snowshoe, horseback, raft, dog team, dugout canoe, and eventually, on the railroad he helped bring into being. By midsummer Flemming had dispatched twenty-one survey parties, totaling eight hundred men.

In *The Impossible Railway: The Building of the Canadian Pacific*, Pierre Berton writes:

> No life was harsher than that suffered by members of the Canadian Pacific Survey crews. None was less rewarding. Under-

paid, overworked, exiled from their families, deprived of their mail, sleeping in slime and snowdrifts, suffering from sunstroke, frostbite, scurvy, fatigue, and the tensions that always rise to the surface when weary and dispirited men are thrown together for long periods of isolation, the surveyors kept on, year after year. They explored great sections of Canada. The first engineers scaled mountains that had never been climbed, crossed lakes that had never known a white man's paddle, and forded rivers that were not on any map. They walked with a uniform stride developed through years of habit, measuring the distances as they went, checking altitudes with an aneroid barometer slung around the neck and examining the land with a practiced gaze, always seeing in the mind's eye the finished line of steel—curves, grades, valley crossings, bridges and trestles, tunnels, cuts and fills. In the first six years of the Canadian Pacific Survey, forty-six thousand miles of Canada were reconnoitered and blazed in this manner.

Twelve thousand of these miles were then laboriously charted, foot by foot, by scores of survey parties. Axemen, following the pathfinder's blazes, hacked the lines clear of brush. The chainmen who followed meticulously divided the distances into hundred foot sections, each marked by a stake. Behind the chainmen came the transit men, calculating the angle of each bend, and estimating, by triangulation, those distances which could not be measured by a chain. Behind the transit, the rod-men and levelers worked, reckoning the altitudes and inscribing them on bench marks at half mile intervals. By 1877 there were twenty-five thousand of these bench-marks and more than six hundred thousand chainman's stakes scattered across Canada. . . . At this point the surveys had cost three and one half million dollars and the lives of thirty-eight men by drowning, forest fire, exposure, illness, and shipwreck.

It is a wonder anybody stayed with the work.

—(Magnolia, Mass.: Peter Smith), 1984

Walter Moberly was one of the legendary men who came to the North American West, egotistical and hard-headed and hugely energetic. He would emerge from the wilderness, dance and drink the nights away in Victoria, then vanish upriver into the great mountains again, his endurance undiminished.

Moberly was first lured to western Canada by the Fraser River gold rush of 1858. When the gold ran out he became assistant surveyor general for British Columbia. Moberly knew the mountain interior as well as anyone alive, and thought he knew the perfect route for the Canadian Pacific. From east to west, it ran up the Bow River from Calgary to cross the Rocky Mountain Front at Howse Pass, looped around or over the great Selkirk Mountains, through the alpine wall of the Gold Range at Eagle Pass, down to Kamloops and the Fraser River, and on to Burrard Inlet (where the great international seaport city of Vancouver was not yet born).

Moberly had discovered and named Eagle Pass in the summer of 1865. As Moberly told it, eagles were coming over the Gold Range by some unknown route; he followed them, and found their pass. He blazed a tree, and wrote: "This is the Pass for the Overland Railway." The idea became his obsession.

By July, 1871, Moberly had gone to Montreal, got himself appointed district engineer, organized his expeditionary parties, and taken charge of the railroad survey through what he thought of as his own territory, the high and extraordinarily difficult country between Howse Pass and Eagle Pass.

As "Commissariat" to the party responsible for surveying Howse Pass he hired R. M. Rylatt, a man he had known as a sergeant in the commissariat of the British Royal Engineers.

That particular group, Rylatt says, "consisted of 4 officers (surveyors), 16 men, principally axmen about one half of them Canadian, 8 Mexican and Indian Packers, and one hunter for the party—a Bavarian. There were 45 animals in the Pack Train, each carrying about 300 pounds."

Rylatt's duties, as he lists them, "being to see to the feeding and clothing of the Party, the supervision of the Pack Trains, and their movements; to have Instruments, tools, clothing and food at the several points required, and to anticipate the wants of a large party, where instructions cannot be conveniently transmitted. To keep all accounts etc."

In short, Rylatt was to supply the glue that kept the party together. The position, he says, "was one full of trust, and taxed my energies at times to the utmost."

Rylatt was just the man for that job. He came from laboring class people, and claimed to have been a dull scholar. At fourteen he was apprenticed, under a "cruel and unjust master" in the trade of stone-cutting. "So unbearable did my life become, I ran away a year before my time expired."

Rylatt enlisted in the Royal Engineers. The Crimean War was brewing. Rylatt was attached to the Turkish Army on the Danube under Omar Pasha, and got to the Crimea "in time for the Battle of Inkerman."

Back in England, Rylatt was stationed in Kent, where he married, then "came out to British Columbia, still a soldier, served there 5 years and was discharged after 11 years service, with an Exemplary Character." In his early to mid 30s in the period recounted in this memoir, Rylatt was an experienced man, his character formed by adversity. He was a true British veteran, engaged in a great enterprise, who clearly yearned to think of himself as a thoroughly decent man, sorrowing for his sorrows, in touch with gentle sympathies and appreciations, and yet a British man, capable of whatever proved necessary ("I leveled the piece, covered him, and told him to throw down the axe instantly, or I would shoot him dead; and God help me, I would have done it").

The force of this telling, as always with great stories, lies in the energy generated by a continual series of collisions between character and fate. In this case, as with so many of the great travel narratives, it is a civilized man in the wilderness, a so-called primitive situation, living out the code of his people.

Rylatt loved the great wilderness from the beginning, and speaks with a natural sentimentality that does nothing to diminish the weight of emotion he communicates. Of the trip in, he writes:

> Flowers of every shade of color burst into existence, as it were seeming to ignore the babyhood of budding, so quickly do they appear; and whereas in the valleys they have their seasons, some in Spring, some in Summer or fall, here they make the most of the short holiday and all leap into existence at once, for soon the icy winds will come, causing them to drop their lovely heads and die, and then the snow king will in compassion spread his mantle over them, and they are gone. I noticed here the Lupine, tall and of a pale blue, the homely Buttercup and Daisy, Hyocinth, Marygold, China Aster (or a flower much resembling it), Convolvolus, Mountain Lily, Tiger Lily, Heather Bell, and others unknown.

The beauty of nature brings him to consider destiny: "These scenes of nature remain fixed, our course is onward, and upward, higher, infinately higher than the towering mountain peaks on our right."

And God, and man, and the paradise we are given on this earth: "How pure and bracing the air we breath, no alloy here, all as God originally breathed it into mans nostrils, when he became a living soul."

These sentiments were not those of a weak man; Rylatt was inflexible, and quite fearless in his determination to pursue his duties, and a rough hand if need be; he was not a man to cross; nothing was ridiculous:

> Gillette, the second in command, in a fit of rage for some depredation done, shot an Indians dog today, and in consequence the savage got not a little excited over it. I have already experienced considerable trouble from this man Gillette, and the result has been, a bitter enmity between us. During our march from Hope to Kootenay, he had charge of the Party, and on more than one occasion he attempted to exchange provisions from my stores with the Indians, for fish, or labor. . . . I fought against any such proceeding: and as the commissariat and pack-train was under my immediate control, I finally gave the Packers strict orders to permit no packs to be molested, save by my orders. One morning

the thing came to an open rupture, and while at breakfast, he got so mad that he threw the bone of a grouse he was picking at me, hitting me on the head. I immediately retaliated by throwing my hot cup of hot coffee full in his face. . . . He swore he would shoot me, and I had no doubt he was quite capable of it: and in the future always had my revolver slung to me. This had the happy effect of staying all further incroachments on my cargo.

The miseries of daily life were unending:

My drenched clothing is taken off at night, wrung out, and I turn into my equally wet blankets. When resuming my clothing in the morning, I shiver all over, and the teeth chatter, as I dolefully reflect how difficult it will be to prepare a meal. . . . Imagine men like these; hard worked, forever wet, and poorly lodged, rising early on such mornings as we are experiencing, and instead of a warm solid breakfast, stand shivering and swallow slapjacks half baked, larded over probably with bacon grease, or maybe a rasher of Bacon, the appetite for such viands stimulated by a muddy compound honored with the cognomen of Coffee, the beans probably placed in a piece of canvas, and bruised between two rocks, and when dished out having neither the aroma nor flavor of that refreshing beverage.

This is, all of it, powerful talk, and part of its effect derives from the clearly intended elevation and nobility of its language. Like so many of those who ventured out onto the proving ground of exploration and adventure and settlement in the nineteenth century, Rylatt seems to have been quite aware that he was engaged in a great conquest. He also understood that he was seeing things that would never be seen again.

Even in the heart of wilderness, an ancient world was ending, civilization was encroaching. In the beautiful valley at Jasper, Rylatt wonders at what we have done with our glories and how our paradise is being destroyed:

Yet why is this beautiful Valley so rich, and yet so empty? . . . Where are the Buffalo herds that should be grazing here? For their whitened sculls lie thickly around. Certain it is they come here no more, and why? Ask the redman; he can answer it. . . .

Civilization drives them [the buffalo] further north, where they become an easy prey during the deep snows of winter; and 'tis then the redskin, nay, whiteman likewise, tripping lightly over the snows crust on his snow shoes, comes upon a floundering, half starved herd of hundreds, half buried in drift, and unable to fly or defend themselves; they are shot, with gun and arrow, or slain with spears; and their slayers, after stripping them of their hides, leaves the huge carcasses to the wolf and decomposition.

The encroachments of civilization have been equally ruinous for the natives:

Many a proud tribe of the red men, who half a century gone carried proudly his Eagles plume, is now content to squat him down by the side of some stream, and fish for food; his game is scarce worth the hunting; his tribe is dwindling to a handful, from a nation of warriors; and his death song has commenced long ago; it has taken the place of his whoop of defiance and war; the scalps of his enemy's no longer float in the breeze before his wigwam of buffaloe robes, but his home is some smoke dried ranch, that scarce shelters him, and a few dried fish hang at his door, out of reach of his half famished dogs.

The end of the adventure comes, for Rylatt, in the form of news from that other country, civilization. Narratives told by runaway boys, making their escape and getaway, to some version of the so-called natural life and territory (*Huckleberry Finn*) or the Pacific (*Moby Dick*), are central in nineteenth-century American storytelling. In so many ways Rylatt is one of them.

He had left an ailing wife behind, but his story is true: he is a double-hearted man of his time (yearning for escape to a life of action and bound to the civilities of his culture); he can't really escape. No doubt he would be offended by this reading of his actions.

On a Saturday, October 19, 1872, Rylatt was handed a slip of paper with a message from one of the packers: "Dear Rylatt, The papers state your wife has passed beyond the stream of time. Dont be too cut up, dear old fellow." He recalls the last words of her last letter: " 'Oh! Bob! do come back, I cannot bear it'—the words cut like a knife."

Numb in his grief, Rylatt endures the winter. In May of 1873, with three horses and a companion named Baird, he sets out for Victoria. The trip homeward is his most vivid pure adventure. The narrative ends:

> And now my reminiscence is done. I might go on to state I found an empty house, my goods intact but stored in a warehouse. My return to my empty home, and the replacing of everything therein as it used to be in the days that were gone. My sad thoughts as I lay stretched upon the bed my poor wife had breathed her last upon. My many visits to her grave, and my final sale of home and belongings, and my wandering away to seek another home, under another government. But to what end?

In North America there was the entire continent to span, sea to sea, primeval, the great rivers, blue distance and beyond to more blue distance, mountains under perpetual snows. And it was theirs, in the urgency of the nineteenth century, more than any other time, to populate and reinvent, to make useful. It was a paradise, holy and terrifying and dying before their eyes, but, nevertheless, for those decades, so they thought, theirs to adore and to use.

We inhabit a different place; it is our heritage from men like Rylatt. His story is a bridge from us to them. We can deplore so much destruction across the ancient natural world, our animal homeland, and yet in our imaginations, as we read Rylatt, we can also understand what pleasure it must have been to take part in the conquest and reinvention of the so-called primitive world that came to culmination in the nineteenth century, driven and so sure of our purposes. What a creature we are: an animal capable of finding its life in dreams.

—*William Kittredge*

Publisher's Preface

From the beginning, publishing R. M. Rylatt's journal has been a delight. The University of Utah Press learned of the journal's existence only by chance. Thomas Huckin in the University's English Department heard about it from Richard Barker of Jackson Hole, Wyoming, who is related by marriage to the Basney family, who had inherited Rylatt's original. When Professor Huckin told us about the journal, we contacted John Basney in Marion, North Carolina, and requested a typescript copy.

On reading the typescript, staff members knew this journal should be published. In order to check the accuracy of the typescript against the original, we asked for a photocopy of the journal. What arrived at the Press was the original. Having access to it allowed us to design and publish a book that represents the journal more accurately than would have been otherwise possible. For this, we wish to thank John Basney for his trust and faith in us. We also appreciate having had the opportunity to see and share with bibliophile friends this extraordinary find.

John Basney is R. M. Rylatt's great-great-grandson through his mother, Violet. Because young Violet was an avid reader, the journal was given to her. She eventually passed it on to her son. And because John's father was a construction engineer assigned to large or unusual projects, the Basney family—and journal—traveled back and forth across the country, circled among several western cities many times, moved in and out of Mexico and Hawaii, and finally settled down in Marion, North Carolina. According to John Basney, "Knowing that my father was not a sentimentalist, I wonder how my mother managed to keep the journal and not lose it and keep it in the condition it is in." But, despite its age and history, the journal is in relatively good condition.

In the opening pages of the journal, Rylatt describes how he came to write an account of his experiences for his mother, who then demanded that he prepare another copy for his children. Whatever became of the copy for his mother, which was sent to her in England, is not known. What is published here is the copy addressed "To my children."

For this copy of the journal, Rylatt used what would have been a common commercial ledger of the period, measuring 10½″ x 14½″. The pages are an ivory, laid-surface, probably cotton-rag paper, printed with faint blue horizontal rules and a single, red, vertical margin rule on the left edge. Stamped on the upper outside corners of the pages are numbers 1 through 286. Several leaves at the back of the book were cut at the binding edge and removed. Rylatt used 254 pages for his journal. Page edges of the closed ledger show faded evidence of marbling. Endpapers are an ivory, laid-surface paper, with one side marbled in a burgundy-veined pattern over a series of dark brown, diagonally parallel shaded stripes. The pages are sewn on tapes and lined with paper strips. There are blue and white striped headbands and laminated binder's boards. The ledger is leather-bound, with hand-tooled decorations. The top and bottom edges, including the spine, are covered with a 2″ wide, continuous strip of dark brown calf-skin with hand-rolled gold decorations. Another continuous strip wraps around the spine at the midpoint and extends 3½" onto both front and back covers. The spine has four raised false bands and two black leather labels, one positioned on the second panel, the other on the fourth panel. Both have hand-rolled gold decorations. The top one is stamped "RECORD" in gold; the lower one is blank. There is no binder's or manufacturer's identification. Handwritten in graphite pencil inside the back endpaper is "J. O. Wilson, Cossurpolis." The leather binding is worn to a suede finish and is torn or worn away in quite a few places. The journal pages are in remarkably good condition. Although there are spots of mildew damage along the bound edges, there is no damage that affected the legibility of the writing.

Pasted in the center of the facing page to page 1 is a newspaper clipping with the heading "Military and Naval Intelligence" (reproduced here facing page 1) that has a paragraph blocked off in black ink which reads:

> Colonel Moody, Royal Engineers, the Commissioner of Lands and Works in British Columbia, sails for that colony by the Cunard steamship Asia this day for New York *via* Panama. He will be accompanied by Mrs. Moody, Captain Gossett, R.E. (late Surveyor-General of Ceylon), appointed Treasurer to the colony, and a number of gentlemen, who are to be employed in the revenue and postal service of the colony. The remainder of the expedition, with stores, 12 months' provisions, &c., are to embark on board the Euphrates, now at Deptford, on or about the 15th of next month, in charge of Sergeant Rylatt, R.E.

Above the clipping Rylatt has written: "This clip was sent out to me 22 years after I sailed by my Mother." Below the clipping he has written:

> Left England for British Columbia January 1859—on barque Euphrates—Capt [Scorgie] of Aberdeen, Scotland—Length of voyage via the Cape Horn was 6 months & 3 days—calling in at no place until Victoria, Vancouver Island was reached.

Corporal Wm Bowden	Royal artillery	wife & children
Corporal Wm Hall	Royal Engineers	____ " ____
Private James Hall	____ " ____	____ " ____
—" —Daniel Dreasy[?]	____ " ____	____ " ____

The wife of Private James Casey & child, being under my charge during the passage.

One child was born to Mrs. Wm Hall during the voyage.

That Rylatt illustrated his journal with colored drawings of exceptional quality only added to our enthusiasm for the book. As evidenced by the few unfinished drawings, he first drew the picture in black pencil, lightly, then used colored pencils over black ink and ink washes. Sometimes he used water colors over an ink base. He added details to the drawings in ink and used an opaque white wash to highlight certain features. One of the unfinished drawings, "Fiddle River," has horizontal and vertical grid lines drawn through the sketch as though Rylatt intended to enlarge the drawing as a separate work of art at some future time. There are many blank spaces left in the body of the journal for drawings, with notations by Rylatt in the margin in pencil of what he intended to draw. Why he never completed illustrating his journal is not known.

He included himself in several drawings, which adds a complementary image of Rylatt to the one revealed in the text. He had a trimmed beard and mustache; he usually portrayed himself with a pipe and wearing a distinctive cap. Other characters in his story appear more than once in the drawings and are easy to identify by facial features and their clothing. The drawings appear in this book as close to their placement in the journal as possible.

The Press is indebted to Professor David Dornan of the Art Department, University of Utah, for studying the drawings and describing the media Rylatt used.

Editing of the journal followed standard practice for such works. Rylatt's spelling was not changed, his punctuation only rarely. Bracketed words were inserted where required to correct proper nouns or to supply missing words. Rylatt's penmanship presented only minor difficulties in checking the typescript against the original. As is the case with most journals and diaries, distinguishing capitals from lowercase letters was often a matter of guesswork. When he neglected to begin a sentence with a capitalized word, we capitalized it. This happened so rarely that we believed Rylatt would have corrected it himself had he noticed. His punctuation was changed—again rarely—when necessary to clarify the meaning of the sentence. Obviously R. M. Rylatt was an educated and observant man who could write with ease of his thoughts, feelings, and actions. There is a strength of spirit in both his writing and drawings as there was in his life.

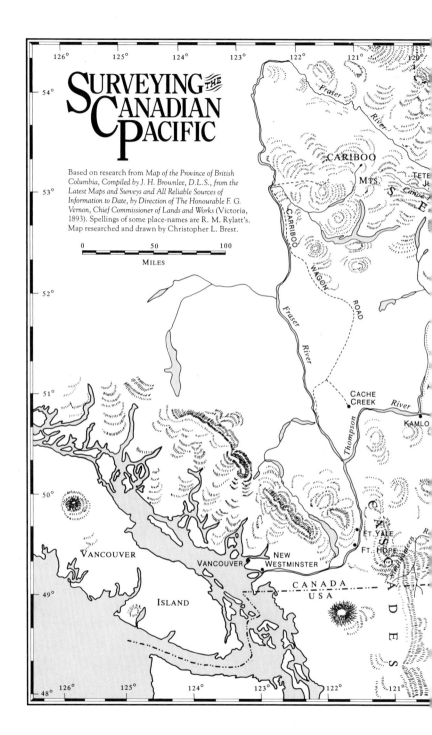

SURVEYING THE CANADIAN PACIFIC

Based on research from *Map of the Province of British Columbia, Compiled by J. H. Brownlee, D.L.S., from the Latest Maps and Surveys and All Reliable Sources of Information to Date, by Direction of The Honourable F. G. Vernon, Chief Commissioner of Lands and Works* (Victoria, 1893). Spellings of some place-names are R. M. Rylatt's. Map researched and drawn by Christopher L. Brest.

0   50   100

MILES

to Fiddle river, which lies a couple of miles off
our route, and by which means I was enabled
to get a sketch of it. Johnny Holding our time here
and insisting upon being included in said sketch

It was on a beautiful Saturday morning we left
our winter quarters behind us, having a train
of 34 Pack Animals in our wake. We made
about half the journey and Encamped, still in
the valley: The night was very Cold, and the
wind moaned its music through the bushes behind
which we had sheltered ourselves with deep and
heavy sighs, each sigh an icy blast.

The valley of the Jasper, as this End might be
named, shows a good feeding ground in the
Summer, and the whole valley is, I should
suppose, about 40 miles in length, by 2½ miles
in width; the buffalo grass, coarse and nutritious
being plenty, and might well be a favorite feeding
ground for this animal. Several small Lakes
are scattered through the valley, some formed by
the widening of the Athabasca; resting as it were; the
it swiftly and silently rolling on, to by and bye
become again a roaring, grand and mighty
Cascade. On Either side of the river grow the Alder
Cotton wood and black fir, blending in a delightful
Contrast, while in our line of travel there is a
freedom from underbrush, making traveling Easy.
Heavy fires have at some period devastated the
valley, leaving the standing timber in places bare
and scathed, bleached white by the winds and
rain since their bark has fallen off, and as twilight
creeps through the silent scene, it wears a ghastly
aspect. Indeed far up the sides of the mountains
on Either hand, even to the snow line has these
raging fires devoured their way, stopping only
at the line of Everlasting Snows. It is a beautiful
valley during the summer months, grand. Sublime
in its Surroundings; an Earthly paradise. That
can only be reached after toil and danger.
A valley not for Every Eye, this valley of the Jasper.
But the time I trust is not far distant when

it may be within reach of all who can afford to travel
by rail, should this route be adopted.. Yet but little
can be realized or felt from a train of cars.. no! to
see it and enjoy it, we must meander through it.
rest in it. after a long and troubled march; this is
to truly enjoy such a scene..

"JASPER VALLEY, ROCKY MOUNTAINS."
OUTLET. EAST END.

Yet why is this beautiful Valley so rich, and yet
so empty?. Why is the devastation by scathing fire?
Where are the Buffalo herds that should be grazing
here? for their whitened Sculls lie thickly around..
Certain it is they come here no more, and why?.
Ask the red man; he can answer it.. But he does
not seem to make his home here now. . No; he
has driven the herds from this place, and as they
depart, so does he.. he goes after the meat..
He it is who has lighted the fires that has devos-
tated spots in the Valley; that has robbed the
mountains on either hand of a portion of their
forest garments.. and the Cause is clear, the Cunning
Savage year after year crept past the herds as they
fed, and attained the upper end, then fired the
long grass during the heated term, driving a thundering living mass in terror to the only out let at
the end of the Valley, where the main body of
their Enemy waited to destroy as many as the

This clip was sent out to me 2 years after I sailed by my Mother

MILITARY AND NAVAL INTELLIGENCE.

Orders from the War Department have been forwarded to Chatham and the other military stations, directing the following reinforcements to be held in readiness to embark for India on the 4th of November, viz.:—30? non-commissioned officers and men of various cavalry and infantry regiments, to embark at Gravesend, for Calcutta; 219 men of all ranks, to embark at Cork, for Bombay; 178 men, to embark at Gravesend, for Bombay; 98 non-commissioned officers and privates to embark at Gravesend, for Madras; and 95 men, to embark at Gravesend, for Kurrachee. The requisite amount of tonnage has been taken up by the Hon. Council for India, and as soon as the vessels are reported ready to receive the troops on board they will be reported at Gravesend by the Commandant of Chatham garrison.

...the 5th Dragoon Guards; and Lord Adalbert Percy Cecil, youngest son of the Marquis of Exeter, has entered the Rifle Brigade.

The report that his Royal Highness the Prince of Wales is about to enter the army is revived in military circles. The Coldstream Guards is said to be the regiment selected for the Illustrious...

Colonel Moody, Royal Engineers, the Commissioner of Lands and Works in British Columbia, sails for that colony by the Cunard steamship Asia this day for New York 168 Passmore. He will be accompanied by Mrs. Moody, Captain Gosset, R.E. (late Surveyor-General of Ceylon), appointed Treasurer to that colony, and a number of gentlemen who are to be employed in the revenue and special service of the colony. The remainder of the expedition, with stores, 12 months' provisions, &c., are to embark on board the Euphrates, now at Deptford, on or about the 15th of next month under command of Sergeant Bright, R.E.

The centre of the Royal Artillery station...

Left England for British Columbia January 1859 - on barque Euphrates. Capt Devigie of Aberdeen. Scotland. Length of voyage via the Cape Horn was 6 months & 3 days. Calling in at no place until Victoria. Vancouvers Island was reached

Corporal Wm Bowden. Royal artillery wife & children
Corporal Wm Hall   Royal Engineers
Private James Hall
Daniel Drury

The wife of Private James every 8 child. being making change during the passage. One child was born to Mrs Wm Hall during the voyage.

"A brief retrospect
by way of a preface."

To my children.—

The following reminiscences and sketches have cost me much labor to commit to paper; we breadwinners find but little time for relaxation, but when that spare time is devoted to a labor of love, we conceive it well spent, and it ceases to be burdensome; and when it is for our children and their children, it takes the form of a duty. I have always thought, the child should know something of the history of its Parants, and yet how many there are who know comparatively nothing. I have the fact forced upon me that as I write these memoirs, I am past 50, and your Mother is nigh 40 years of age; while our boys are as yet little children, and God only can tell if our ernest prayers to see them grow to manhood will be granted. We should not like to pass away, and leave them in the years to come ignorant of some little knowledge of us. The child who can grow to manhood, and can look back to his boyhoods home, and not include Father and Mother in the picture, is no true man. He may become a father himself, and the same strong hope will be, to him as to us now, "That his children shall remember him tenderly, lovingly, when he shall have passed away." These feelings are inherent in our natures, and are sacred; they are our hearts yearnings as we see the little prattler advance; and we watch, ever so closely, to ward off the shadows that creep athwart his sunny hours of childhood, and as his young mind developes, and we do our duty; we instruct him in the fear of his God, and his duty towards us, and all mankind.

To my children, when it shall become your time (god willing) to instruct your little ones, have a care how you perform your duty towards them, and they will place a better Epetaph over your graves than polished marble can testify.—

"A tearful remembrance."—

These reminiscences were first penned for my mother, and are now, together with several sketches, in the possession of your uncle Henry's family. I thought it quite an undertaking (for me) to begin enlarging from notes taken while in the mountains; but it was a mothers wish, and had to be obeyed; and I must admit, I was not at all sanguine of completing the manuscripts, or that I should draw them out to any great length, after making the commencement; but the family in England gave me no rest after I had begun to forward by instalments, and were so well pleased, that all contributed their mite to have them handsomely bound in book form.

I had no sooner completed my task, however, than another claimant arose: a claimant who generally comes out winner at the end of an argument—your Mother.— I must write it again for the children, and I must illustrate it likewise; it will have so much more value in their eyes.— Mothers argument was very strong, "Surely your own children have a right to know something of you, if any one has!"—and so the book was procured; and as I had fortunately preserved the sheets I had penciled out while writing the other, I set to work: of rough sketches I had a plenty, although some of the most interesting had gone with the originals.

Do not think I attach any merit to my work! —I do not. It is faulty, very faulty, but I have endeavoured to portray as faithfully as I knew how each incident. If I have rendered any absurd ideas, if I have misrepresented anything, it has been the fault of judgement.

I have not written a book for the general public. I have written it for my children, and their children. A heirloom to be preserved.

I have little doubt in the years to come, you will carefully read all I have written, for I know how I should have prized any writings of my father. Hence, I write and sketch cheerfully, satisfied my little history will be preserved as a treasure.

My retrospection shall be very brief; an outline merely, which I deem will be suficient.

First then, with your Mother. One of several children,— the parants in very moderate circumstances. The father a clerk in the employ of a large shipowner. Her maiden name— "Fanny Morrison"—birthplace, Hull, Yorkshire. Having the misfortune to loose her mother at a very early age, she was destined to come under the control of a harsh stepmother, who, having a son from a former husband, had no love for the helpless ones she had adopted. On the contrary, they were treated with cruelty. The consequence was, your mother was placed in service at the tender age of eleven years; and after service with several families, at length aspired to the position of cook, and as cook in respectable families she remained until married to me at the age of 34 years. What remains will appear presently.

My father was a laboring man: a boatman, or fresh water sailor, if the term applies. My birthplace Lincoln, Lincolnshire. So you see we were both English, although I am now a naturalized American. At the age of 7 years, my Parants were fortunate enough to have me entered as a Blue Coat School boy. So until I became 14 years of age, I was entirely off their hands; our family was a large one—I being the oldest of eleven. I believe I was but a dull scholar; for I remember well the head master remarking to me on the night previous to my leaving the school, that he should miss me for nothing but my singing.

I was then apprenticed to the trade of Stone and Marble Cutting, for another 7 years, or until I became 21. My master was cruel and unjust. There were two other apprentices, whose parants were in easy circumstances; and they were the favored ones. I, a poor boy, was made a drudge of and had more cursings and blows than I deserved. So unbearable did my life become, I ran away a year before my time expired, and after working at several places for limited periods, I finally enlisted in the Royal Engineers. And the Crimean war shortly afterwards claimed me. I became attached to the Turkish Army under Omar Pasha, on the Danube and elsewhere, then to Crimea in time for the battle of Inkerman [November 5, 1854]. Having served through the whole of this bloody war from beginning to end, a matter of two years, I returned to England, was promoted to Serjeant, and wore on my breast 3 medals and a clasp. While stationed in Kent I married my first wife. "God bless her memory." Came out to British Columbia, still a soldier, served there 5 years and was discharged after 11 years service, with an Exemplary Charater. These memoirs will tell you the end of my poor wife.

After being a widower 7 years, I remarked in a letter to my Mother, I should be induced to marry again, if I had a good English wife. Although I had no real meaning in these words, my brother Henry had a lady member in his Sunday class he had a great regard for. He told her some of my history, and my remark to my mother. She replied, "if he is your brother, and wants me, I will go to him."— I was greatly surprised, but knowing nothing but good could come from my pious brothers recommendation, we exchanged pictures, were satisfied, and out the lady came, in the depth of winter, and alone, crossed the contenant in the cars, and I had her on my arm on the twenty eighth day after her leaving her friends in England. In 4 days we were quietly married. That brave little woman is your Mother, who alone, came across the seas to a stranger, whom she had never seen, and on the recommendation of that strangers brother. I had previously left my situation as clerk at the Neah Bay Indian reservation, not liking to take her to so much isolation. We have had our ups and downs, but thank God we still live for each other, and for our children. Henry was born at Seattle, W.T. Ernest at Quinaielt [Quinault] Reservation, while I was Teacher there.

This I think is sufficient, beyond this we have nothing to tell, and all we hope for, is to see you good citizens of your country, and God fearing.

Your affectionate father

RM Rylatt. [signed]

Montesano W.T.
May 16, 1885

FOOT OF HOWE'S PASS, WEST SLOPE.
ROCKY MOUNTAINS, B.C.
from an elevation of 4500 feet.

"LEAVES FROM MY DIARY."

TWO YEARS WITH THE CANADIAN PACIFIC RAILROAD SURVEY.

ROCKY MOUNTAIN DIVISION.

To My Mother:—

July 25, 1874.

    I but recently told you why I ceased to communicate regularly with you and the rest of our family: and furthermore, as you have several times requested me to give some account of myself in this new Country, I may as well gratify you by a history of my past two years experiences in the Rocky Mountains, and return.

    The date given above being the one on which I left my home, and gazed for the last time on the sweet face of my Wife, as she lay unconscious on the bed:. for the painful hour of parting had come, and the words "Oh! Bob, I shall never see you again". the last words uttered as she fainted in my arms; the last words as I laid her gently back upon the pillows, imprinted a farewell kiss, and was gone: words of prophesy as fresh after the lapse of more than "seven" years, as they were on the morning of the day of our final Earthly parting;- and which, as I write, brings the tears welling up, and the sad memories of the years that are past before me in array so palpable, that I feel bowed down

"Leaves from My Diary."

To My Mother.—

I but recently told you why I ceased to communicate regularly with you and the rest of our family; and furthermore, as you have several times requested me to give some account of myself in this new country, I may as well gratify you by a history of my past two years experiences in the Rocky Mountains, and return.

July 25th.

1871

The date given above being the one on which I left my home, and gazed for the last time on the sweet face of my wife, as she lay unconscious on the bed: for the painful hour of parting had come, and the words, "Oh! Bob, I shall never see you again," the last words uttered as she fainted in my arms; the last words as I laid her gently back upon the pillows, imprinted a farewell kiss, and was gone; words of prophesy as fresh after the lapse of more than "Seven" years, as they were on the morning of the day of our final earthly parting; and which, as I write, brings the tears welling up, and the sad memories of the years that are past before me in array so palpable, that I feel bowed down while I write; and though I ought to submit to my makers will, I cannot, but must rebel; and these memories, and the knowledge of how hard my lot in life has been for many years, seem to have soured me, and too frequently the chain of memories unite themselves, and hugging them to me, in spite of myself, leaves me at times gloomy and unsociable. You have ever believed me truthful dear Mother, and I am truthfully laying myself bare to you now: Had I married again, I doubt not I should have forgotten to feel so acutely after this lapse of time, and only deep, tender memories would have remained.

I have nothing very serious to upbraid myself with, for God knows, I tried hard to be a good and faithful husband, and I loved her dearly in all her years of suffering. You remarked on our marriage, you did not think she would live long; and that I must be prepared to loose her. Yet she was with me "fourteen" years, a great sufferer, a God fearing woman, and a devoted wife.

I have often blamed myself for having left home at all, and yet how could I avoid it? I had struggled hard to keep our little home together, and to the time of leaving we had kept out of debt; but times were dull. I was required constantly at her side; Doctors charges were enormous; and year after year, as the monotonous struggle went on, myself often worn out in body, returning frequently from a hard days toil to Wash, Iron, and Cook, besides the general attendance upon a sick bed; and on two occasions laid down sick beside her. We were some distance from neighbours likewise; and during these early times in a new country, hired help was almost impossible, even had I the means to engage such.

It was therefore, after my wife had lain bed-ridden nigh "six years," that the tempting offer was made me to join an expedition in the shape of an exploration party of Surveyors, to search out a practicable route for a Railroad through the continent of America. A Railroad to connect British Columbia with Canada; or in other words, a line of railway to belt the Continent from the Pacific to the Atlantic; a distance of some 3,000 odd miles. Can you wonder, dear Mother, that I accepted the situation, and tore myself away from wife and home, in spite of her entreaties to the contrary, more especially, as I was fortunate in securing the services of a lady to live with and attend upon her, on payment of a monthly stipend; and which I could well do from the salary I was to receive, as well as furnish my poor wife with many comforts she had of necessity been debarred from. It was simply a change of nurses on the one hand, with many added comforts; yet when placed in the scales beside a womans love, how light in comparison; but stern necessity was likewise added, and then, spite of love, the scales had to go down. And thus it was, after six years of incessant struggle on my side, and of patient suffering on hers, I hastened away, fearing each step to hear her cries, and but barely reaching the steamer as she was casting off her lines. May I never have such a parting experience again. Had it not been for the helpless creature I had left behind, who was dependent on my exertions for support, and who hitherto had not received the half necessary to an invalid, and had it not been that I felt the parting but temporary, and that for her sake I could endure all things, I would gladly have had an end of it; life without my crippled darling was not worth the having, and as the steamer, with every stroke of her paddles bore me further from her, I felt as I had ruthlessly abandoned her. How I longed for a letter, and how rejoiced when I received it. Poor thing, she spoke cheerfully; spoke of our seperation, and the comfort she should derive from my letters, and what nice letters she would write in return; spoke of all with only one end in view, to try and make me less unhappy, while her own dear heart was breaking. Had I known then that opportunities to forward and receive letters were to be months apart, I would have assuredly remained by her side, or had I thought never to see her again, nothing should have seperated us; she should have died in my arms, and I would have comforted her in her death hour as best I could. I had promised to be back within "twelve months," and although, with a sad yearning look in her eyes she told me I should only find her grave on my return, I had seen her as then year after year, no better, no worse, and I could not realize it. Poor Jane.

I stated that I left home (New Westminster) on the 25th July 1871. I joined the expedition with the understanding my services should not extend beyond a year; and I had every reason to believe I should be enabled to return at the expiration of that period of time. I had but however a faint idea of the nature of the unexplored regions through which we had to toil, and the many impediments in the way of moving through wild, untrod forests, and mountain passes, and which could be done with any chance of success in bodies, and at certain seasons. So that when I would have returned, I could not be permitted to resign my position of "Storekeeper and Clerk" to the party, and when I would have resigned, the 500 miles of mountain and forest which lay between us and civilization could not be traversed without much risk, save as I said, by men in large bodies. Consequently I did not again arrive home until the end of June 1873 or a year and eleven months from the date of leaving.

I do not purpose to go into any great length in recounting my wanderings while attached to the Canadian Pacific Survey, and yet as this is absolutely all the history I have to give (you being made acquainted with my life pretty correctly through our communications), I cannot do better than dot you down such portions of my diary as I think will interest you, and which will give you at home some idea of the hardships and annoyances men have to endure who penetrate the wilds of this Country. And you are to consider my experiences were under the most favorable circumstances; unlike many pioneers, I had plenty food and clothing, and had also in general the cover of a small cotton tent at command, also the means of transporting my Blankets &c. and that really I suffered no hardship until I had left the party, in company with one other man. The time I allude to is when I commenced my homeward march, during which I suffered somewhat, being sick with scurvy, and having had some narrow escapes from drowning. But that will all come in turn, as I follow my diary through its pages. Therefore in commencing I would impress upon you I shall confine myself to what strictly concerns myself, and avoid as much as possible any theories or views of this railroad scheme. I am not an engineer, nor was I expected to render any service as such, my duty being to see to the feeding and clothing of the Party, the supervision of the Pack Trains, and their movements; to have Instruments, tools, clothing and food at the several points required, and to anticipate the wants of a large party, where instructions cannot be conveniently transmitted. To keep all accounts &c, and in this capacity I had all the work I could contend with, and frequently some what more. In fine, the position was one full of trust, and taxed my energies at times to the utmost. To follow the expedition over mountains, through swamps, with large trains of animals, is no easy matter, true, the Packer does the actual work; but to produce just such articles as may be in want in the midst of a tangled wilderness is no easy matter, to superintend and keep in control a set of cursing, half savage Mexican Packers, and when beyond the limits of all law, is also no easy matter, and decidedly, by no means to my taste.

Walter Moberly, being Engineer in charge of the Party, which was but one of several, although much larger than any of the others, and with a larger outfit, having a more difficult section of country to traverse, and more distant likewise. This gentleman had formed my acquaintance when I was Serjeant in the Royal Engineers, and as I had the care of the Commissariat department at that time, he picked upon me to undertake the task of being the Commissariat for the party under his command.

The Party was named "Party S" and to it was consigned the Survey through the Rocky Mountains.

Three other Parties left for the interior at the same time, to explore the Selkirk and Blue ranges, their duties to commence almost immediately, while our survey was not to commence until the foot of the Rocky range was reached. And at the foot of the Howe's pass the instruments were first adjusted. (See Sketch at the commencement.)

Man in his hunt for gold had established a rough mule trail from Fort Hope, through the Similkameen Valley, and over the Cascade and Selkirk ranges of mountains, to a large Mining Camp, or several Camps in the Kootenay country, on the borders of the British possessions. Taking this trail as our route to the field of operations, we had not much difficulty in reaching Kootenay, a distance of about 450 miles, and probably 140 miles distant from the point at which our work was to commence.

I shall give but a short retrospect of our journey to Kootenay; the same route has been traversed by hundreds of gold miners, and pack-trains laden with necessaries for their use, but at the time of which I write, these mines were no longer sought, were in fact about worked out, or had ceased to be sufficiently remunerative, and the trail was no longer required. The government had long ago withdrawn the means of keeping it open; the miners had left for other fields; and [with] no supplies passing over the route, no taxes were to be collected, consequently no money to be expended. Moreover, there was another and more direct route to these mines from the United States side, or from Walla-Walla, a distance from Fort Colville of not more than 420 miles, and as the American people (the most thorough go-a-head people in the world) could lay down supplies of all kinds both cheaper and quicker than their British cousins, the long stretch of country through which we had to pass was left to its original solitude. It was not a farming country, and had it been, the distance from civilization was [so] great, and without roadways, which could not be made only under enormous difficulties and expenditures, that anything raised would have had no market value.

It would be difficult for you, in England, to form any conception of American forests; of the density of the undergroth; the great size of the trees; for though their original position is an upright one, many of these towering giants lie prostrate, either broken off by storms, or torn up by the roots. Often piled one upon another, forming a massive network, and the tough and thorny underbrush, adds greatly to the difficulty of cutting a passage for the loaded animals. At times the trail winds round the steep sides of mountains, through swamps roughly bridged or corderoyed by the limbs and branches of trees, and where many a poor cayoosh horse or mule mires deep, and at times is left to his fate, his pack stripped off him, and the additional burden borne by his fellows. The underbrush grows very rapidly; and an abandoned trail in a short time becomes impassable, in many places unrecognizable, save for the axe marks made at some former period. Huge trees again are felled by the elements and obstruct the way, the undergroth stands high above the heads of those who are cutting a way for themselves and their animals.

Upon starting, our party consisted of 4 officers (surveyors), 16 men, principally axeman about one half of them Canadian, 8 Mexican and Indian Packers, and one hunter for the party—a Bavarian. There were 45 animals in the Pack Train, each carrying about 300 pounds.

The old adage "A merciful man is merciful to his beast" would scarcely apply in such a country one would imagine, it would read better if worded will be "merciful as he can". How horrified would be any member of a humane society, could he see the treatment animals in Pack Trains receive, where the animals themselves are only a secondary consideration, the open sores on their backs, through hard and incessant packing; angry, and running with humour, over which the packer, too often, if not closely watched, without washing throws the heavy apparajos or Pack saddle, and as the sinch is tightened as only a paker knows how to tighten it, the poor beast groans, rears and plunges, and not unfrequently sinks down under the pain, only to be whipped again into position, while his heavy load of 300 or 400 pounds is secured to the saddle by lash ropes. Ten of the mules in our train had been driven in a distance of 110 miles in two days; having accomplished 70 miles the last day; arriving at midnight, worn out and hungry. They were nevertheless packed early the following morning, and had to travel 16 miles 'ere they were unloaded and turned loose to find feed as best they could. They were more-over unshod and footsore. I could not help noting all this, and feeling pity for the brutes, but 'twas not long 'ere I could look upon this sort of treatment, if not quite as callously as our Mexican comrades, yet with an amount of indifference I should not have judged myself capable a short while back. It is hard on the animals, but in the wilderness, when far from releif, the labor must be performed, the goods must be advanced, and the animal can only be releived of his load when he lies down to die.

A rather remarkable incident and escape occurred on our third days march. We were moving in single file on a narrow path hacked out of the side of a mountain, a mere nitch cut into the face so to speak, when one of the mules missing his footing, was in an instant rolling down the steep slope, and bidding fair to go over the precipice, when by a streak of luck his body came in contact with a jutting rock; and what is more singular, this was the only obsticle apparant in the even face of the slope; and the only thing that saved his carcase from being dashed to peices, as also the loss of his pack, con-sisting of 300 lb. Flour. By the aid of ropes he was safely drawn up again, and the march resumed; and if curses had been oats, that animal would have felt distressingly full.

On the 4th day we reached an altitude of 5000 feet, the trail of the roughest description, and although sterile, in fact con-sisting mainly of hard rock, yet for many miles our path lay amid Rho-do-den-dron Bushes, the large rich flowers looking like huge full blown roses. We felt the cold very severely dur-ing the night, and mosquito's very troublesome. Traveling over the Hope Mountain is hard on the animals, there being no feed of any kind for many miles, and the poor brutes suffer hunger in consequence.

What a view bursts on the sight from the summit of Hope Mountain; while standing on its broad flat crown, the vision takes in one of the wildest and grandest scenes in nature, down, down in the far depths, so deep in some of the immense gorges, that night seems to eternally dwell there;

OVER THE HOPE
MOUNTAIN.
A CLOSE SHAVE.

while in their depths are roaring cascades, heard by none, and in appearance tiny threads of silver. The dark firs bristling from the base to the snow line, overhanging and waving their branches from giddy heights, in solitude which may never be broken; above all are the glistening summits as the sun plays upon them, and 'erewhiles canopeed by whirling snow clouds as the fierce tempests strike them, for they are for ever hooded in snow, and their rugged sides varied by dark lines, or pale blue, where immense glaciers of solid ice choke them, the birthplaces of the rushing angry waters of the Cascades.

But if I stand longer drinking in the most magnificent scene that it has ever been my fortune to look upon, I shall have the train out of sight; I am already far behind, to remain is hardly the way to bring me nearer to the end of my wanderings. While upon this topic however, on which I delight to linger even at this distant day, I may state that this march of eighteen miles over the summit was to me one of rare pleasure, a panorama of unsurpassing beauty; soft, and breathing of Mother Country, the trees standing in clusters; at times singly and stately, reminding one of the Parks of the rich in dear old England, and all that is wanting, the deer lazily enjoying their shade. The rich carpet giving no sound to the step, save the rustling as the bright and many colored flowers are trodden underfoot, contrasting with the bright green, which so admirably contrasted with the sombre green of the fir clusters. No sooner does the snows leave the ground exposed to the suns rays, usually about the end of May, than nature decks herself in far brighter hues than she does on the lower levels: Flowers of every shade of color burst into existance, as it were seeming to ignore the babyhood of budding, so quickly do they appear; and whereas in the valleys they have their seasons, some in Spring, and in Summer or fall, here they make the most of the short holiday and all leap into existance at once, for soon the icy winds will come, cause them to drop their lovely heads and die, and then the snow king will in compassion spread his mantle over them, and they are gone. I noticed here the Lupin, tall and of a pale blue, the homely Buttercup and Daisy, Hyocinth, Marygold, China Aster (or a flower much resembling it), Convolvolus, Mountain Lilly, Tiger Lilly, Heather Bell, and others unknown to me, all lovely to the sight, but having no smell; in fact very few wild flowers in Northern America throw out any fragrance. By a simple turn of the head what a wondrous change! No flowers, nature reverses herself instantly, and as with a flash, the mild, the innocent is lost sight of; and from the winsome smiles of a gentle maiden, the stern and scarred warrier stands out to view. Equally beautiful, but in what a contrast, the Creator has here surely spread before us mortals the two extremes of nature. Now we gaze again upon a solemn, and save to the strong winged eagle, a silent and inaccessible scene of grandeur. Mighty mountains, towering upwards, their peaks almost in the blue of the sky, so well does their pale snow lines blend into the blue above; then down, far beneath us, their bases buried in gloom, their sides rent and worn by natures convulsions, and the mad streams ever leaping in foam and tumult from their snowy starting points, gathering force continually, until a river, a huge rolling troubled volume is sent still plunging onwards, forming barriers in the way of puny man, as he threads through the chaos of the lower levels amid difficulty and danger. It is impossible to do other than stand and gaze with awe, and sigh as we are reminded of our own littleness, and turn the head for releif, and see again our pretty companions the flowers, rearing their tiny heads in a waving welcome, and we think "The lilly's of the field, Solomon in all his glory was not arrayed like one of these," and then the one passage of scripture sends our thoughts, maybe inadvertently, to "Not a sparrow falleth to the ground, but he knoweth it, are ye not of more value than many sparrows?" and we think we are not so puny after all. These scenes of nature remain fixed, our course is onward, and upward, higher, infinately higher than the towering mountain peaks on our right. How pure and bracing the air we breath, no alloy here, all as God originally breathed it into mans nostrils, when he became a living soul.

After we had made the descent on the East side of the Cascades, and had entered the valley seperating these mountains from the Selkirk range, we entered upon a stretch of country much infested with the Rattlesnake; and after crossing the Columbia, and while marching along the banks of the Kettle river, we killed several of these deadly reptiles, some having as many as 9 rattles. The animals appeared very much afread of them, and whenever they heard the ominous rattle of their tails, would snort and leap aside, and leave the dangerous vicinity as quickly as possible; such is brute instinct, warning them of the danger, and to avoid the same in a hasty retreat. An ordinary garter snake gliding accross their path does not startle them. Deer have been known to destroy the rattlesnake by leaping with lightning quickness, and coming down with all four feet close together upon the snake, their sharp pointed hoofs crushing and cutting through the reptile 'ere he can make his deadly spring.

The rattlesnake strikes only in self defense; when cornered, or when basking in the sun, he is suddenly disturbed, he assumes the aggressive; but if he sees a way to retreat, he generally takes advantage of it; or when gorged with food, and too indolent to move aside, he causes his tail to vibrate, the

"BRUTE INSTINCT."

formation of which gives out a rustling rattling sound, usually having the effect of giving him a wide berth, for when once heard, the sound is not easily mistaken. If attacked, he fights viciously, making quick deadly springs at his enemy, throwing forward the sharp long fangs as he strikes, through the centre of which he ejects the deadly poison, leaving it at the bottom of the wound he makes, and even if quick remedies are applied, it generally prooves fatal. Such remedies as dosing the patient with whisky until made drunk, burning deep into the wounds with a red-hot iron have at times saved life, but these means are seldom to be had in the haunts of this snake. I have seen two or three cases (or rather the facts came to my knowledge), while employed on the Thompson River, where these reptiles are abundant, of Indians, who have been cured of their bite. The remedy is severe. Two of the cases were on the lower part of the leg, and one on the hip. In each case they were in company with other Indians, who at once had the bitten man on the ground, and proceeded with a knife to cut out the flesh to the bone, making a circular sweep with the knife, then filling the hole with healing herbs which they chew to a pulp in the mouth for the purpose.

The party to which I was attached at the time, while in this vicinity, soon discovered that a camping place was not by any means the safest from these snakes. The camp fires were an attraction to them, and we took the precaution before retiring for the night, to arm ourselves with long sticks, and after beating the outsides of the tents, to scare them away, we carefully examined the interiors; on more than one occasion, we had dislodged snakes, on two occasions rattlesnakes had esconsed themselves in the blankets. These creatures love warmth, and now, while on this expedition, I invariably took the same precaution when in a rattlesnake country.

Within half a mile of the summit of the pass we were traversing (Selkirk range), one of the party, on going to his tent (we had camped early), observed a rattlesnake on a comrades blankets: The noise he made on entering disturbed the creature, which raising its head, was the signal for a hasty retreat on the mans part, when it quietly coiled down again. As the door canvass was open, it could be seen from the outside, and was quickly dispatched. Being much gorged and swollen, curiosity prompted some of them to desect it, when a full-grown squerrel was discovered.

One of our animals died through eating a poison plant while crossing the Selkirk Range. The Packers name it "Poison Tobacco"; it has a leaf much resembling the Tobacco leaf.

I tasted "Porcupine" for the first time while in this Pass. It eats very tender, and in flavor not unlike sucking pig; but the unsightliness of the animal took away all enjoyment of it.

The summit of this pass is about 6000 feet, while on either hand the mountains rise, and to appearance we are as far from the snow line as when picking our way through the foothills.

Jack Cox reminded me that six years ago to day he was married, and it brought to me the fact that my poor wife and I were at the wedding. Jack was also a Sapper and Miner.

August 29th

[1871]

19

The following day we began the descent of the eastern slope; for some hours we traveled through hard packed snow, then through loose trap rock, very tiring to the animals; and towards night entered a deep and contracted canyon, and had to camp, the trail being choked with loose boulders from the heights above, while in places the animals mired to the girth in mud-holes. On the following day we found the mud holes so bad that several of the animals had to be unloaded before they could be got out. And 'ere we had proceeded two miles had to give it up and encamp. The axemen, who are always ahead, had to return and corduroy the worst places for some miles. (To corduroy is to cover a soft place with logs and branches, so that it will bear a loaded animal on the surface.) In places where the distance to be covered is short, or where mere holes have to be covered, this is not difficult, but when a long stretch has to be covered, it involves much time and labor.

After considerable delay, the axemen again started to the front, and after they had got out of the canyon, and had attained a higher grade, they found comparatively little to stay their progress, and so pushed on to a distance they antici-pated the train would be able to reach: but unfortunately for them, they were out of their reakoning, having done their work so poorly, it was found impossible to advance the train out of the mudholes, and had again to encamp before we had made an additional mile. Sending an Indian on to bid the Party return, we prepared to make things as satisfactory as possible. Again, unfortunately for the axemen, the Indian lost his way, and struck off on a blind trail. As all the provi-sions and cooking gear was with us, we had nothing to com-plain of; but the Party ahead, after waiting until dark, and no pack-train appearing, had to pass the night supperless and blanketless. The night was extremely cold likewise. About noon the following day they came straggling back, and curses were loud and deep—they had not broken fast since the pre-vious morning.

Having charge of the train, it became my duty to have a row with the person in charge of the party, but being somewhat of a philosopher, I held my peace, knowing that while they had their mad up, I should assuredly get the worst of it. I contented myself therefore, by being glad the circumstance had happened, as it contained an Excellent Moral. "Never do a thing in a hurry"— again, "That which has to be done, had better be well done."

It passes beyond the endurance of even "Ye gentle packer," animals miring deep, and having to be unloaded while in this position, men and goods become plastered with slimy mud; the animal likewise is apt to sprain himself in his struggles, under the lash of the exasperated packer, to extricate himself. Volleys of Oaths roll out of the mouth of "Ye gentle packer," a choice selection of English, Mexican and Indian, while the whole train is brought to a stand. These drawbacks, therefore, should, as much as possible, be avoided, for when a body of men make merely a pretence of overcoming such obsticles, and the packer, in all confidence, urges his animals forward, only to find the leader in the train flop in up to his neck in black stinking mud, it is to be expected he will get angry, and he invariably releives himself by loading the atmosphere with execrations.

The animals have had nothing to eat for two days, and this morning they came into camp, and attacked the aparajos (heavy pack saddles filled with hay). We expect to reach feeding ground however some time today. Most of the animals in our train have done packing to the Cariboo gold mines, where a good waggon road has been constructed for a distance of nigh 500 miles, and where owners of Pack Trains have grain houses for their animals. Many ranches are likewise on the route now, and the country is well adapted to the growth of Barley and Oats, but in this wilderness no such conveniences are to be had, and it is impossible to carry a pound of feed along; hence all that remains is to depend upon

Sept 3d.

71

nature's bounty, in the shape of feeding spots of wild grass or swamp rushes and nature's hand has dealt out such spots very sparingly hereaway, and when a halt is called for the night, with only bare rocks, or may be dense timber, moss covering every thing with the humidity, it becomes hard on the over-worked animals. It is not unfrequent, that after being turned loose, the mules will come back to the packers in a body upon finding no food in their vicinity, and with ears pricked for-ward, form a line, and stare their masters full in the face, ask-ing with mute appeal, more effective than language could be, for food. Packers in the main are rough customers, and are apt to be cruel and passionate, yet they are human, and in his rough way is fond of his animals. No wonder that he will hang his head, as I have seen them do, and curse the luck. During these times the animals have to be carefully guarded, or they are apt to make back tracks for the last feeding place, be the distance ever so great, and a mule will travel a long distance during the night—the old saying is he sets his ears forward, and never knows when to stop.

Sept 7th
[1871]

There are a number of married men in the party, a few of them being old Sappers like myself, and they are very anxious to have some understanding with our chief, "Moberly," on our arrival at Kootenay, with reference to regular remittances being established, so that their families be put to no incon-veniences during their absence. As clerk for the party, it becomes my duty to lay before the chief the necessity of some definate arrangement being made. Everything being under the Canadian Government Control, becomes entangled in Red-tape, and as the "mills of the gods grind slowly," we do not feel the confidence we otherwise should were the expedi-tions under the immediate control of some private company. I mention this circumstance here, because our leaving was so abrupt, that no definite conditions were entered into, only the surety given that our families should have regular remit-tances so soon as we were on our route, and classified, the chief in each party upon reaching the last limit of civilization forwarding proper lists of each mans salary, the amount he wished to remit, with the address &c.

But, had we known, or even suspected how our claims were to have been abused, our families neglected, and that the urgent appeals of the women left behind to the tender mercies of the government agents, for their rights unjustly withheld, not a man but would have turned his face homeward at once, and have hastened back to his loved ones. To liberal did the government show itself, that all a mans salary, if he desired it, save a per centage, could be remitted to his family, or if single, deposited in the Bank to his credit, hence all fear of any unfair play was hushed, and full confidence established. Poor deluded fools, it was many months 'ere a dollar was doled out to these suffering families, and even then in trifling amounts. The officials in Victoria threw the blame on the Canadian Government, but later on the Charge de affairs in Victoria B.C. was superseded, and recalled to answer grave charges preferred against him, for it was found upon investigation the wretch had been withholding just claims not only of the families of the men in their employ, but the merchants generally; and that certain of these sums he had deposited in the bank, the interest thereon appropriating to himself. Nor was this the only charge against him, our mails lay for months in the several Post offices, and no arrangements had been made for forwarding the same to men isolated as we were, and hungering for home news. And while upon this matter, I may say, that this brute's successor was but little less a brute; a hard, unjust, and arbitrary wretch, who withheld the claims of others as long as he dared to do so, and who was likewise suspected of the same criminal acts his predecessor had doubtless been guilty of. Methinks the Canadian Government could have picked upon a more trustworthy servant than this "Marcus Smith."

Moberly, the chief did not travel with us, having left us before starting from Hope, and going to Kamloops, proposed to cross on the Hudsons Bay trail from thence to Karameas, in the Similkameen Valley. Karameas being the name of a trading post of the aforesaid company.

On our reaching Karameas, we were augmented by ten additional animals, and left one there badly sprained.

Sept 14th

[1871]

Reached Kootenay today, and encamped about three miles from the Mining Camp of Wild-horse Creek.

At wild-horse creek I came upon an old friend "James Normansell," and we spent a few happy hours together. Dear "old Jim," he was then constable at Wild-horse. We had gone through many ups and downs together, were together through the Crimean War, belonged to the same company of Sappers at Shorncliffe in England, came to British Columbia together, and spent together our five years in the Royal Engineers (nee Sappers), and taking our discharge together, finally went our several ways. The last I heard of my old chum, he was in the far North attached to the Hudsons Bay Company. Jim is a Birmingham man.

I had a very busy time of it at Kootenay, receiving supplies and animals just in from the Walla-Walla country, making up the accounts of the Party for mailing, and storing for future use several Train loads of supplies, to be brought forward eventually by our animals. Thirteen head of cattle were also purchased here, and hired one white and two Indians to drive them after us. These cattle are intended for winter use.

I had not much time for observation while at Kootenay, but as it is one of several mining towns (so called), it may interest you, dear Mother, if I give a slight pen picture of it.

Wild-horse Creek mines, together with Perry Creek, a few miles distant from each other, were among the favored of the gold mining districts, so far as the necessaries of life were concerned. Although more than 400 miles from civilization, good mule trails existed from Colville in the walla-walla country, and much opposition had for a length of time been felt by the Packers, owing in a great measure from the working out or failure of the mines in Montana, thereby concentrating more Pack-trains than the demand called for. And as the Carriboo

Mines were at a great distance, and the transportation of trains was costly, many Packers and their animals were idle, moreover, there were as many trains on the Carriboo route as could find employment, more especially as the merchants doing business on that route had many of them Teams and trains of their own. Goods, therefore, could be laid down at Kootenay very reasonable. In the early days of these mines however, this was not so, and it was well for the few business people here that such was the state of affairs now, or these mines must have been entirely abandoned: for the diggings paid but little, and if men could not live comparatively cheap, they could not live at all. The days were past when men took out their big swags of the yellow dust; when speculators made fortunes, and gamblers were rich today, and broke tomorrow. When a man carried his life in his hand so to speak, for the days had been when a word was not a blow, but a bullet-hole. To call a man a liar was deemed sufficient provocation to seal the lips of the utterer forever; and for the bully, who hurled his fellow being into eternity, to swagger up to the bar, and drink damnation to his soul in Chain lightning Whisky. Nay, indeed, so bad were many of the mining camps when in full blast, and especially during their early period, when a big rush was made to some far off gulch in the mountains, that many a dark deed has been done. At any of the mines can always be found some of the worst characters on the face of the earth, and frequently women too, women who have not only unsexed themselves, but are often worse, if possible, than the men, long past all shame, irredeemable. So soon as trails are made, some few of these will make their way, in the company of gamblers or rascals of some sort, dressed while travelling in mens clothes, bestriding a mule like a man, and outvying him in cursing, gambling and drinking.

It is thus that during early days in these gold mines, so ungovernable would this portion of the community become, so many lives be taken on the merest pretence, and for plunder, and when no man felt himself safe, that the miners would mass themselves, and hang two or three of the worst characters to the limbs of trees, post up notices to others to leave the mines in a given number of hours, or share the same fate; then holding a general meeting, form a "Vigilance Committee" of thirty or forty members, and punish crime with stern determination in the absence of a proper court of justice, by appointing from among their number Judge and Jury, giving the accused the form of a trial, and a short shrift.

These Vigilence Committees are carried on to the present day, and of necessity I am sorry to say. In many of the large cities throughout the United States can be found these Vigilence Committees, in some cases called by another name; but the same, and for their necessity much is attributable to gross corruptness in those whose duty it is to administer justice; rascals in high places; rascals on the very bench, and not a weekly paper of the present day but proclaims that this or that Jail has been broken by armed and masked men, criminals dragged therefrom, and hung. This is not the doings of a lawless mob—far from it—these men are law abiding citizens, carrying out the law, and taking upon themselves what they feared would not be otherwise, strictly defending justice, that and nothing more.

To return to Wild-horse Creek. It did not take a very close observer, to see these mines were not paying well. The small community, the empty clapboard stores, the tumbledown shanties, all proclaimed the fact. The magestrate (Mr. Haynes) with whose wife, since dead, I knew well, lived in the midst of the camp, and his house and office combined had a more domicile appearance than most others. Built of logs certainly, the joints between chinked with mud, hewn somewhat into shaplines on the inside, giving the walls a flat appearance, the fireplaces built of rough rock, mud or clay, and the whole covered with shakes split from the Cedar. Such dwellings, though not very attractive in appearance, are snug during the severe winters to the occupants. The miner generally cannot boast glass windows, but substitutes in lieu calico, generally empty Flour sacks. My wife and I lived happily for many months in one of these cabins, while at Port Douglas.

The only unpleasantness we experienced in this style of window being, that the mules would occasionally take a fancy to our window, and tear it off with their teeth, possibly scenting some faint sign of the Flour once contained in the sack versus window.

The community at Wild Horse numbered about 50 whites and 150 Chinamen. Of the claims then working, was the—

" Nip and Tuck	paying	about	$ 3.	per	diem	per	man.
" Price Bros	____"	____	$ 6.	___"	____	___"	____
" Griffiths & Evans	____"	____	$ 3.	___"	____	___"	____
" Dietz, Sanders & Co	____"	____	$ 3.	___"	____	___"	____
" Quirks Hydralic			not known				
" Woods Bed rock flume Co	____"	____	$ 10.	___"	____	___"	____

Chinamen were averaging $ 3. per diem.

I did not leave wild-horse Creek until the Sunday after the departure, and by some mismanagement, being alone, I lost my way, riding in a wrong direction for several miles; the country hereaway being open bench land, and the trails numerous, it was easy to mistake ones way. Fortune favored me however, for coming accross a Rancher, he not only offered to put me in the right direction, but gave me the choice from a band of horses in a corral in exchange for mine, which was quite used up. At once clinching the bargain, I struck out again, the good hearted fellow riding some miles with me. Traveling until late, I took a drink of water for supper, and stretched myself at length at the root of a tree, tying my animal by a long rope to let him feed. The following day I came up with the party.

As I am writing from my diary, wherein I had a habit of dotting down in brief any trifling incident that might occur during a days travel, I shall be found to insert more or less of them here. Many of them may appear trifling, and unworthy of note, but I am recounting circumstances which occurred (however trifling) for my relatives alone, for their edification alone, so that having no fear of the uncharitable remarks of a very uncharitable public, nor the cutting's up of a set of critics, I shall tell my tale with simple ungarnished facts, and as such I know they will be received by those who love me, did I think otherwise, I should drop the pen at once.

Occasionally I shall give dates, so that you may be the better enabled to follow me; you will know which of the four seasons the narrative moves in &c.

Today we passed several piles of stones, a thing in itself of no significance, had they not a history. There might be probably five or six tons weight in some of them; the stones were small, of an almost uniform size, and were apparantly kept clear from the growth of weeds and creeping plants. At a glance it could be seen they were placed at these spots for some particular purpose: and why they should be so placed in the wilderness would to a stranger to Indian customs be a puzzle. There were likewise piles of small fir branches, also placed with care and neatness, the upper layers were in some cases green, showing they had not long since been placed in position, while below these decay had set in, and at bottom, rotten with age, or reduced to a pulp. Upon enquiry, I found they marked spots where savage warriors of the Kootney tribes of redskins had fallen in battle many years before, when these tribes were a great and warlike nation, their enemies being the Assinaboines, a powerful tribe, whose hunting grounds are further north, and on the eastern slopes of the Rocky Mountains.

This old battle ground is on the trail to the fishing grounds of the Kootneys, on the upper Columbia Lakes, and each redskin, as he passes the spot, places a small stone of a certain size on one or more of these piles, as a mark of respect for the brave dead of his tribe, or else a green fir branch, carefully crossed in a way manifest to the whole community, and though more than fifty years have elapsed since these warriors found bloody graves, the custom is most religiously adhered to. And yet we are not to consider all this is done solely out of respect for the dead: superstition has more to do with it than any other feature. The American Indian, like all savage people, or people in their primitive state, are steeped in superstition; these people have the dread, that did they neglect, or relax any particle in this observance, ill luck would befall them; their fish would abandon them, and hunger and sickness, and death be the result. And whenever the season's catch has been unsatisfactory, or any epidemic has taken hold of them, it is attributed to the spirits of their dead being angry.

There are many ways of disposing of their dead by these northern tribes of Indians. Some tribes wrap the bodies in cedar bark, and hang them in the trees. Some make rude boxes, and in the absence of nails, fastening these boxes together with wood pegs, or tying them together with withes, and placing them in the trees, resting on branches. Some tribes bury them, with only sufficient earth over them to cover the body. Some bury them by laying them on the surface of the ground, and building rough houses over them, while again, other tribes build a stage, and resting the dead mans canoe upon it, place the body in it, cover him with his Blankets, mats &c. and also surround him with all his worldy possessions, pans, guns, paddle, Beads, no matter if he has a family of children and a wife, all goe's, and as a natural consequence these last are often reduced to great straits. The Quinaielts and others, not only go to this extreme, but will frequently slay the Horses, Dogs, Cats, and even cattle at the grave, sprinkling the blood of the animals over the bier.

The tribes I am at present residing among (as Clerk at the Indian agency) the Makahs and Quillehutes, bury their dead almost before the breath leaves the body (and rumour says, instances have occurred before life was extinct), doubling them up, and tying them neck and heels together, force them into a rude box, and so dispose of them two feet below the surface of the ground.

I may have more to say about these people at a future time, and so will digress no longer, save to remark, that on two occasions I believe, forest fires have licked up the accumulated branches of the Kootenays, only to be commenced anew.

All hands suffered more or less about this period through drinking water impregnated with alkali.

On September 25th we reached the head waters of the Columbia River, which takes its rise from two lakes, and at its starting point is not more than five feet in width. I let the train pass on in the early morning, and in solitude I watched the sun guild the tops of the lofty mountains on the opposite shores of the lakes, watched its bright rays creep down the rugged sides; now below the snow line, lighting up the sumber forests of bristling firs which darkened them from the snow to the shores of the lakes, and as at last it threw its silvery sheen over the black waters, my eye swept along to the tiny river, as it stole silently through a swampy valley, and I enjoyed a train of thought none can follow nor appreciate who have not wandered in primitive wildernesses, and through scenes of natures rudest grandeur. I pictured in my mind the many scenes through which this river must pass on its way to the Pacific Ocean, as like a monster serpent, it wreathes, doubles, and winds itself along for some 1500 miles 'ere it looses itself in the salt ocean. Through silent valleys, solitary and beautiful, smiled at by the god of day, through deep gloomy canyons, where the sun never shines; now calm and trusting, now tearing, thundering, white with fury, over huge boulders hurled from dizzy heights in former ages, and finally, reaching the haunts of man, civilized man, its bosom becomes ploughed by ocean ships, and giving a last proof of its turbulent and treacherous nature, its broad breast, with its bed of shifting sands as it empties into the great ocean, has been the grave of many a good vessel, broken to peices by its waves, while being in the embrace of its shifting, ever varying sands, and where the dying cry of many a doomed sailer, passenger, and fisherman has been heard without the power of aiding.

The Columbia River Bar, who can forget the horrors on the wreck of the Passenger steamship "Brother Jonathon"; only a week prior to my writing this the large steamship "Great Republic" went on the sands, and is now being broken up, and is fast disappearing by the fury of the waters from this river. She was a vessel of 3400 tons regester, and had 1500 passengers and crew, by Gods mercy all save 7 or 8 reached shore; the last numbers were drowned, little besides life was saved however. Her case was a more fortunate one than some; but few were saved on the "Brother Jonathan." I never did like the Columbia river. Away in the mountains she starts on her course a frowning child, and her playful moods are short-lived. I came near passing in my checks on her fretful bosom, it was touch and go, to use a common expression.

Our chief thought it good policy to potlatch (give) to the Indians dwelling here, as a peace offering, some Flour, Calico, Sugar, Pipes & Tobacco &c.

Gillette, the second in command, in a fit of rage for some depredation done, shot an Indians dog today, and in consequence the savages got not a little excited over it. I have already experienced considerable trouble from this man Gillette, and the result has been, a bitter enmity between us. During our march from Hope to Kootenay, he had charge of the Party, and on more than one occasion he attempted to exchange provisions from my stores with the Indians, for fish, or labor. Now as our supplies were only destined to serve the expedition as far as Kootenay, and were cut so close, that no surplus remained (to save packing), I fought against any such proceeding: and as the commissariat and pack-train was under my immediate control, I finally gave the Packers strict orders to permit no packs to be molested, save by my orders. One morning the thing came to an open rupture, and while at breakfast, he got so mad that he threw the bone of a grouse he was picking at me, hitting me on the head. I immediately retaliated by throwing my cup of hot coffee full in his face. "Green" and "Rheaume" interfered and prevented further trouble. He swore he would shoot me, and I had no doubt he was quite capable of it: and in future always had my revolver slung to me. This had the happy effect of staying all further

Sept 29th.

71

incroachments on my cargo however, or in interfering with my Packers.

When Moberly joined the party, he reported a very strong case to him; and all the satisfaction he obtained was "You had no right to interfere," and ought to have known better, that man is an old commissariat, and knows the responsibility of getting short of supplies; that was why I placed him in the position.

From that time forth harmony never existed between us, and the only words we ever exchanged were when duty demanded, and that of necessity was very frequent.

But I transgress, let me go back to the dog business. It was a very foolish act on the part of Gillette. The Indian is glad at all times to have some pretence to compel his beloved white brother to loosen his purse strings, but the dog was a valuable one, at least to the Indian, and the tribes in this region would not become more hostile at a white for taking liberties with their women; and an Indian I believe would rather his woman was abused than his dog. These animals are avowed enemies to the white man, and are very treacherous. They have such a comfortable way of sneaking quitely behind, and making a wolfish snap at the leg, making their fangs meet in the flesh, then off like a shot; they are large, half-starved, mangey looking curs, most frequently of a dirty yellow color, or black, and not unlike the wolf in appearance with long heads, small eyes, and bushy tails, and with formidable rows of ivory's. They are nevertheless invaluable to the Indian in hunting his game, which they are taught to drive from a distance to a given point, probably some lake or open sheet of water, where they can be dispatched by their masters lying in ambush. And these savages may be induced to sell wife or daughter, but not their dogs.

Octr 2d

[1871]

Day before yesterday we started down the Columbia river (no longer a small stream) on rafts and in canoes. It is astonishing how soon this stream assumes proportions, fed by tributaries from the mountains on either side; it was at our starting point a respectable sized river. The raft I was on contained Jack Cox, Jas Malloy, [sic] myself, and two Douglas Indians. All went well for some time, but coming to some rather dangerous rapids, which took a somewhat sudden turn in their course, we were forced too near shore on our unweildy craft, and being in danger from projecting snags, and while straining to our utmost, we broke an oar; this caused some confusion, lessening our chances of getting into midstream again, onward we were bourne, and before we could avoid the danger, came full tilt against a fallen tree, half submerged, and projecting out into the current. All leaped for dear life when close upon it, and clung desperately to the slimy log. Jas Maloney leapt short however, and he and the raft were both sucked under. We never saw him again; in all probability he was held down beneath the surface by snags and sunken underbrush. We also lost a quantity of Provisions. After creeping along the log to shore, we made our way below the rapids with difficulty through the matted undergrowth, and were picked up.

The lagoons and swamps on either side of the river swarmed with wild fowl; Swans, Geese and Ducks in flocks rose with a loud noise as we passed. Myriads of these birds come into these northern mountain streams to breed and hatch their young, and the time had not yet come for their migrating southward. The tracks of Bear, Mink, Martin, and Muskrat were also very numerous, and very plain in the soft mud on either bank; scarcely a hundred yards intervened in accessible places but were marked with bear tracks, as they scrambled up or down the banks; it was evidently high carnival with them, as many dead salmon lay along the shores. It seems almost incredible that these fish could force their way to such a remote distance from the ocean, but such is the case; and many were seen swimming aimlessly near the surface, their flesh torn and hanging in strips, bruised and beaten in their wondrous journey through boiling currents, through leaping cascades, and the thousand dangers and all but impossibilities that beset their course to reach the head waters.

A young fellow, by the name of Porter shot an immense Black Bear in the river, but only wounding him, he reached shore and got away.

On either side of us are the mountains of the Selkirk and Rocky ranges, and through the narrow valley seperating them, the upper Columbia forces its way. I observed that during freshets the river all along bursts its banks, and spreads itself over more or less of the entire valley, and I calculate at this place the rise and fall between the melting of the snow and the winter season to be from ten to fifteen feet.

We also experienced a terrific storm of wind and rain while rafting down, and as we were ashore at dinner, we concluded it was best to remain there. So violent was the wind, that its roar, with the crash of the immense trees as they fell, could be heard long before it struck us; the lightning played about us in a very vivid and most unpleasant manner; and the peals of thunder was absolutely deafening, rolling away, the sound striking and reverberating through the mountains in a grand yet awful manner. Branches and tree tops were sent whirling through the air, and the giants of the forest bent like whips; however we escaped without some casualties, is more than I can tell. Crouched on the river's bank, with no means of moving through the thick underbrush, and destruction all around us. The water a mass of white foam. It is hard for you to conceive the force of these mountain storms; they are most appauling, especially situated as we were.

We reached the mouth of a large creek on the 2d which takes its rise in the Rocky's, and in "Howes Pass", and as the survey of this Pass was to be the commencement of our work, we landed at the mouth of said creek, with the intention of camping, but after cutting passages through the dense undergrowth in different directions in search of moderately dry ground, and night coming upon us, we had to go back to our landing place, and cut down a quantity of wet branches to lay upon; it had been raining heavily the whole afternoon, and

SUCKED UNDER. DEATH OF JIM MALONEY.

every man was drenched; and now we had to sleep on ooze (or slime) a foot or so in depth. The rain increased rather than diminished during the night, and we felt the cold keenly. To cap all, our tents were not with us, so we were about as badly fixed as it was possible to be, or at least so we felt it.

It was the intention to commence from this point and cut our way back towards the point from which we started in the boats, distance being about 80 miles. Some of the party were left at the latter place well provisioned, and they are now working their way down, cutting a mule trail. After working a limited time, the agreement was with either party to fire three shots in rapid succession upon leaving work, so that they would have some idea when they were closing upon each other. As soon as the trail should be cut through, and sufficiently good to permit, the pack-trains were to be hurried in with sufficient Provisions and stores to last the winter.

I would here state that Sundays were never observed on this expedition—no Service, no Prayers, but when things had to be rushed, or when traveling, Sunday or Monday, it made no difference. You are probably shocked at this, more particularly as such orders were supposed to proceed from the Government. The term "necessity knows no law" applies somewhat here, although many Sabbaths might have been observed as a day of rest, which were not.

We were heartily glad when night at length lifted her sable mantle, and a dismal dawn broke upon us; as soon as we could discern surrounding objects, we made preparations to seek some more hospitable resting place. Sore and stiff were we, an unwashed, growling community, partaking of no breakfast; we committed ourselves to the river again, and about two miles lower down stream we landed at a suitable spot for camp; all hands and the cook helped prepare breakfast, and after our hearty meal of Slap-jacks and Bacon, washed down with Coffee, we prepared to enjoy ourselves for an hour, with the smoke from our Pipes curling upward. Jack Cox and I related our mishap, and poor Jim Maloney's fate; and the hour up, the boys started in, hacking a passage through the hitherto untrodden forest, while I turned my attention to what stores we had brought down, lighting additional fires, and drying such as had suffered from the heavy rains. The chief divided our party, one half being detailed to cut the trail to meet the advancing party, the other half cutting a way to the foot of the "Howes Pass" proper, about five miles back from the river, and on the 7th October I moved up to the foot of the Pass, (See Sketch on page 5 [of the original journal]), leaving two men behind building a log-hut for Stores and Provisions. The following day, being Sunday, I passed my first day in solitude in these mountains; all hands were some four miles ahead in the Pass cutting their way towards the summit; myself and stores to form the depot here. A camp equipment of Tools and two weeks Provisions had been taken by either party on starting.

This being my first experience in being alone in such a wilderness; I have to admit my feelings were strange. I knew that here animal life and nature had been undisturbed by man: Since Doctor Hector and a party of explorers cut their way through this pass some 25 years before; I imagine the solitude had not been disturbed by a human being. This evening as the sun went down, the tops of the mountains alone were tipped with his rays, and the glaciers of ice were distinctly marked. The picture was a grand one. The sun set red in the west, as I could tell by the tint on the snow, while the ice in the gorges, in long streaks of pale blue appeared transparant and beautiful. I watched the rays slowly die out, until the golden gem had left the highest peaks; then gloom and shadow filled the valley; twilight came, and night succeeded with its canopy of stars. The sky was perfectly clear, and although very dark below, the mountain tops shone with a clearness most wonderful, and pale rays of the Auroro Borialis flitting through the starry firmanent, threw softening hallows of light around these everlasting snows. The night was very cold, and as I watched and shivered, I felt very lonely. Not a leaf stirred; not the hum of an insect, not even the noise of the water in the creek, being too distant. I made me a blazing fire, and the crackling of the burning wood was at least some company.

You in England cannot understand all this. You may think you can, but you cannot. Your sense of being alone in the heart of a city, or even a village, or within easy distance of fellow beings, the intervening thoroughfare being a known path to you, which you can thread with safety by night or day, gives you no claim to use the term, –alone. You may have the feeling peculiar to being alone, and that is all. Listen sometime when you think you are alone, try it if you are alone now, as I did. I listened for some sound, but I did not hear the rustle of even a falling leaf. Can you hear a footfall? a door slam in the distance? a carriage go by? or the rumble of one, however faint in the distance? a dog bark? have you a cricket on the hearth? or even the ticking of a clock, is the cat purring? Any one of these is a feeling of releif, and the sense of knowing your own species are at no great distance is even a greater [relief]; but here, with these great white mountain tops looking ghost-like in the distance, and in the valley where you nestle, darkest night, made darker and more weird as the fitful flames of the fire lights the circle of a few yards. I got well used to this kind of thing however, before I quit these mountains.

But I must quit soliloquizing, and as I love to dream, I find it somewhat difficult.

Note: The original manuscripts sent home were illustrated by a number of Sketches, recopied from pencil sketches taken at the time, and which I flatter myself were pretty correct. As I have destroyed nearly all the pencil sketches, I cannot reproduce them. I have a very few however in my folio, and shall introduce them in order. My original intention had been to present them to the Canadian Illustrated News, but on my return, I found that paper had colapsed, so sent them home with this little history, and am better satisfied to have done so.

The men cutting the trail along the valley, having met the party from the other end, and having completed their work, came in, followed by a train lightly loaded to test the trail. They lost two mules on the way down, one by miring so deep it was impossible to extricate him, and he was therefor shot, the other by loosing his footing while crossing one of the many creeks flowing from the mountains, and being swept down stream, pack and all, was seen no more. It is very trying on the animals, making their way through the wet bottoms; and as this trail will have to be used considerably, the party will return and corduroy the worst places.

Moberly sent down from the party in the Pass a young fellow, a half breed "Donald McLeon," so that I had a companion; the poor boy (he was no more than a boy), was far gone with consumption, and the rarified mountain air prooved too much for him, so that the desease made rapid strides. He shared my tent, which the train brought down, and I must say he was anything but a pleasant chum; it was distressing and annoying to lay awake and listen to his groaning and coughing during the night hours. I should much preferred to have been alone. He was finally sent with the Train to Wild Horse, where he died.

Hurt my leg today: I was assisting a sick animal over a small gulch, to a place where scant feed could be picked up, when, being too weak to climb the opposite bank, the brute fell over on me; at first I feared my leg was broken, but nothing more serious than a sprain, which pained me much, and set me limping.

Octr 28th

[1871]

All hands came in from the pass today, the snow being too deep for further progress; and the boys will now start in and build cabins for our winter quarters; the stores in the pass have been cached, as the trains cannot be spared to bring them in. These caches are as follows, rough enclosures are made of logs dovetailed together, and high enough to contain the supplies, which, having been placed inside, the whole is covered with logs, and so left until spring. A cach is simply a rough storehouse, made solid to prevent Bear and other large animals from destroying the contents. Master Bruin will scent Molasses, Sugar or Bacon afar off, and hasten to the feast; Bears were, during the whole time I remained in the mountains, especially when alone, a great greivance to me; so

Novr 1st.

71

much so, that I frequently had to keep a light burning after dark, which shown very plain through my calico tent. It was not always necessary to see or hear them. Bears in their wild state are often like a scent-bag, probably owing to their diet.

The men were glad enough to get out of the Pass to the Bank of the river, where we are more sheltered by the timber. the cold in the pass was intense, and the high wind, at all times sweeping through it, made it so cold that the boys had to keep up fires all through the sleeping hours to enable them to endure life under canvass so late in the season; but here I err, they had no tents, simply their blankets, and but a scanty supply of those.

Novr. 2d.

71

My birthday. My poor wife will be thinking of me today, sadly I fear.

Several large canoes, manned by Indians, have made two trips with stores and provisions, but they are now blockaded by Ice, so I do not expect their return for the winter. Worse luck, the animals are in such a weak condition, they are unable to pack, and will have to be sent off empty 'ere they become snowed in. No food for them here, their only chance is to reach Kootenay to winter, where a sufficiency of bunch grass can be had by pawing away the snow. Snow, by the way, doe's not generally lie very deep in that section. It is therefore expected by the chief, and has been impressed on the packers that the animals ought (if properly attended to) by spring to turn out in fair condition, and with the sickening sores on backs and withers healed.

As regards ourselves, we have a tolerable supply, not the least item being fourteen head of Beef Cattle now in camp, and which will be slaughtered without delay, or as soon as the frost sets in permanently, and the quarters will then hang frozen and sweet until Spring; these 56 quarters Beef with a goodly quantity of Salted Beef and Bacon will give us all the meat we shall need. We shall be short I fear of some articles, sugar and Dried Apples being the most conspicious; the train masters neglected the orders given on their last trip: they were told to load with provisions only; but instead of which they brought a quantity of stores we have no immediate need of, hence, through these noodleheads, we shall have to make the best of it.

Why did the expedition start so late, I expect you will say; and it is certain it might have started a month earlier, but things were not got ready in time: I may state for the benefit of you at home, that, it is May at least before the mountain trails are passable, and considerably later in some of the deep ca-ñons through which our route lay; it is not really safe to travel with loaded trains before June, and even then the streams are crossed with much difficulty, being swollen with the melting snows from above.

The men are daily hard at work felling trees and squaring the timbers preparatory to building the Log Cabins, and the blows of the axemen have a cheery sound. The trail party have also worked their way in, and work advances rapidly, but none too rapid, for it is bitter cold in cotton tents, so that every back is bent to the task of securing warm quarters; the snow is falling heavily, an additional reason why each man should put in his best licks.

On the 13th inst two men came down the trail from Wild Horse, accompanied by two Indians. They report having had a hard time of it; and as they state they are bound to French Creek, about 100 miles beyond this, a harder time is in store for them in all probability. They had preferred this route, with the advise of their Indian Guides, in the belief they would find the river frozen over, or, in the event of its not being frozen over, they would try [to] throw themselves on our hospitality until such times as travel could safely be made upon the ice. There is a suspicion rife with us, these men are flying from justice, and so have taken this hazardous route; probably thinking it safer with its dangers than the clutches of the law would be to them. However, the river is frozen over, and they have passed on their way, well supplied with dried meat and fish, by Moberly. The wilderness makes men what we find them, and we ask no questions, it brings us to one common level, and whatsoever the appearance of a man may be, if he be hungry, and we be human, he must be fed, if out of supplies, he must not starve, while our larder holds out. When they struck our camp, they were pretty hungry, as they had not tasted food for two days. Pistols were their only fire-arms, poor tools to depend upon when supplies fall short. Starting down stream in a canoe, they had, after vainly trying to force a passage through the mush ice in the river, to abandon this mode of travel, and upon landing, and striking our trail, they followed it, and with some difficulty footed it down.

<u>Novr 16th</u>

[1871]

The two men above alluded to have returned, and state it is impossible for them to get through, as the river runs through a deep cañon some miles below here, and the country is so densely timbered, and mountainous, a dog could not force his way through. Moreover, the snow is so deep, that to attempt it would be to perish.

<u>Novr 17th</u>

[1871]

The two men and their Indians were gone when we turned out this morning; where, or at what time, no one seems to ken. They made no sign, and left none, for it is snowing hard, and their tracks are covered; it is impossible to say in which direction they set their faces.

George Rana, a Greek, in falling a large tree today, let it drop accross my tent, smashing things to splinters generally; fortunately I was somewhat streaky about it, and had turned out of it, or I should have concluded my diary somewhat abruptly. Knowing the man was no axeman, and not having more brains than the law allows, I had no faith in his ability; as a sailor, he may be all O.K. He was told the tree would fall in camp, but George knew better, and the result, somewhat frequent in my case, "I came to grief." I had a nice improved Winchester Rifle in the tent, which I prized, as it was a gift to me from my old friend Jim Normansell, and by some lucky accident, that was spared me intact, but my Stationery

Box, and everything else breakable, was knocked into a Cocked Hat.

Dupois, one of the packers, and an Indian, came in on snow shoes from Wild Horse, bearing with them a few letters, but none for me. Poor wife, are you dead or alive? Has the two deposits of money sent reached her? It may be easily understood in my case how hard it is to receive no word, no sign, and altogether I am very miserable.

Moberly, and a party, mostly Indians, have left us, striking down the now hard frozen river, and well supplied with the necessaries of life, snowshoes and firearms. The trip from hence to civilization will be a hard one, the distance to be traveled 500 miles, or thereabouts; a great part of their route will lay through the rugged Selkirk range, and at about 350 or 400 miles, they may expect to reach the first habitation. One of the party named Verdier, a Frenchman, also left with him: his case is a sad one, news having reached him of his wife having deserted her home and little ones, five small children roughly tumbled into the cold world by their inhuman mother, who had eloped with some rascal, and the father so far away; no wonder he was like a crazy man, and was eager to depart and protect them. We all felt sad for him, even the roughest of us.

Decr 4th.

I took this opportunity to send a further remittance to my wife, or about $200 to date, and as it will be impossible to hear or communicate until Spring, that is to say May or June next, I have sent every dollar I had earned, after deducting expenses for outfit &c.

On the 6th a party of men were sent up river to the first landing, to sleigh down certain articles; as the river is now hard frozen, it is anticipated the trip will be made without much difficulty.

What little things at times make one have the blues: having cut my thumb today, I had to open a little roll of linen my poor wife had stowed away among my traps; I had hitherto had no occasion for its services, hence it remained as her thoughtfulness had fixed it. When I saw scraps of Oiled Silk, fingers of old gloves, and the softest of lint, how tenderly I felt towards her, but when a slip of paper came to light, on which were the words "God bless you Bob", it made me feel very wretched, being so far away from her bedside. I fancy, had she known how her little love token effected me, she would have been sorry she placed it there.

Our Christmas day passed very quietly; the weather clear and cold, 34 below zero. On the following night (26th) the mercury became frozen; it was contained in a glass Ginger Beer bottle, and is used for the artificial horizon, and was, save a globule the size of a pea, frozen solid. Eating dinner, and more particularly Breakfast was a matter of difficulty; the cook house was snugly built, and the cook kept up a roaring fire, and yet, the food, served hot, would be frozen on our plates before we could consume it: all have to be well wrapt up when out in the air; force the breath from the mouth, and at the same instant strike the hand through it, and a slight resistance can be felt as it comes in contact with the frozen minute particles.

The night of the death of the old year was not pleasant to a few of us. Jack Cox, Brafield, McKenzie, Porter, and myself sat the old year out, and although our cabin, well chinked, was kept warm as a rousing fire could make it, it was necessary to constantly change our positions, as the side furthest from the heat became numbed with the cold. We talked of our wives, of adventures &c; but there was no mirth; and when the new year was announced by the watch, we crept each into his blankets. It was quite a time before I slept; my brain being busy with past remembrances: This was the first time the anniversary of the new year had not been kept in the company of my wife; we always sat until 12 oclock; had prayers, kissed each other a happy new year, and side by side sank to slumber.

Evidently there is but little game in this vicinity—a few wild fowl being about the limit; there are plenty Bear to be sure, but bruin is dozing his winter away, and is never seen, a small band of wolves come in sight at times, and at a safe distance sit gaunt and hungry, howling dismally: we shot one a day or two ago, his comrades vanishing at once 'mid the dense undergrowth, then after a time returning, they devoured their dead comrade. But we do not care to shoot wolves, but reserve our ammunition for more useful purposes. There is no knowing for what our powder and ball may be required 'ere we are through.

That sneak thief "the Wolverine" is also an habitant and a pest in every part of these mountains, and their daring is something beyond belief. A few cariboo tracks have been seen, and some Rabbit tracks.

January 5.

72

Our three dogs (one mine) made a terrible noise during last night near where the body of a dead horse lies, and close to camp. Nobody cared to face the cold however, and this morning, on going to the spot, one dog was found dead, while tracks prooved our visitors to be two large Panthers, probably male & female; the remains of the horse had been removed to a greater distance. But the quarters Beef suspended in the midst of the camp cause the wolves and kayotes to hover about us, making night hideous with their noise.

On January 6th, and while the sky was beautifully clear, we had a splendid phenomenon of a mock sun, which remained in dazzling brightness for full two hours. Two suns, almost equal in splendor, were in the heavens, one about south, the other southeast: in fact, so dazzling was the mock sun, that the naked eye could not gaze upon it; while, at the same time, a beautiful arch of rainbow colors lay athwart the sky, not striking from the earth, but lying flat against the sky, so to speak.

On the 30 January, Mr Green and two others left camp to try [to] reach the summit of the Pass, the weather having moderated. Their object being to ascertain the depth of snow at the summit, and along the pass. Gillette and a party at the same time proceeded down the river on the Ice to explore, so we were left with but eight men in camp; ten inches [of] snow fell on the night the parties left.

Green and party returned today; they report such a storm of wind in the pass they could not make headway against it, and that the snow drifts were in places very deep; that owing to the extreme cold the snow would not pack, being dry and fine as flour, so that snow shoes would not keep them up. They have taken more provisions, and again left. Moberly picked upon good quarters for us, the storm in the pass not having been felt by us.

My dog Nip, a huge brute, although but a pup yet, shows signs of viciousness, and I have to chain him up at times to cool his ardour.

Gillette and party returned on the 8th February, not being able to force their way through the deep snow; they returned minus their tobogan and cooking traps.

That man Gillette is not only a fool, but an unmannerly cur, deserving the sympathy of none, and the power that pitchforked such a being into even our rough society, and placed him protem at the head of it, ought to be blackballed; he was crazy at one time in Carriboo, and he shows strong symptoms of again becoming so. It may be inferred from this that no very friendly feeling exists 'twixt us; in fact, we are at daggers drawn, and so great is his love for me, he fondly declares his intention of drilling a hole through me 'ere we part.

I was much amused today watching the manouvers of two large ravens: These same two birds have kept about our camp all winter. Today I threw an ox head on the river ice; and Master Nip, my dog, took possession of it at once; the ravens, after circling a minute, alighted near the coveted meat, when first one, then the other would make a dart towards it, and as quickly retire; Nip disdained to take heed to these sham attacks other than by an occasional growl. Tiring of this, or finding it had no effect upon the dog, they suddenly changed their tactics: one of the birds remained in Nips front, claiming his attention, while the other went around to his rear. Suddenly, the latter hopped nimbly up, and gave the dog a peck with his beak, upon which he wheeled round and showed his teeth; the other raven then gave him a peck, when Nip wheeled again, but stuck to his meat; they kept worrying the dog in this way, until finally his rage got the better of him, and he made a lurch after his last tormentor; this appeared just the object desired, for the other bird at once took possession of the head, and tried to carry it off; being too heavy, he did the next best thing, made an attack upon the frozen meat; observing this, Nip tore back from his unsuccessful chase, and drove him off; but it was only to be harressed as before, until in desperation he had to defend himself from their sharp beaks; I finally called the dog away, he had worked himself into such a frenzy; and I thought they had earned the head.

Five Indians came into camp from French Creek; they were of the number employed last fall canoeing down the Columbia. They report McClellen and his survey party wintering at Kamloops, also that they have lost all their pack animals— 125 head: being out in the field too late, the snow overtook them before they could get out, and, the animals had to be left in an inhospitable region, and starved to death; as little reliability can be placed in Indian reports, we did not credit it, but subsequently found they were correct in their report.

Sunday
Feby 25th

They also report that Mohon and his party are wintering in Eagle pass, in the Selkirk range, and that they have been on half rations, and have had no meat of any kind during the winter, having been caught by the ice king before they had got in their winter supplies. This also was found to be correct. Now, such being the case with other parties nigher the settlements than ours, we ought to be thankful for having great plenty; and I think Hall and myself are deserving of credit for our exertions and foresight, and save for sugar and dried apples, our larder is well supplied with as follows.

Fresh Beef	Syrup	Currants
Salt Beef	Curry Powder	Raisins
Salt Pork	Farina	Candles
Bacon and Hams	Yeast Powders	Matches
Flour, plain & selfrising	Mustard	Castile Soap
Beans, white and brown	Pepper	Common -do-
Split Peas	Salt	and other articles.
Tea and Coffee	Vinegar	
Rice	Pickles	

And withal, blessings on them, they growl. There is no issue of stipulated rations, but allowing of no waste, there is no stint, no limit, yet their grumblings would lead a stranger to believe, starvation was staring them in the face; this spirit of dissatisfaction is caused in a great measure I fancy, through inaction; the men are growing rusty for want of activity, and billiousness has soured their tempers. Unfortunately we have a few hard cases with us, and under the old maxim, "Evil communications corrupt good manners," they in part contaminate the would be contented. There are seven or eight roughs in our midst who are bully's of the first water, and would as leif cut a throat as a purse I take it, as however, is very frequently the case with bully's, they are, I am certain, cowards at heart, for so I prooved them to be. My diary of March 13th 1872 contains the following. It is high time some movement was made to have the men actively employed! or that some one was at the head who would assume authority. Some of them have been long in a state of insubordination, and now the roughs of the expidition are in open mutiny. Growling at their food, and cursing me for being out of sugar; all this I care little for, and have turned a deaf ear to idle words, but my long pent up feelings have found vent today, and the leader of these roughs will carry my mark to his grave. I have passed through a somewhat exciting scene, and don't care to have it repeated.

Finding I bore their taunts, and that they could not incite me to retaliate, they waxed bolder; and as I always take my meals after they have left table, today they collected in a body around the cook house door; Roberts, the ringleader, big Reilly, Jackman, Reynolds, Rainier (a Greek), Keating, and Joe Reuff (a Bavarian). They were evidently waiting for me, and I knew things had about come to open rupture: On my going to Breakfast, one of them asked me if I would let them go through the store, and proove for themselves whether or not I had sugar there? Also telling me they were about tired of the Beef, that the Salt Beef was no other than stinking salt horse &c. I told them they could have Bacon and pork only in turn, that if issued to them every day, these articles would soon run out, and then what? Simply Beef alone, and a wider field for discontent, as I had Beef in greater proportion, Beef must necessarily be issued in excess of the others; Roberts made reply "Damned if we dont have what we want, or there will be somebody sorry." I told them they were eight to one, but so long as I had control of the supplies, I should neither allow them nor their abettor "Gillette" to take the issues into their own hands, much less permit them or him to dictate to me what I should or should not issue. I told them truly that Gillette was the cause of there being no sugar; he it was who stopped the Indian "Young Joe" and party going to the first landing for Sugar; he would not let Foster and party go up the pass, simply because I desired it, and probably thinking this muss would be the issue, whereas, at that time, the way was open, and sugar could have been sleighed or packed down from the Cache. If their Coffee and Tea had to be sweetened with syrup, the blame lay not with me, but with him; I further told them they were just as discontented when the table was well supplied with sugar, that they had hatched up something to keep up an incessant growling during the whole winter, that they were acting a very unmanly part: first, in beleiving Gillette, when he told them there must be sugar in store; and again, in waiting until they found all the officers away on duty, and with only myself and the cook to contend against. They told me I had best look out for myself, as they had a heavy score to settle with me; I told them I did-nt care for their threats, I'd do my duty, did the devil himself stand in the way. I passed into the cook house, when Jack Cox, the cook, an old sapper like myself, told me big Reilly had snatched the fry pan off the fire, and had thrown my steak out of doors. I asked the great ruffian what he did it for? He answered, d—d if you shall eat unless you let us go through the store, and see for ourselves; I told him I'd see about that, and told Cox to dish me up some Beans and Bread; he went to comply, when Reilly tried to stop him; I snatched up a hatchet, and told him if he did'nt stand back, I'd brain him; he glared at me, but thought it safer to keep off. Cox placed my plate on the table, when Roberts said, there are seven of us, and we will see you d—d but you shall not have it, and he thrust his hand forward to take the plate. I was thoroughly roused now—down came the hatchet, and he left portions of three of his fingers on the table; I guess I aimed for the whole hand, but he was too quick, yet not quick enough, the hatchet passed through them clean, and buried its edge in the pine board, such was the blow I dealt. I now made a rush for Reilly, hatchet raised, but the whole cowardly crew escaped to the door. Roberts they led away crying like a big boy, while they threatened me with some choice oaths. I ate my Breakfast, and taking the Hatchet with me, left for my hut; after an hour or so they came down in a body and told me Roberts had lost much blood, was very weak, and asked me for medicine and bandages. I gave them what they wanted, when they asked me to go and dress his hands; I told them I should leave that to them, he was one of their gang, I was'nt! Reilly had an axe in his hand, and as it appeared their object was to get me out of the way, he said, come boys, let's smash the store door in! if he wont open it. I jumped back, got hold of my Henry Rifle, and as Reilly was then at the store door (not 15 yards away) I leveled the peice, covered him, and told him to throw down the axe instantly, or I would shoot him dead; and God help me, I would have done it. He took in his chances at once, and threw down the axe. I told them I had stood it as long as I could, and that the next of their number who insulted me, or used threats to me, I'd have his blood on my hands. They knew I was a sure shot, having seen me shoot Duck in the river with this same rifle, and they concluded I meant it. They left slowly, taking their hang-dog countenances out of my sight. I moved my bed into the store, and slept there, and I never went out until the officers returned without my rifle, not even to my meals. These men would do no work afterwards, and gave me a wide berth. I am convinced, had I not made this stand, I should have come to grief. I have found this a fact; place a number of men together in a camp, give them little or nothing to do, throw discipline aside, and the result will be something like the above; it may be, perhaps, not so violent; but rely upon it, the better the treatment, the better the feed, the sooner the discontent; you may not be convinced of this, but men in the wilderness are not the same men they are in the heart of civilization, and I speak from personal knowledge, as this was by no means my first experience.

My esteemed friend Gillette had been particularly careful to leave this set behind when the others were taken from camp, expecting doubtless, a scene, and inwardly praying I might have my brains knocked out. I am told he affectionately expressed himself afterwards to that effect. He was the prime mover in all this trouble, and had urged these men to act worse than they would have done. However, my time came with him, and the tables were turned upon him when Moberly returned. I subsequently found out the man Reilly had served a term in the chain gang at Victoria B.C. and that Roberts had been a convict in Australia.

And when the proper time came, the fair ungarnished tale of truth was convincing, and he (Gillette) and his cowardly pack of hounds were turned adrift minus a considerable portion of their salaries. But of that hereafter.

I had forgotten to mention that during the winter, two of the men, sawyers, had cut with the whipsaw a quantity of lumber, and that a boat builder, engaged for the purpose, has been building boats for our future movements in the summer.

The ice on the river gives signs of breaking up, the water showing on the surface.

Since my fracus with the mutineers, I appear to have gained considerably with the better disposed of the party, and with all save the discontented ones, have the sympathy of both officers and men. The winter is drawing to a close, the ice King slowly yielding place to the smiling face of spring, the sun warms with his rays again, the party are being actively employed, biliousness and ill humour are disappearing, and good feeling and merriment prevails; my stand, and general management of the grub department is approved, and with chagrin the blackguards are fearing the pit they have dug for themselves: They are quite convinced I shall report the circumstances, Gillette knows I have kept a record of all that has transpired, and he goes on with the work with apparant dogged indifference. He no longer interferes with my concerns, directly nor indirectly, and his orders to the men are obeyed with reluctance; in fact, at times, not at all; he is held in contempt, and spoken of as "The Government's Bundle of Rags," or by other expressions too vulgar to mention here; Mr Green is the one to whom the men look, and tacitly place at the head of affairs, as he is without doubt the most capable. All save four of the black sheep have returned to work, they are now quarreling among themselves, and blaming each other; occasionally condecending to ply me with soothing syrup; but I have suffered too much and too long at their hands; and am determined to have redress, if redress is to be had. Moberly had strictly enjoined upon me before leaving to keep the commissariat and other stores in my own hands, and he should hold me responsible on his return if anything went amiss with the supplies; he also informed the officers of this. As I have endeavoured to be faithful to the trust, I feel already compensated in a measure. We may expect now daily the breaking up of the ice, in which event we can secure fresh supplies by canoe.

Mail arrived; the first after so many weary months of wait-ing, but strange to say, not a word from my wife; not a line. I had one letter only, and that from my sister Betsy; a letter making a bitter attack upon me; and for what? God only knows. Telling me she wanted none of my assistance &c. It was a most unkind letter, and hurt me a great deal. I thought it a poor return for all my hoping and waiting: I had never written to her, therefore had never given her cause to insult me! I cannot forget it, it seems so strange, and withal, she enclosed her photograph, and those of her children, three innocent little pets. I gazed sadly at these pictures, her sting-ing words of abuse sinking down deep the while; I may state, this letter is the only one I had ever received from her, and I have no desire for another.

We were informed that the white man who undertook to carry down the mail from wild horse creek to Hope last fall, did not reach; and that this spring his body was found some-where on the lonely route, the mailbag beside him. Ah, well; he had gone the way of many others, and all that can be said "He perished in the mountains."

I cannot understand how it is no line having reached me from my wife: Is she dead? I must go on remitting my earn-ings; but this suspense is terrible; what papers did reach us told nothing of this, to me, vital question; I can think no other than that death has palsied her dear hand, and this the cause of no letters; yet surely some one of our many acquain-tances would have let me know; any news were better than suspense; and generally people are ready enough to signal bad news! My chum Jack Cox had some bad news, his house being burned down; his wife, it would appear, was enjoying herself at a Ball, leaving her children with a neighbour: I am thinking had she been my wife, and the mother of my little ones, I should have thought somewhat hard of her; I certainly think a married woman, with small children depending upon her, and her husband from home, would respect her husband

and herself more, and have her helpless children closer to her heartstrings, by remaining at their side, than by walsing with another mans arm around her waist, and her pets (or rather his pets) deprived of their proper rest. The house being isolated, he lost everything. Cold comfort Jack. I remit by return of the mail $150. to my wifes address.

My diary here covers several pages of gloomy thoughts, which seems to me out of place at this late date, and which could find no interest for you, dear Mother, save to feel sorry for me probably; but at the time it seemed my only relief. I had no one among our party to whom I cared to confide my troubles, and my diary was a silent, yet sympathizing witness. This much however, I may state, ere I pass on: I subsequently found out, when too late, that the parties who had been entrusted with the special charge of my wife, and who were bosom friends, had done so most nobly, God bless them, but that the parties paid for giving their attendance, failed to perform their duty, and that she was more or less a victim to their unscrupulous natures.

I had nigh forgotten, that in Betsy's letter was a likeness of you, dear Mother; my Mother, well advanced in years; and oh! how striking the change from what I remember you to have been.

Joe Rueff (a Bavarian,) and one of the mildest of the malcontents, tries every means to get into favor with me again, and I freely forgive him his share in the troubles; he is fond of spinning laughable yarns; and the night following the arrival of our mail, Joe was indulging his hobby, and some of his twisters were hard to digest, to say the least. I listened listlessly, being in no humour for company; but one of his yarns tickled me so much, I burst into a laugh in spite of me, and that broke the ice, doing me heaps of good; as the tale he told was quite feasable, and is a true touch of Indian character, I will dot it down for you. But first let me say, that Reuff was engaged as hunter for the party; and he was not a bad hunter, a good shot, and a native of the Bavarian Tyrol.

Joe stated, that on one occasion, while hunting in the Similkameen country, he was quitely sitting by his camp fire in the evening enjoying his pipe, when three Indians came upon the scene; as usual with them, the first thing was to beg of their white brother. They were hungry, and wanted supper; their apetites were sharpened doubtless by seeing a large buck lying at a little distance, and which Joe had shot and packed into his camp; Joe complied by giving them a good hunck of the dead animal, probably, says he, 18 or 20 pounds. They then asked for Flour; a little was supplied them from his slim stock of that article, and a kettle to boil the meat in; next in order, they asked for salt; thus supplied, they boiled their venison, and ate all their big stomachs would take; for savages are great gluttons. Joe, fancied a drink of the water the meat had been cooked in, and rising to his feet, dipped his tin cup into the liquor with that intent; one of the redskins however, did not see his way quite clearly, he thought his white brother was going rather fast, and told him so, telling him if he wanted it, he could have it by paying for it: and demanded to know how much he (Joe) would give for it, and all in sober ernest, mind you. I certainly thought the yarn a tough one, but far from impossible. You must understand, that during the many years I have resided in this country, I have seen much of Indian character, and have been acquainted with many tribes, yet never once have I seen the slightest gratitude in any one of them. Gratitude is not in their nature; it is simply a virtue they do not possess. You may take up a missionary work and find it; I have read of the nobleness of the red man, but gratitude I have failed to find in the first mothers son of them; others who ought to know have failed to find it, in fact no gratitude even with their own people, or kindred exists.

On the 6th May our first supplies reached us, also a few letters for some of the party, yet nothing for me from the source I was hungering to hear from. My time honored friend, Jim Normansell, writes me from wild horse creek, stating he has noticed I have had no letters from my wife (Jim is Post Master among his other duties); he also knows my wife's writing, but he says Johnson the Expressman told him my wife was improving in health. Now how in the world can that man know, he is not acquainted with my wife, nor with me in fact, and if she is getting better, how is it I am left without letters?

We are beginning to find the Mosquito's very bad here.

I have somehow got it into my head my wife is not dead, but out of her mind, this thought haunts me.

On the 20th May Chisholm and a number of Indians came down, the latter to help man the boats built here during the past winter. Chisholm had been informed that Moberly and Hall were last heard of at Portland, Oregon, on their way up, and that it is rumoured Howes Pass is to be abandoned, and that a way is to be cut to the Leatherhead, or by some called the Yellowhead Pass.

I have written Moberly to relieve me; I feel I must return; and I trust my letter will reach him, and enable him to bring along a substitute. The River is rapidly filling by the streams carrying the snow water from the mountains.

On 27th May Gillette gave me orders to stop the pay and Rations of the men who refused to work. He says he will starve them into obedience. Surely this is characteristic of the man; they have been his willing tools, have served his purpose, though not with the result he had hoped and anticipated, and this is some of the compensation. No Gillette, you may try to pile it onto their shoulders, but not by any means shall you escape, if justice is to be had. As regards these men, they cannot starve, so I have notified them, that I have orders to stop their pay, and that they will be charged each at the rate of $2. per diem for their food, to come out of the pay already due them; and this to continue until they make up their minds to resume work; and this has brought them to their senses, they having concluded to go to work.

The first Pack Train of the season arrived today, bringing in about eight tons of Provisions. We are also augmented by a number of fresh hands, whites and Indians.

On the 15th Moberly arrived, and, better than all, I had news of my poor wife. The letter when handed to me was without envelope; the address only was preserved and was pinned to the letter. Moberly informed me he got it at Colville, Oregon, and that having no means of forwarding it to me, he had carried it in his pocket until the cover had worn out. It was dated on the 9th of the previous October. Only 9 months in reaching me. It bore bright hopes, intended to set my mind at ease; but no better, not able to leave her bed, and begging for my return soon. Ah! me. Moberly is determined to keep me, he says it is impossible to replace me at this stage of the route, that there is abundance of work he must have me take up, and poor Jane will have to wait God only knows how much longer 'ere she sees me: if she knew how anxious I am to be at liberty, and hasten homewards, but it may not be, at least at present.

Moberly tells me there is a large supply purchased, and that several Pack trains are on their way up from Walla Walla, with more to follow; also a small herd of Beef Cattle are on their way up to us, and more men have arrived; among their number being one, an old hand in river navigation, and formerly Captain of the steamer "forty nine" running between Colville and the Dalles, on the Columbia River. This mans name is Pingstone, he is to take charge of the boating parties, and is now busy making preparations to leave with his crews; these are half breeds and Indians, a hardy looking set, used I believe to shooting rapid streams, and men reliable in difficulty and danger.

On the 19th June I handed my books to the chief for inspection, at the same time presenting a somewhat lengthy report of the abuses I had been subjected to during his absence. In preparing said report, I took special pains to dot down not a word I could not substantiate by evidence, avoiding everything where witnesses to the same could not be furnished: hence, a very great deal had to be omitted which would have added considerable weight to the charges preferred against these worthy's.

I knew the man with whom I had to deal, a thoroughly just man, and a dare-devil of the first water. Not easily roused to anger, but very bitter when angered, and I knew that to report circumstances I could not proove by testimony, would lesson my chances of redress, and might tend even to throw a shade of doubt upon the whole.

Mr Green later on informed me, Moberly read my report without any remarks, but that as he laid the paper aside he remarked, "If Gillette has sown the seed of this discontent, d—n him, he shall reap the harvest."

Gillette and the party being still in the pass, nothing further can be done in the matter until they come in. So I must bide my time.

On the following Sunday we moved down the river several miles, and as near the first Cañon as convenient; thus leaving our winter quarters, to which we never returned. The four new boats were loaded with men and such stores as were needed for present use. Old man Smith being left in charge of the balance, to be hurried along as quickly as possible. We experienced a second of those short but violent storms while running down the swollen stream, having to put in shore until it passed.

Today we were joined by an old Indian who had been with us last fall, but had been discharged for creating trouble with his brother redskins in the employ. His name is "Old Joe," and is a petty cheif of the Kootenay tribe. The interpretation of his Indian name is I understand "Eagle of the light." This high sounding name, nor his chieftonship availed him nothing however, for he had no sooner presented himself, than he was ordered into his birch bark canoe again, and told to "Git".

The provisions cached last fall in Howes Pass are doomed to remain there to rot, about 3000 pounds in all. Too much valuable time and labor would have to be consumed in getting them out.

While preparing our camping ground here, and while cutting away the underbrush, some of the men observed a grouse sitting on a nest of eggs, and under a bush they were about to cut down. Strange to say, nothing alarmed at the intrusion and noise, she stuck to her nest, merely ruffling her feathers on too near an approach. She became a favorite with the men at once, and her bush was left standing, and as she is within five yards of my tent, I can see her bright eye watching me. The dogs have been taught to respect her, and they go by, without giving her any uneasiness. All who come are told not to molest her; I take her soft bread, and she stretches out her neck, and pecks it up. She leaves her eggs once a day, and with a whirr is off into the forest, remaining a time, then returning, and with all the bustle and worry of an old hen, and acting as though the cares of the whole grouse family were upon her, she settles herself for another twenty four hours. She is a pretty little mother, but alas for her, tomorrow I expect a cat I have had all winter, and which came to me in a box from Wild horse creek, and whose name by the way is "Diddlems," and on her arrival, a very sharp look out will have to be kept if no harm comes to little grouse mother. It is amusing to observe some of our rough and tumble fellows come as near as they may without annoying our little bird pet, and trying to put on a winning aspect, pucker up their mouths, with a chuck, chucky, chuck, and stand watching her. I have particularly observed this in a few whom I thought had no spark of gentleness in their natures, and yet surely, there are none so bad but a tender chord can be touched, did we but know where to strike it.

On the 26th June I find this entry: Train or a portion of it came in today; and my esteemed friend Gillette with it. It was not long before Moberly had him in his tent, and I surmised for what reasons. I was informed later on he (Gillette) had been ordered off somewhere, although I cannot learn where; but I was to rest assured we were to be rid of him. Let me repeat it. Rid, rid, rid of him. Green, my informant, tells me he supersedes him as second in command, and that I am to make up his account at once, which I do with undisguised pleasure.

Experienced another of these mountain Blizzards today, with the accompanying crash of trees, deafening peals of thunder, and blinding lightning, and in the midst of it the arrival of boats from Howe's Pass, and my cat "Diddlems."

Moberly has had serious thoughts of running the Cañon as soon as the trail is cut through to this point; it is a case of going it blind if he does, for no one knows what it is like, nor the difficulties in the way; all we can see is the river, now much swollen, turning sharply as it enters a yawning mouth beteen two perpendicular faces of the mountain, dark and forbidding; he argues the thing would be a great saving of time and labor, and that the chances are favorable with the river at the flood. I cannot say I for one admire the prospect ahead, it he adheres to it.

June 27th

[1872]

Have again made a move of two miles, and to within a short distance of the Cañon. The river is rising very rapidly, and the immense volume of water, not finding free passage below, its rise hourly is plainly observed. Great care had to be observed in making these two miles in the swift current; to have missed our landing place, would have compelled us to take the Cañon, for beyond us no landing could be made. So far Captain Pingstone and his halfbreeds have behaved admirably.

Let me here mention a peice of heartlessness on the part of one of our party. As we were about leaving our last camp ground, and after several of the men had held a last cluck, cluck, interview with our feathered pet, a man by the name of Benson, who had arrived with Moberly, and whom he had engaged as a Leveller, took it into his head to kill the bird; and acting upon the thought, he deliberately fired at her with a loaded shotgun. Luckily he missed her, she had won the hearts of as rough a set of men as need be, she had escaped the deadly claws of the cat, and now narrowly escaped the cruel clutches of a cowardly wretch who would have taken her life through mere wantonness. He did not get a chance for a second shot, his gun was wrenched from him, and by the furious gestures and not very choice language of his comrades, I expected non other than to see him get a thrashing. From that hour he lost the respect of all hands; it was looked upon by men, who were not over particular themselves, as a dastardly act: and all felt that none but a man of cruel instincts could have done it. This man was well connected in Canada, held the position of an officer with the party, in fact well educated, and for one act of foolhardiness he had branded himself among men, rough as god permits them to be, as a "dirty scrub." I placed a good store of food near her nest, and so we left her to hatch her young in peace.

From our new ground we have a better view of the entrance to the Cañon; that, and nothing more. Its appearance is anything but inviting; the huge throat appears choked with the mass of water seeking a passage, and we hear the dull hoarse sound as it forces its way. Moberly remains undecided what course to take: if he could only get some point of observation, have some idea of what hidden obsticles lurked between the walls of gloomy rock; and he says if he could only bring himself to think a passage could be made, he would no longer hesitate. Pingstone says he will run a boat through if he says so; and so it rests at present.

Friend Smith, or "Old Man Smith," as he is called by the party, is my Commissariat Assistant, and is quite a mechanical genius: he came to British Columbia as Engineer on the Gunboat "Forward" now eleven since, leaving a wife and family in England. As I move forward, Smith remains to clear out the last camp.

My feline friend Diddlems was my sole companion during the first night I (or we) passed in this camp. The Party of men who came down returned to help get the boats up stream, and so we were left to console each other, but I must say he proved most unsociable, or probably he may have thought me so. I think I have intimated "Diddlems" is a Thomas Cat, to report to you his wretched behavour; I had no sooner released him from the Molasses Keg in which he was brought down, than he gave his tail a jerk by way of emphasis, and scurried away. I cooked my supper, and saving his share, waited for his return, but during the whole evening I saw nothing of him, while through the silent night hours, I could faintly hear his melancholy call of "Maria,- Mariar- Mariar-r-r-." I smiled as I fancied his Maria was as far off as mine probably, unless it might be a Maria untamed: in which case he would be likely to get a little too much of Maria. Well, I thought, it is lonely, and I dare say he too feels it so.

June 29th

[1872]

The goods being now all brought forward from the last camp, the same was vacated, save by four of the worst of the malcontents, to wit, Reilly, Roberts, Reynolds, and Jackman. Moberly told them he would take them no further. That sufficient food would be left them to suffice until the trail was cut through the bottom, and the mule trains were in and ready to return; they would then be sent on to Wild Horse Creek, and turned adrift, that the pay of Roberts and Reilly would cease from the date of their breaking out into mutiny; that of Reynolds and Jackman, from the present date. In the case of the first named, Roberts and Reilly, I felt only that it served them right; for the other two, I felt sorry; sorry they should have been so foolish. Reynolds was quite useless anyway, but he was getting well on in years, and Jackman had been an old Sapper, and had a wife and family.

I cannot forget the look of hatred on Roberts face, as, upon my leaving in the boats, he held up to my sight his mutilated hand, as he exclaimed, "You see this? It will help me to remember you."

And so these men were parted from by their hitherto comrades with scarce a "good bye"— their growling propensities, and dirty habits had made them a byword among their fellows, and no man extended the hand at parting to help wish them God speed. Did they feel it? Doubtless they did; how could it be otherwise. Three of them were quite sick with scurvy.

It may be well to observe here, that, each man, upon entering into his engagement for this service signed articles binding him to certain rules and conditions. The government on their part of the Contract were to comfortably feed him, have a sufficiency of Clothing, Tobacco, and other extras he might require to have by purchase, within easy reach of him, and at cost price on the spot at which the purchase was made by the government, and no matter to what distance said articles had to be conveyed through the mountains, the price list should remain the same. That, on completion of service, or if from accident or sickness he should become incapacitated, he should be safely brought back to his starting point, or place of his engagement.

The man, on his part, agreed to faithfully serve two years, if required, that any infraction of rules laid down (and open for his perusal), should be punished by forfeiture of Pay, or if a slight offence, in such other way the Commanding officer should suggest. That mutiny, inciting to strife, threats, refusal to obey commands, and several other of the major conditions, should be considered, if proven guilty by his officers, sufficient warranty to discharge him on the spot, with forfeiture of all pay while serving.

These, doubtless, were strict conditions; but it has been already seen how necessary they were, and whereas, no man need render himself a subject for the rod, so that the government fulfilled their terms of the agreement, so therefore, such conditions were not applicable to the orderly numbers of the party, and our chief was just to his men.

The boats receiving orders to go up to the first landing, I sent copies of their accounts to these four men named on the preceeding page. Two of them were the losers of nigh 3 1/2 months pay, and must negotiate, or proceed to Victoria to receive what was their due: They would be enabled to pay their way from Wild horse Creek, where they were dropped, by an order on the government, if necessary, and which amount was deducted from them on settlement. To effect this, each man was in possession of an order from Moberly, to all whom it might concern, that money (amount stated) was due from the government to the bearer, on his order, and that any assistance rendered said bearer, on his way to the lower country, would, upon presentation within a limited time, of the authority in question, and upon being endorsed by said bearer, be paid forthwith.

The pay of these men had been $50 per month.

Gillette still remains with us, but inactive, and performing no duty. What Moberly's intentions are in his case I cannot say.

June 30th

[1872]

Gillette came to me today and demanded stationery, and as I have strict orders not to issue the same, I was compelled not to comply with his request, or rather demand, but referred him to the chief; in fact he was quite aware of the order, and I suspect took this means of promoting a quarrel, for he at once poured forth such a vile string of abuse as no Billingsgate could equal. I was engaged at the time checking stores, and knowing the man to be desperate, I made him no reply, but kept steadily on with my work. Failing to acquire his end by rousing me to an exchange of like civilities, he came close enough to touch me, explaining at the same time, I've the d—ndst mind to shoot you, you ——, at the same time carrying his hand to his revolver, a heavy Smith & Wesson he invariably had slung to him. Not doubting but he meant business, I turned quick as a flash, and struck him a violent blow in the face which staggered him; Hall at the same instant leapt upon him from behind, and pinioned his arms to his sides, while another man jerked the pistol from his side. He was perfectly livid with rage. And that was the last time he and I exchanged a word with each other. In fact I had few opportunities of again seeing him. Moberly hearing the rumpus, and ascertaining the cause, sent for us both, and upon the whole case being explained to him by Hall, he told Gillette he had made an unprovoked attack, no matter what his objections to me personally might be, he was quite aware I was but doing my duty in refusing stationery. "Rylatts life has been threatened by you more than once" he continued, "at least so I am told, and today you grasp your pistol with a probable deadly intent. I will simply say, that had his case been mine, self preservation would have led me to have made it impossible for you to have needed a pistol at all by this time, for you would have been among the absent. Had Rylatt been armed, and taken the drop on you, shooting you in your tracks, he would have been justified in the act." And so it ended; upon my word, I wonder at my forbearance when I consider the pains he had taken for so many months to make life so intolerable to me.

The Party during all this time have been busy making trails for the animals, one body being engaged ahead cutting a way over the foothills to the outlet of the Cañon; luckily for my peice of mind (I only speak for myself) Moberly has concluded not to run the gauntlet.

On the 10th July a mail arrived, but brought no letter for me. Jim Normansell sent me a couple of papers from Wild Horse, and a few lines, telling me not to be downhearted. He is now in the service of the Provisional Government, and is Collector of Customs at Josephs Prairie, and for which place and duties he was just setting out.

Have had to again move all stores to higher ground, the water is rising so rapidly.

July 22.
72

Pay sheets and accounts for the past 7 months have left for the lower country today, and I have remitted a further sum of $200. £94.17.6 3/4 to date, or $416.16.

The first train ran through direct from Wild Horse Creek two days ago (Mexicans), and the animals are looking well after their winter's rest.

July 25th.
72

Today to me is a memorable one. It is 12 months today gone that I engaged myself to the present service. Today I had promised my poor wife to cheer up, for was I not coming to her, yes, I should surely be home today, God sparing me. Today— Oh! I wonder will she be looking for me, and straining her ears to catch the familiar footstep crunching the gravel. Today I have the blues most sadly. Poor wife, poor Jane. After sending a trains supplies ahead of me, I mount my Cayoosh, and with dog Nip at my heels, I strike into the forest. I am glad somehow to be away; Smith was at the Depot, and he was one to many in my present low spirits. At last, night drops her mantle, and hides me as I sit with my back against a tree in gloomy thought. Nip lies beside me without a care, my horse is browsing at a short distance, tied by a long rope, and my scant supper disposed of, I seek what consolation I may in my pipe. Quite late into the night I sit thinking of wife and home, the dying firelight throwing ghostly shadows. Chilled at length by the night air, I roll myself in my Blanket and try to sleep: but my mind has been too disturbed through the day to give me dreamless sleep. I felt dead tired, but could not sleep. Gradually, stealthily the glad forgetfulness came o'er me at length. I could not have slept long I imagine (I had no watch), but long enough to travel back to wife and home again. We were parting again. I was laying my poor sick wife back on the pillows after fainting in my arms: I was kissing the two big teardrops from her closed eyes, and with a groan I started up, staring around amid the total blackness, the beads of sweat stood upon my forehead, and I had somehow a terrified feeling. What did it portend I asked myself. It was still inky dark, I could hear only the rustle of the leaves, Nip was lying against me; but I shuddered at I dont know what, it was like an ague fit. I lay down again, but got no more sleep, and was glad when it became sufficiently light to make my fire.

Breakfasting from a cake I had made last night, and a drink of water from a noisy little brook hard by, I again mounted, and passing the Mexicans Train, also 3 men repairing bad places, I sauntered on until night overtook me, when I camped as before.

PLACID RIVER

At about noon the following day 27th July, I came to a stand at a River; (Placid River the party called it I afterwards learned, on account of its smooth surface, although it was tolerably swift). The 3 men I had passed yesterday told me where they had constructed and tied a light raft, and having found it, I started my Horse over, halloing at him to insure his not turning back, and was preparing to follow, when my voice brought friend Rheume to the opposite shore, and from out the undergrowth; shouting to me to "hold hard a bit," I had the satisfaction of seeing him carry a birch bark canoe to the bank, and cross to me. Getting very carefully in this very frail bark, I was soon wafted to the other shore.

Rheume informed me Benson and he were stationed there waiting my arrival. That the goods, on the arrival of the Trains, were to be depoted there, on the opposite shore; and that I, of necessity, would have to remain with them. Benson, he informed me, was on a little hunt somewhere, trying to knock over something for the pot. The party moreover, were not more than 5 miles ahead; as soon as I could conveniently wedge in my jaw, I gave him to understand I was faint with hunger; and would like much to scrape acquaintance with his larder. By Jove, Rylatt, I have nothing cooked said he. That to me is the hardest task of all. Benson and I spar each other who shall get meals; but as you are hungry, we won't wait for Benson, but get us up a jolly good dinner. I am glad you have come, we both wished you would come, you are such a stunning good cook, and so he gabbled on, and strutted around, fighting the misquitoes, but making no attempt at a dinner. Suddenly he took breath, and turning to me in the coolest manner possible, asked if I would'nt make dinner for us two, you know. We'll let old Benson scurry for himself, letting me into the secret that he had caught a wild gosling, a plump little chap, all meat, but as he had no bread, would I make some bread first, and he would make the fire, and so he rattled on. I felt my dander rising at his infernal impudence, and told him in no very measured terms I would see him hanged first, that he had eaten often enough at my table, and I had cooked many a meal he had partaken of, but I had an idea he had eaten all he ever would eat of my cooking, unless he turned to and took a hand at it, and his equally lazy chum, Benson likewise, at which he took the alarm, and with his french shrugs and grimaces, said, being such an excellent chef-d-cuisine, he thought I would prefer good cooking to bad, but he would get some Tea and so forth in a jiffy. Simply telling him to go to the devil, I determined to strike out for the party 5 miles ahead, and so started on foot.

This man Rheume, whose christian names, by the way are, "Louis Napoleon", is a Canadian Frenchman; his father is a Lawyer, in pretty good circumstances I am informed; he is also a member of the Canadian Parliament, and the son is a little high strung in consequence.

Knowing the Train could not reach the river until the following day, I had no fears on that score. As I again struck into the forest, I turned my head, and could not help laughing to observe my friend Rheume trying to dodge the misquitoes, wishing evidently to cut a figure by his dainty walk, only the misquitoes would'nt let him; he would stop every few paces, and slash right and left with the pine branches he held for the purpose, then daintily stepping out again in his lack-a-daisical manner, as anxious apparantly to impress the trees and undergroth with his importance and petit-maitre manners, as though he were in his own dear Quebec, and his girl watching admiringly from an opposite window. I still paused, it was cheering to observe him, the lazy begger; I reasoned, he is compelled to work at something in spite of himself. At length the clouds of buzzing insects fairly drove him from the field, and I heard his anathama's as he darted under the protection of the heavy smoke of the slow gum wood fire burning for the purpose.

I was not a great while on the trail 'ere I regretted I had not stayed at the river, and even cooked the dinner; the path was thickly studded with the sharp points of Salmonberry stems. The trail having been cut through closely matted Salmon brush, the stems of which were probably not more than 9 or 10 inches apart, the brush hooks had left the short stubs projecting 2 or 3 inches, and as I was in mocassins, the pressure of these sharp points became very painful. True, I had the usual blanket strips next my feet, or I could not have endured the pain. The misquitoes too, beat everything I had heretofore experienced. After a time however, I reached better ground; and eventually, my friend Jack Cox and supper.

Obliged to wait until the boys came in from their work, in order to take their orders for Clothing, Shoes, Tobacco &c, and being further detained by Moberly, I had to travel back by the light of the moon, now about full; but upon reaching the dense timber moonlight availed me but little, for it was with difficulty I kept the trail; and having to step at random through the Salmonberry stubs, my feet were peirced in several places, and pained me terribly. My face, hands and even my legs were blistered and sore by the stings of the clouds of misquitoes that beset my path. Upon reaching the river I was scarce able to walk. I found Rheume and Benson turned in, and the fire out. Searching for my Blankets, I coiled myself within their folds, and in spite of the dreadful throbbing pain in my feet, was soon sound asleep.

This morning Rheume and Benson again suggested my doing the cooking, stating they were willing to undertake any portion of my work if I would only comply, but I felt in no humor to comply. My feet were swollen, and pained me so dreadfully I could scarce stand upon them, and I moreover lay my present trouble to their confounded inhospitality last evening. I therefore determined not to oblige them; and during the day I crossed over to my own side of the river, to wait the arrival of the train and my own tent and cooking traps.

Before leaving, I had the satisfaction of seeing Rheaume try his hand at getting up a Breakfast. It was positively amusing; he would have some Farina patties, as he called them. In mixing his batter, he let his spoon disappear to the bottom of the substance, and instead of taking it out with a fork, he plunged his hand in to the mess (nigh a pailful); securing the spoon, he slapped his face with the same hand to kill a misquitto breakfasting upon his blood, by which act his spoon again disappeared, while now his face and beard were plastered, while making the attack upon the misquitto. Once more he dived after the spoon, and transferring it to the other hand, he proceeded to wipe off the mess upon his pants. By this time he had a piebald appearance. His chum was equally busy; he had made Coffee, and taking it from the fire, he placed it in a somewhat ticklish position beside the embers. Rheume by this time had all things ready to sail in as he termed it, and with the bubbling Bacon grease in the fry-pan, he dropped in some of his mixture, laying the balance down beside him to attend the first batch of patties; when now, by some unlucky accident, the coffee pot was upset, and the scalding contents penetrated through poor Rheume's mocassins; with a howl of pain he jumped aside, only to plunge his foot into the pan of batter, upsetting it at the same time. frantic with rage, he caught up the unoffending pan, and flung it

"Chef d' Cuisine."

far away from him. Benson during this time was busy cutting some rashers of Bacon, dropping his knife he came close to Rheume, and in a threatening manner wanted to know what the devil he was doing, whereupon poor Rheume told him he could cook his own breakfast, as he did not want any. Benson stood looking at him for a moment, then burst out laughing, and I joined in until the tears ran down my face. One side of the poor cooks face was white with the batter, also one leg of his pants, and one foot; and as he stood there, drawn up to his full height, with a look of insulted dignity, it was too rediculous for any thing.

As it was now 11 o clock, and as I had regained my good humor, and being hungry to boot, I turned to and got Breakfast, after which I left them to do the best they could as regards the culinary department until called away by the chief.

The train arrived in due time, also John A'hern, Cargodore or head packer. John A'hern is an Irishman, or rather an Irish American, a little wiry chap, smart as a steel trap, and does not fail to impress upon all new acquaintances that he is a down-easter. He is the possessor of an immense gold watch, about as big as a small fry pan, and for which he says he paid $300. As he and I may naturally expect to do considerable business together, I had been watching him pretty closely, and I concluded he was no fool, but thoroughly understood his business. He apparantly had also been taking an inventory of me (so to speak) although I was not aware of it, until he stept up to me, and said, I see what you are after, guess thats all proper, at the same time holding out his hand for my acceptance. I shook his hand, when he mounted and rode away.

The train also, after discharging, left again; somewhat contrary to the usual method pursued by the Mexicans, who have in general a hundred excuses to loiter their time, but I presume the presence of A'hern accounted for it in a measure, and probably they were glad to get away from this misquito infested spot.

These Mexicans have a poor train however, compared with our American train of animals. The Mexicans have a number of Cayoosh horses in the train, and they are slow travelers, necessitating their having the poorest and slowest mules to match as nearly as possible. On the other hand, our American train is comprised of large powerful mules, packing heavier loads, and traveling much quicker, save in very marshy ground, where the large broad hoof of the horse has a decided advantage.

Rid of the train, and the goods snugly packed, I proceeded to make myself as comfortable as possible. My little tent had been made to my order, and with a misquito net to cover the front, I could sit within and write or whatnot, while the bloodthirsty little wretches darken the front, and keep up an incessant hum in their endeavours to get at me.

Ward, one of our packers, came down from the front, and informs me Gillettes condition is a most pitiable one; he eats by himself, and sleeps in a small tent by himself. The men shun him like a leper; he still hopes to resume work, and it is a puzzle to all hands why Moberly keeps him with the party. What misery this man has heaped upon himself. I cannot help having some pity for him now, and could I do him a kindness, I feel as though I would do so.

Augt 1st.

Price's train arrived today. 52 animals, of which 43 were packed. They had to leave again at once, the misquito's literally covering the poor brutes, making it impossible for them to camp here, although there is abundance of feed.

One of their mules was left with me, with his feet badly graveled. We swam him accross the river, but he soon swam back, and tore after the train.

Webster also came in with a small train of Cayooshe's, and has crossed over to pack to the front.

The heat today was intense; finding it impossible to take comfort in the tent, no alternative remained but to face the misquitoes on the outside: and even here but two alternatives remained, either to be half choked in the smoke of the gumwood fire, or run briskly up and down, whisking about in a lively manner with fir branches.

Augt 3d

[1872]

On the following day another train came in, reporting the forest on fire behind; and Green sends me word the same is the case ahead, so between heat and smoke we may expect to be pretty well stifled; already the atmosphere is becoming obscured.

I was sitting in my tent today, when one of those sudden tempests came tearing through the gorge in the mountains; before I had time to secure anything my tent was torn from over me, leaving me still sitting; my blankets quickly followed; jumping to my feet it hurried me along, thumping me up against the cargo, the covers of which had disappeared likewise. The rain poured down in a stream, and the thunder rolled around the heads of the giant peaks majestically, and with a sound almost deafening. In four minutes all was quite still again, save the thunder, scarce a leaf stirred. The misquito's having now an open field, turned to with a will, getting into my mouth and nostrils, so dense were they. And now again, with only a moments roaring sound, and a sudden crash of the trees, came another fierce blizzard, stronger than its predecessor, and I had to hold on to the cargo ropes in order to save myself from being blown away. Fortunately, my Stationery Box, although rolled over and over, was not injured; as to my cooking traps, they were carried clattering before the gale, and were hidden somewhere in the thick underbrush. It was a very fortunate circumstance that the wind set towards the timber, and not towards the river, or the loss would have been serious, as much of the lighter cargo had been carried off. After a time however, I recovered all property, having to scramble amid the undergrowth to get at a great portion of it, but glad to get it anyway.

My friends Rheaume and Benson left the river yesterday, and are with the party.

<table>
<tr><td>August 5th
[1872]</td><td>Feel quite poorly.</td></tr>
</table>

August 5th
[1872]

Feel quite poorly.

Sunday
Augt 11th
[1872]

Have been very sick for several days, and not a soul has been near me, save two redskins, strangers to me; they told me they were Shushwap Indians. There were, in fact, four of these interesting strangers, two of them being women; but the ladies of the party were not introduced to me, remaining in fact on the opposite bank of the river. One of these redskin rascals, with a countenance ugly enough to hang him any day, and a very powerful Indian to boot, asked me for something to eat; I gave them a share of such as I had cooked; while eating they appeared very anxious to know how far the whites were away, how many there were, what things I had; if I would sell to them, and in fact a heap more, all spoken in the Chinook jargon, which I understand pretty well, but I did not reply to their questions. I pretended ignorance of the language. I was anxious to be rid of them, and was too sick to entertain guests. Fortunately, they evinced quite a terror of dog Nip, and I dont blame them for being on their behavour; the faithful brute I verily believe scented danger, for he sat squarely in front of me, eying them in the most wicked manner. The big fellow spoke coaxingly to him once, and only once, Nip grinned, and displayed as pretty a set of ivory's as any canine could be the possessor of. They said they were afread to go away, for fear he might fly at them, and asked me to tie him up, but I did'nt see it, nor would I understand. I knew so long as Nip was between us, there was little danger, and I knew likewise the slightest sign of encouragement from me, or of hostility from them would be the signal for his attack. I called him to my side, and holding him, made signs for them to go, and taking the hint, they quickly had the river between us: I saw no firearms upon these fellows, only Knives, and for ought I know, they may have been honest enough in their intentions, but I have no faith in a savage, in his own wilds, and with the power on his side, and no fear of the law before him. However, they passed down the river towards the mouth, and I saw no more of them. In all probability they had been trapping small game somewhere here abouts. I found afterwards, none of the party had set eyes on them, and that they had been visible to no one but myself.

On the following Friday the Mexican Train again put in an appearance, dropped their cargo, and left again immediately. Five miles back, as the trains return, there is high bluff land, not infested with misquito's, and where plenty feed and water can be had, and there the trains betake themselves after discharging.

On Saturday I had another Indian visitor, Old Kimbasket, the head chief of the Kootenay Indians, a daring, little shriveled up old fellow, but whom I was glad to see, and with whom I suddenly became acquainted with the Chinook jargon again. I questioned him about my late visitors; he told me he had no idea who they were. After smoking a pipe with me, the old fellow crossed over, and was at once swallowed up in the forest underbrush; he left his horse with me, and as I could not have the poor brute eaten alive, I started it back to the bluffs.

This old chief Kimbasket is in the employ at present, and his principal occupation is blazing; that is to say, his duty is to be in advance of the party, and blaze the best route to be followed in making the trail, by blazing trees within sight of each other; or, should this not be clearly understood, blazing signifies chipping the bark off the trees for about a foot, so as to be clearly desernable to the party following.

And thus it is, for days I see no one, and when anyone does put in an appearance, they leave again as quickly as possible, and the main cause is these infernal little pests, the misquito's. My brow aches, and my neck, arms and hands are raw and sore: I have smothered myself with misquito muslin, smeered my face and hands with bacon grease, but bah— nothing keeps them off, and the heat only melts the grease, and sends it beneath my clothing. The days are fearfully hot and sultry, making life in the tent not to be thought of, but the nights are deliciously cool, and then I am able to keep my enemies at bay. I soon retire however sore and tired. Today I have handled, and had to lift and place in order 19 tons of goods, in heavy packages of from 175 to 200 pounds each, piling them tier upon tier, until the topmost tier is 7 feet high. I am compelled to do this in order to make my scant supply of cargo covers eke out. I feel weak for the work, and having overdone myself, I retire feeling miserable.

Sunday
Augt 11.

[1872]

Took a purgative last night, but feel wretched this morning; I turned in supperless, and dont care to rise and cook breakfast. My teeth have a feeling of looseness, and my gums are so sore, to touch them with my tongue gives me acute pain; am wondering if it is a touch of Scurvy; it is not very comforting to be sick in the mountains, but to be sick and all alone makes the chills creep down my back. These mountains are inhospitable enough for a man in full vigor.

I have wondered how these men who were discharged got Scurvy, and although it was the opinion of the party generally the dirt and discontent had a deal to do with it; yet I remember one Taylor, our boat builder, and a very clean man, left us on account of Scurvy.

I suspect want of vegetables is the chief cause. Everything I eat must be sopped, and even then it appears to become jamed between the teeth. It may be, that having had general good health throughout life makes a coward of me when I feel at all unwell.

Ward came in today for a few Stores, he had only a couple of animals with him. He tells me the party are now 20 miles ahead of this point: and adds that Moberly looks thin and quite unwell, that he is working very hard. Moberly considers he is not more than 45 miles from the Big bend of the upper Columbia River, when we shall leave this bottom land, and take to the mountains.

I had quite neglected to state that at Pingstones suggestion, and with a view of ascertaining how far it would be safe to run the Cañon with the boats, Moberly stationed men at the outlet of the Cañon immediately above the mouth of this river, and had a canoe sent adrift at the upper end, before spoken of. The men were to releive each other, and keep close watch: but no canoe ever came through. Nor any portions of her. The supposition is that she either got into some eddy, or got jamed between rocks, or equally likely, that a jam of drift logs exists in the Cañon, rendering it impossible for anything to pass. This has rendered our chief somewhat uneasy; it is absolutely necessary that the boats run the Cañon, or that new boats be built somewhere near this point, which latter is considered out of the question. The delay would be so great that we should be compelled to winter near the Columbia, with probably a loss of months. Word has gone up to Pingston and his half breed crews to run through at all hazards, as we must have the boats. Seven miles beyond here the river opens up into a lake, which has been named after the old chief "Kimbasket Lake". This lake is some 20 miles in length, and using the boats over this surface would be a great saving of time and labor, and would rest the animals considerably.

Our goal, or laid out winters quarters, is far away in the distance yet. Our chief seems determined we shall winter in the Leatherhead, or as it is also called, the Yellow head Pass, and as in the mountains snow falls early and deep, every exertion must be put forth so we may not be caught unprepared, or that our animals share not the fate of those attached to McClellans party, previously spoken of.

Prices train arrived today, and have gone back to the bluffs to camp. There they will remain until the boats arrive (always providing no accident occurs to them), when the goods will be sent accross, and packing commence from this [point] on to the lake ahead. Price told me his animals had made a forced march, and were dead tired, and that he had half a mind to camp here, and save them a weary five miles return to the bluffs. I told him his animals could get no rest here, and would be more tired in the morning than they were now, that they would stampede, or some of them might take to the river, and instead of crossing, swim down towards the mouth, and probably be lost. "I should like you boys to stay right here, I want your company. But you can't do it." So having taken off the animals Aparajos (pack saddles) they were driven back to the bluffs. However, Price, like a good samaritan, sent his five men off with the mules, and himself gave me his company for the night, by sharing my tent, and I felt it quite a treat.

Upon closer acquaintance, I found the men of Price's Pack Train very pleasant and sociable, and to appearance void of that ungovernable recklessness, and want of feeling, half brutal, so characteristic in the Packer.

Old man Smith has been removed as my assistant, and his place filled by Richard White, one of the party who joined us this spring, but whom I have not yet seen since his arrival.

White is not an entire stranger to me, although I know but little of his history; I knew him as a government officer, and Toll Collector at Port Douglas B.C. some four years ago, and while I was employed as clerk for E. T. Dodge & Co. of Port Douglas, and other places, who were Merchants, Packers, forwarding agents &c. We had several Teams and Pack Trains in the employ, transporting goods to the Carriboo mines; and as a heavy Toll charge was imposed upon all articles transported, I saw and transacted considerable business with this Mr White. I was not long in discovering he was a heavy drinker, in fact he was rarely other than half seas over, go to his office ever so early. How the man got through his duties was a puzzle to me; he was always scrupulously clean in his appearance, and during summer, dressed himself wholly in white, was some what haughty with those with whom he was unacquainted, and I put him up as an exceeding excentric individual; he was always well bejeweled as far as rings and heavy fob chain could make him, wore an eyeglass, which he applied on all occasions, and spoke with a lisp. To sum him up, he was a swell of the first water. He and I got along famously together however, and he took me sufficiently into his confidence, as to at times disgust me. I knew at that time he was heavily in debt, and in truth, on my entering Dodge & Cos employ, I was told to look out for him, and on no account to credit him, and as he luckily never put me to the test, I am safe in saying, I never trusted him. White had been a Major in a Militia Regiment in Ireland; had got cast loose somehow, and had emigrated to British Columbia, one of the very many broken down gentlemen office seekers under the British Government. So far as education and manners were concerned, he bore the stamp "Gentleman" unmistakably. A rale auld Irish Gintleman, and a broth of a boy.

Unfortunately probably for White, another rale auld Irish Gintleman was a office holder at Port Douglas, in the person of J. Boles Gaggin, the local magestrate, and a pair of more reckless, rollicking blades it would have been hard to find any where I fancy. Such men as these would have been their country's idols a century ago, when gentlemen were expected to not quit the festive board until they slipped under the table, and had to be carried gloriously drunk to their beds. Gaggin was also very warmly disposed towards me, and had I sucked the bottle as frequently as they offered this peculiar friendship, I should possibly have gone to ruin long ago. Ah! Rylatt, my boy, Gaggin and I had a divil of a night of it; or, White and I had a glorious time; but I'm awful shaky this morning; these, and the like expressions were so frequent as to be almost quoted, always.

Ah! well, poor fellows, both are now in their graves; they played with the whisky fiend, and he run them to earth. Poor Gaggin was transferred to Kootenay, there to take up his duties as magistrate; the journey is a long one, the road of the roughest, the route traveled being the same as ours. Gaggin was at the time almost a wreck, and in no condition to travel, but go he must, or leave the service, and as a consequence, after reaching his new field of duties, he was prostrated; and too fond of the ardent to the last, he sank into his grave. I believe the Doctor told him if he quit drinking, he would go off like the snuff of a candle, but no need to recommend him to continue taking a moderate quantity to keep life going. The advice was given a patient unable to quit. At last he could not longer swallow the poison, and so the end.

Of White, all I know is, that upon my resigning my position in the mountains, and returning to the lower country; he succeeded me as commissariat and clerk, and that upon the return of the S. Party some two months later, and the discharge of its members; he had a brief period of "Comet of the season" with a certain class, as swell of the period, but his savings were soon squandered; and nothing else offering, and how should it? he accepted a position of an ordinary Policeman in Victoria, the only position that could be found him by those in power who had known something of his happier days, but all power to be a man had gone from him I presume; he could not let the bottle alone; and his reign was a short one as a peace officer. Again adrift, and pennyless, some pitying hand tried once more to lift him from the degridation into which he had sunk, and secured him a position with the Hudsons Bay Company, who transported him to one of their isolated stations far north, and where the tempter could not reach him, and where he sickened and died. Peace to their ashes, they made no man their enemy. They were their own enemy.

Such deaths are numerous enough on this coast and are not classed as suicides. Your old men in England who can boast of being tipplers 30 or 40 years, would few of them be living to make such a boast had they tippled in like manner in the far west. Even the stolid German will too frequently leave his beloved Beer, and taking to more ardent and hurtful drinks, loosing his rotundity for emaciation; and like the vast multitude who travel this road of death, will become such a lover of the ardent, that the stronger and more firy the mixture, the better it is appreciated, and "I dont surprise my stomach with water, let me have my Liquor straight," says the Inebriate. I tell you, the best saloons keep some terrible tangle-leg. The cemetary's and Lunatic Asylums are filled with dead and living-dead victims of this curse. And tell me? are they not suicides? 'Tis true, they do not place a pistol to their heads, and leave an empty skull, nor do they hurl themselves before their maker by way of the river. And yet, herein am I wrong. Hundreds of king alcohol's adherants do pass in their checks in this way. How often may we hear men say "I've got to stop it, or I shall be getting the jim-jams," meaning they will become delerious. Others affirm "If I could only give up drinking before breakfast, but I feel half dead until I get three or four drinks"—and so the mad whirl goes on.

Pingston ran two of his boats safely through the Cañon, arriving here today; he told me it was the wildest run he had ever made; that it took him 7 1/2 hours from the time he started; and that twice he thought they were gone sure, as they had to shoot the boats between huge boulders, through which the water rushed at a terrific speed, with barely space sufficient to admit the passage of the boats. That the danger was augmented by the depth of the Cañon, and the contraction of its walls. So much did the cliffs overhang in some places, as to almost join far over their heads, leaving them in the gloom of twilight, and the war of waters dashing madly against obsticles, made commands given the crews at times unheard. At other times the river was so lashed into foam, it was impossible to discover the black forms of the boulders in time to avoid them. He said he had no idea even yet how he succeeded in getting through; and is convinced he could not

Augt 13th
1872.

do it again and come out alive. And as nothing, he says, could induce him to try and run the other boats through, they will have to be left to their fate, to rot by the side of the river at the upper end of the Cañon, and their crews I presume will be sent to Wild horse, and discharged.

Tomorrow Pingstone commences transferring the supplies to the opposite shore.

Augt 14th

[1872]

Boats were busy all day, and have ferried the greater portion over. Prices Train also crossed today.

No difficulty exists in swimming a train of animals, when once the Bell horse is induced to lead, every mule or horse would follow that bell if going to certain destruction. The bell horse is, when practicable, ridden by one of the Packers, who manages to tinkle the bell as they proceed accross. All trains have a bell horse, which takes the lead, and can be heard coming through the forest often long before the train comes in sight, or the shouts of the Packers are heard, urging on their tired animals.

After all stores are crossed, Pingstones crews will cut their way to the river some short distance below here, to examine what kind of obsticles they may expect in getting their boats through some bad looking water they observed on entering here. Their object is to make for the Lake as soon as they can get away. The Mexicans are on the way here with another load, which the boats must cross before they proceed below. In fact, besides the Mexican train, the Cayoosh Train of 60 animals has yet to come in, having gone up to clean out the camps above. I shall be glad when they are all over on the other side, and I am permitted to leave this dreadful place.

As I write this for my childrens benefit, and 13 years has elapsed, it may appear strange that I feel the desire strong within me to revisit these scenes of so much difficulty and annoyance; and this spot especially. I verily believe that, had I no one dependent upon me now, and an offer were made me to join a like expedition, I should close with said offer at once, and this feeling does not rest with myself alone; it is quite true that men who have been much in the mountains or wilderness, frequently become restless spirits after their return to civilization, and the yearning for the old life comes over them, and in many cases drives them back to their old haunts. There is a strange fascination in the weird gloom of the primival forest, the roar of the cascade, and in natures solitude; where danger lurks in many forms, and where often hunger knaws. The more the hardships and exposure to be surmounted, the greater the desire for a renewal of the old life.

When I first started to pen these reminissences, I determined to make them as concise as possible. In submitting them to the loved ones at home, I knew they would have an interest, being something totally different from anything they would be likely to experience; but when my boys shall, please God, be old enough to read the pages I am at so much labor to prepare for them, how much interest they will feel in them, living as they probably will in this country, is another matter: I only trust they may feel sufficient interest in them to preserve them, in memory of a father who dearly loves them, and who, as he sits in his little Teachers room at the Quinaielt Indian Agency—Wash. Terr[itor]y—and removed from them for a short period; I only trust that in the days to come, they may sometimes think of that father and that mother who thinks no trouble they may take for their welfare is labor lost, but is a labor of love for them. God bless them, and make them good men and good citizens. Amen.

As the packers invariably go back to the bluffs to be out of the way of the misquitoes, I still pass my nights alone; the insects have no terrors for me when my days work is over, and supper eaten; as I before remarked, my little tent, with its coarse muslin curtain in front keeps them at bay, once I kill off the stragglers who have found their way inside my den. I can see their vast array without, and can lie back and smoke, and enjoy the delightfully cool evening breeze, after the burning heat of the day. I would not have it quite understood I am entirely alone. Dog Nip is always with me, although not inside the tent for obvious reasons. And again, there are other living things in the vicinity not very companionable; Bears are very numerous; and that theif of theives, the Wolverine or Glutton; and as I cannot leave, I have to endure them. I keep a light burning in my tent the whole night, which I find effectual in keeping Master Bruin at a distance. I see them occasionally on the banks of the river, or swimming accross, for there appears to be a great many of them. And I not unfrequently hear them during the silent hours of night, forcing their way through the thickets, snapping the dry undergrowth beneath their feet, and drawn my way doubtless by the scent of Sugar and Bacon, of which they are remarkably fond; and as I listen, I hear them express their discontent at sight of the bright light through the canvas tent, which has a formidable appearance to them no doubt; and I hear them retreat again with a half whine, half growl. As I have become so used to them however, they no longer give me so much uneasiness as at first, save for the cargo. I have not yet come accross any save the black species; and my experience of them is, they would rather run than fight, save when flight is impossible, or when wounded, or when having cubs, in any of which cases they are dangerous. I should in all probability sleep soundly with their near vicinity, but for Nips answering growl, which is sure to wake me; for faithful Nip is always lying at the tent door, save when he makes a sudden rush through the cargo after a sneaking Racoon or Wolvereen which his quick ear has detected on a marauding expidition. Listening for a moment, I court sleep again, lulled by the droning him of the misquitoes on the outside, and the purring song of Diddlems my cat, snugly curled up at my feet, and I am content, with my faithful guard outside.

Pingstone reports very bad water between here and the lake, the river being full of boulders, and a very angry current; portages he says will have to be made, as there are places through which a boat could not be navigated. One of his men, Charles Labba, a French half-breed, has left him, and gone above to the other crews about to leave for wild horse, and receive their discharge.

Sunday once again, and my diary bears this entry. Alone as usual! The misquitoes are so unendurable I cannot have my usual gamble with my dumb friend Nip. I have to keep my tent in fact, and as the day is comparatively cool, I can endure it. I have been trying to draw Diddlems into a game of play, but Diddlems is too sedate a cat to be given to frivolity. I can no more than elicit a blink of her large eyes, as she calmly eyes my efforts at play. So I lay back and think; and think aloud for pussy's edification. I am thinking it is the day God has ordained to rest, and he expects it of me here in these lonely mountains, but I shall hear no bells chime this day, nor no face shall I recognize in the crowds who walk and talk, or among those who go to worship, for this sinner will no sermon be preached, no prayers said. But I pause here, well I know if god has spared her, one feeble voice will be raised for the absent one. God bless her, and I take great comfort in the fact that although out of the pale of society, I am not beyond the reach of a loving heart.

Poor old Chief Kimbasket has come to grief. He was in his place a day or two ago, or in other words was somewhat in advance of the party blazing the route, when of a sudden he was set upon by a bear, and having no arms save his light axe, his bearship took him at advantage; the rush to the attack was so sudden, and the animal apparantly so furious, the old chief had barely time to raise the axe and aim a blow as the brute raired, 'ere his weapon was dashed aside like a flash, and he was in the embrace of the monster, the huge forepaws around him, the immense claws dug into his back, the bear held him up; then fastening the poor chiefs shoulder in his iron Jaws, he raised one of his hind feet, and tore a fearful gash; commencing at the abdomen, and cutting through to the bowels, he fairly stripped the flesh and muscles from one

KIMBASKET AND THE BEAR.

of his thighs, a bloody hanging mass of flesh and rent cloth-ing. Thus he was found the following morning, being too weak and torn to attempt to reach camp. What a night of suffering he must have had. Green, who by the way has stud-ied medicine, and is considerable of a doctor, says he hopes to bring him round all right, but that he has had a narrow squeek for it. As soon as he can travel, he will be sent off with the Indians who will shortly be leaving us.

Bruin may not be attacked with anything short of a Rifle, unless the hunter is tried of his life, and adopts this method of passing out of existance. A long keen blade may do the busi-ness, but the chances are in bruins favor by long odds in a rough and tumble fight. He may be a clumsy looking animal, but he is quick as a cat, and his strength is immense; let him once get to close quarters, and get a hug at you, even though your knife arm be free, your chances are slim in coming out victor; he can ward off a blow so quick, that the motion of the huge paw can scarce be observed, and that terrible hind foot, with its powerful claws, can disembowel its assailant with one downward stroke.

Tonight the misquitoes fairly drove me to bed supperless, they got into my eyes and nostrils; and when I opened my mouth to bestow my blessing, they were hurrying down my throat to meet it. Seizing my water can and a crust of bread, I made a shoot into my wigwam; Ah; but they are nimble on the wing, a cloud of the little wretches accompanied me in, and as I closed my curtain they had their insinuating little needles drove home, and were bleeding me merrily for supper. I had quite a lively time killing them off—they are precious cute; they have a very small head, but a heap of sense, seems to me. When they are corraled in a limited space, and are getting the worst of the fight, the little vampires will dodge most dexterously, and will retire to the darkest corner, or hide behind a fold of the canvass, and keep perfectly dark for awhile. There; say you. I guess I've about got rid of you, and you prepare to enjoy yourself after the slaughter, just then—Ping—ping—ping, and you whisk up the towel, and face a dozen or so more. They dodge, you hop around on your heels like a cat on hot bricks, and, yes, you have them this time. Lie down now, my boy and take a smoke. Ping, and he settles on your ear, ping, and this one is on your nose, and so an hour passes 'ere you can take any comfort. Probably, after being quite awhile, you are again assailed, and find that the enemy is perceptibly increasing in numbers. A small hole the size of a pea has been found in your fortifications, and an assaulting party of the enemy are entering, as fast as the passage will admit. You find the weak spot, repair damages, then commence the fight anew. Yet so intent are these amusing little creatures upon the work before them, that when once fairly at work filling themselves, you can slap your hand upon them, or even lay your finger upon them, and crush them. I have watched them many times upon my hand, and it is astonishing how quickly they will draw your blood through their little tubes, and fill themselves. I have frequently imagined I had not one in my tent, and yet in the morning I could count from twenty to forty of them, like a red blotch upon the sides of the tent, their bodies blown out, and looking like minute bottles of blood through the transparant skin. Sluggish and no doubt content, my first care was always to clap my finger on each, and exterminate him, at each attempt staining the canvass with a very large drop of my own blood. I presume no lessening of their number propelled me to the act, that would be futile, but I wanted revenge, and the power given me through their gluttony pleased me; did these wretches not compell me to seek my blankets at sundown?

August 22d

[1872]

I got away from the river today, leaving behind me only eight mule loads of stores, with Johny Ahern on guard until the train arrived to remove the same.

Dick White (my assistant) also arrived today, bringing up the last of the stores, a few packs. Not having seen him since he was Collector of Customs at Port Douglas (previously referred to), I felt somewhat glad to renew the acquaintance. I saw him standing on the opposite shore, and as soon as he saw he was observed, he hailed me with a graceful wave of the hand, and even at that distance I could see the glisten of his eyeglass. Still keeps the goggle at work, I observed to myself. He was evidently in a hurry to get over to me; and I could see he was not at home in the frail craft in which he was soon embarked. Lanware, one of the Packers was ferrying him over in the birch bark canoe, which through constant use had become quite unservicable; it had been packed in many places, and leeked like a seive. I had crossed myself daily at the risk of being drowned (the river being very deep) and it was all I could do to get accross moderately dry, but now there were two men in her. I hallooed to them she would not carry them both, but no use. Lanware carefully paddled, White baled with his hat, and all went merry as a marriage bell until near my shore; White baled in a very uncertain manner at best, he had strong fears of tipping over, when within about five yards of terra firma, down she went. Both men struck out at once, and landed, White shook himself, turned towards me, and performed another graceful curve in the air with his hand, as though to say—You perceive, I shall soon be with you. Now unfortunately for them, as they had to make the shore as quickly as possible, they had landed some distance up stream, and between me and them lay a pretty deep creek. By the way, Dupois, a packer had previously landed, and being unaware of the creek, had likewise landed above, and now in order to reach me and my goods on this side, White and Dupois straddled a log, and with a couple of sticks as paddles, started manfully accross said creek: as luck would have it however, when about midway the log rolled over with them, and both were soused overhead. Making the shore finally, Dupois, like a true frenchman, stood cursing all nature, filling the air with his Sacre's. —Not so White; he came dripping to meet me, and his soaked clothing hanging limp upon him, he performed the indispensible florish, adjusted the eyeglass it was impossible to see through, bleered as it was with water; and with a smile half comical, yet serious withal, he held out his hand, and Ha! Rylatt my boy, glad to meet you once again—you know. My heart went out to him at once, and if I was ever glad to see a face I knew in other days, and mid other scenes, it was then. Not having any change of garments for him, he was perforce compelled to tramp to camp five miles ahead, soaked as he was. And so at last I turned my back on the river, reached Strawberry Camp (so named from the quantity of wild strawberries found there) and supping with the packers, White and I slept the peace of the just, quite free from misquitoes.

Poor White told me a woeful tale as we smoked our pipes over the camp fire. His lot had not been cast in pleasant places during the past three years, and he did assuredly look the worse for wear, the same beaming face was there, the same devil me care manner when casting aside the dignified, but there were hard lines not to be mistaken. He had worked hard at any employment that offered—that twice he had determined to profit by Gaggins death example, and become a sane man, but that each time his little earnings had been snatched from him, once by fire, once by robbery.

A quarrel occurred in camp this morning, and which might have had a fatal termination. Price the packer boss of the American train, became incensed at his cook, a Spaniard named Parma, for oversleeping himself, and upon going to where he was lying, gave him a savage kick, calling him a d—d greaser (term given to Mexicans) and bade him hustle out and hurry along the breakfast. The Spaniard rose at once, and coming over to where I was lying asleep (we were not in tents), he quietly and deftly possessed himself of my Revolver, and walking over to Price, began calling him names. Price seeing he was bent on a quarrel, and suspecting he was ready with his Knife, stooped to pick up a club, and while thus bent, the Spaniard fired; fortunately the ball grazed Price only, causing but a slight flesh wound, and in a part which would prevent him sitting with comfort for some time to come. Price at once thought he was worse hit, and dropped the club, and the Spaniard not following up his advantage, and being apparantly satisfied or afread to proceed further, order was restored. Had the man taken my Rifle his aim would probably have been more deadly, and we should have had warm work on hand.

Augt 28th
[1872]

I reached the head of Kimbasket Lake today. The ground in the vicinity of the lake here is low and swampy; but the journey has been interesting in the extreme: so wild, "so grand." I scarce experienced fatigue while watching the suns beautiful effect upon the glaciers of Ice and snow high up, upon the rugged mountains on my left, the contrast being the more striking from the dark and sumbre pine forests reaching as far up the jagged slopes as nature would permit. What silence deep must reign up yonder, save when the howling storm whirls away the snows in blinding clouds, or a crashing avalanch of Ice vies with the thunder peal.

The following evening I reached the foot of the lake. I am told Bear are very thick here: We saw one immense black fellow from the boats, and were pretty close upon him before he observed us. With startled mein he reared, wheeled, and rushed under cover of the favoring thicket. He was a monster. Yet when first observed, he looked like a big black flea upon the sandy shore. The Mexicans report that a portion of their train was stampeded yesterday; a couple of Bears crashed through the underbrush, crossed the trail right through the train of mules, causing a temporary panic. I guess the Bears were as badly scared as the mules. It was on the shores of this lake Kimbasket was so fearfully mangled, it remains a mystery to me why the brute did not quite finish the poor chief 'ere leaving him.

I hear Moberly has left the party for a brief time; has gone in advance accompanied by three Indians, exploring the line of route.

Gillette, our mutual friend?, has at length left us. One of the Trains returns via Kootenay to the Kamloops country to winter, and the precious carcase of our quandom friend accompanies them. Gillettes account will be forwarded at the same time, with our mail matter, as also a report of his behavour and general uselessness. Gillette being an officer in the expidition, and second in command, all evidence in his case has been carefully taken down, and submitted to those whose duty it is to investigate the matter. I have never heard how the man came out of his difficulty. The last I saw of him, he was reclining on the shore of the lake, raised upon one elbow, and was gathering pebbles in his hand, and lazily throwing them from him, his broad rimmed hat was well pulled down over his eyes, and as our boat shot from the bank into the stream, I kept my eye upon him, for I was well assured he was furtively watching me with hatred eating at his heart. He had then joined the Packers preparatory to leaving.

I have again sent my letters, also an order for all that is due to me to my dear wife: We have had no mail now for months, and I, I have had no line of any kind since February last. Oh! this suspense!

Hall, the Paymaster of the party passed up the Lake today in the boats, and the Mexicans are to start at once, he, as well as friend Gillette accompanying them.

Augt 31st

[1872]

Hall informs me my Salary has been raised, also, that Moberly, who had promised me I should be allowed to leave the service this fall, now declares I cannot leave until next summer, that my appeal will be in vain; but that in order to show some appreciation of my services, and to make some amends, he has raised me another $15. per month. Let me add here, the salaries were a fixed thing, and that mine was the only salary raised of our party during the whole period of service.

Hall further told me our winter party would be comparatively small; that Moberly will remain with us, also himself, as he only goes a portion of the way with the train; but that we have some heavy work before us before esconsing ourselves for the winter, as the determination is to push forward to the other side of the Rocky's, if possible. I had become quite convinced I should be held with the party for the winter, and had been trying all I knew to school myself to the disappointment, but the telling of it to me had an unusually harsh sound, and saddened me. Thus it is ever; who cares for anothers sorrows? The heart of one will ache, while his neighbour at his elbow rejoices, the one mourns, the other dances. Even death severs loving bonds, and as the hearse bears the sorrowed for to the grave, the bells are pealing gayly, as bride and groom are joined. Who cares. Whirl on, mad world.

I should have mentioned that my assistant, Dick White also brought a cat along, and which we have named Toddlams; this cat, by the way is not Whites cat, but belongs to the outfit, and as it is considered fitting that Diddlems should have company, Master Toddlams has been consigned to my care. Now, one would naturally conceive, that there would be joy with the feline members of our party; that Diddlems would sit himself down, and relate to his friend Toddlams how lonely he had experienced it, and that Toddlams would have not only condoled with him, but have responded by relating his own adventures, and the solitary hours he also had passed while having been conveyed so many weary miles to become a member of the party. But, alas, for cat nature, such was not the case, and I begin to fear they too are not good sympathysers, for they met, they smelt noses, their backs and tails went up, and the fur rose, and sad to relate a pitched battle ensued; their claws were of the sharpest, for the fur flew, nor were they on amicable terms for some little time, nor even then always; there were times when Diddlems would chastise his brother, and sad were the wails and cries they raised. It will have been observed 'ere this both were Thomas Cats, and I am told they never do become very fast friends, but eventually my pets did improve upon acquaintance, and become very dear to each other. How it might have interfered with that friendship had a lady of their species been introduced I may not say— Such an unlikely thing did not occur.

The party have taken quite an interest in my sketches; poor I must admit them to be, but as I am the only one who has the slightest gift this way so far as I can ascertain, I am honored with the cognoman of the Artist. I have enclosed a sketch of Kimbasket Lake to my home, sweet little wife and home, and as a relief I have dotted in the foreground of the little love token an Indian in a birch bark canoe.

Have been suffering from Rheumatism for some days past, my shoulders being the most effected; and I found yesterday I had the greatest difficulty imaginable to rid myself of my coat. I turned into the blankets early, but could not sleep, and this morning when I would have risen and dressed myself, I was unable to do so. The pain in shoulder and shoulder blades rendered me perfectly helpless, while rain and wind made the weary hours additionally uncomfortable, and my mind also was racked about the safety of the cargo; fully alive to every sound, I could hear the covers flap in the continued gale, and knew that some portion of them had become loosened, and perishable goods were probably being rained upon, but I

Sunday,
Sept 8th

[1872]

could not stir to repair damages. On the mountains at either hand of me avalanches of Ice and snow thundered down the precipices, loosened from their hold by the steady downpour of rain; which also found its way through the thin cotton material of my tent, making everything within uncomfortably damp. Many times I tried to rise, but only to sink back with a groan of pain—it was impossible to move my arms to clothe myself, and I was moreover unusually hungry. Poor Nip whined pitifully, he too was hungry, and he— yes he had far more sympathy than our species can boast of.

During the afternoon of the following day one of our Indians came into camp for something or other, and assisted me, or rather dressed me, and cooked me and my dumb companions some supper, having been two days fasting. He shared my tent, and left early the following morning for the front again.

I dont remember ever feeling so lonely as during those two days. I lay all that day, after the redskin had left me, but the following morning I felt much better, and was able to rise, being already dressed, and late on that day the boats arrived with the last load, as also White, Benson, and Price the Packer.

On September 17th Pingstone and his Boats crews left us for the lower country, their services being no longer required, and at about dark Prices train of animals was stampeded while on their way here. For two mortal hours the thunder claps were deafening, the lightning blinding sheets of flame, and the rain a deluge. The affrighted and bewildered mules left the trail, perfectly frenzied with fear. The Packers, could only remain near the spot where they stampeded, and await daylight; by noon next day, every animal was recovered, and by night they arrived here, recovering every pack, but some of the goods seriously damaged. But I am slightly wrong here. Two of the Aparajos with their loads were never found. By some means they managed to hide this loss from me, and it was only afterwards I discovered it. Here in the mountains I only knew what the loads consisted of very frequently, when I saw them; for unless my assistant was on the spot, I could have no waybill.

Antonio Plant, a half breed Packer, declares I caused that storm. I had the bad luck thrown in my way yesterday morning to shoot a wild cat, and when I laughed at his folly, he grew angry, and said I must never do such a thing again, as something serious is sure to occur if a cat meets with a violent death, no matter if it be a wild cat.

Matty Sherratt, a young fellow attached to the trains, and herding some sore backed mules, and the cattle we are bringing along for Beef by and by, came into my camp this evening from his post some 5 miles away, and says the Bears have fairly driven him out. After furnishing him another man from one of the trains as a companion, and an additional Henry Rifle & ammunition, I told him he had best return at once, and not leave the animals to be stampeded and lost, but Sherrett was unwilling to return, and told me that yesterday, while baking his bread, a large Cinnamon Bear frequently showed himself, making him feel anything but comfortable; that finally it rushed out of the timber, and made for him open-mouthed; having only his pistol handy, he thought the better part of valour under such circumstances was to take to his heels. I fancy such a move would never have saved him, and told him so; he said, he knew that too, and that had the bear not stopped short on reaching his tent, he was sure no shadow of a chance existed in getting away. Master Bruin had it appears been tempted, even while in mad wrath, by the smell of warm bread and other edibles; and coming to a sudden halt, lost no time in eating up the poor fellows supplies. Camp kettles were turned over, and the contents quickly demolished: in fact, Bread, Cold Meat, Apples and Sugar, was cleaned out in short order. Matty had betaken himself to a small tree, and as soon as his bearship had returned thanks, and sauntered off, he lost no time in hurrying here, and reporting progress. He was about as badly frightened as he could well be. I fear I did not help him out of his difficulties much; I told him that Bruin would, like the tramp, remember the place he had fared so well at, and had such an easy victory; and that he might rest assured he would receive another visit very shortly, &c.

The Cinnamon is in my belief the worst and most dangerous of our North American Bears. The Grizzly is no climber, but a Cinnamon is; hence, once up a tree from a Grizzly, it rests with the one who can out endure the other. The mans position is certainly the most uncomfortable, but you see, if he comes down he will die of a surety. While the Grizzly has simply revenge or a desire for the destruction of a supposed enemy to gratify, let the man hold out long enough, and his bearship will find it necessary to leave and search for food. When the man comes down, hungered too, no doubt, but taking good care to go in an opposite direction to Bruin for his food, or if he has to go that way, will make a detour. But a Cinnamon is a very savage beast, and can run at a very lively rate, spite his clumsy appearance, out stripping a man two to one, and especially in the Timber, and he can climb like a cat.

I remember well, when we (the Sappers) first came out from England, we were all anxious to see Bruin in his wild state: and by our camp fires we were a brave set; this was in 1859, and it so happened, that I, together with four or five of my comrades were out in the woods, along a trail that had been made, and were probably a mile or so from camp, when somehow I got ahead of the others, and knowing none of them had fire arms, something put it into my head to try and scare them; getting off the trail therefore, I crouched down behind some underbrush, and as they came abreast of me, I growled as deep as I could, and then gave a short whining grunt; then another deep growl. It is likely they had not noted my absense, however that might be, they took the alarm, and let out towards camp at a terrific rate. I stood and laughed after they were gone, enjoying the joke immensely, and seating myself on a log by the side of the trail, I commenced filling my pipe; suddenly a cracking in the timber behind me caused me to turn, and through the thick undergrowth I could see his bearship nosing his way directly towards me, unconsious of my presence I make no doubt. Just about that time I had no curiosity to see Bruin in his native wilds, although I had repeatedly expressed such a wish. I was off that log, and dancing along that trail at a lively rate, more frightened I dare venture than those other fellows. Just as I panted into camp I met a dozen coming out armed for a bear hunt; and instead of letting them go on a wild goose chase, and laughing in my sleeve, I joined them, but we did not get him; he heard or scented us, and made off.

Matty also says he saw a large Moose feeding with our animals; fortunately for his peace of mind however, as he was leaving with his mate, orders came to move him down to the lake.

Weather continues wet and cold, and on turning out this morning, I found the snow had crept down the mountain sides considerably.

Sunday
Sept 22.

[1872]

Leaving Kimbasket Lake today, I started along the trail towards boat encampment, with Nip by my side, and the cats in a box on a loaded mule. being a long march, and an exceedingly bad trail, we got belated: and long 'ere we reach camp, I was quite hoarse yelling at the poor jaded animals; in fact, it was so dark, I had no alternative but to keep the tail of the last animal of the train in my hand. I had no fear of the animals being able to keep the trail, although I could distinguish nothing at a distance of two feet; we finally arrived all safe however.

Sept 26th

[1872]

Starting again on the following morning, we made boat encampment at sundown, the distance from Kimbasket Lake being about 25 miles; and here I once more came up with the party, and received a rough, but hearty welcome. Some of the boys were kind enough to pitch my tent for me, and after a hearty supper, we all gathered around the camp fires, lighted our great consolers, the pipe, and started in upon tales of adventures, some I doubt not mythical, some bearing fact. How I enjoyed all this company; and it was quite late ere I sought my blankets, remaining by the embers so long as one would remain with me.

The men have been enjoying a few days rest, but start ahead again tomorrow; opening out a path towards the foot of the Athabasca Pass; for here we bid adieu to the upper Columbia, turn off at right angles, leaving the valley for our way through the Rocky's.

Tonight, to wind up the little recreation our men have enjoyed, we had a grand Ball; think of it. A dance, an enjoyable dance at that. And the ladies; well, we shall see about the ladies. In this respect as in all others, we adapt ourselves to circumstances, avail ourselves of such means as we have at command. True, I may not introduce loveliness, grace and beauty, fairy forms, and costly dresses, yet I fancy none of these could have added enjoyment to our Ball; to be candid: ours was not an elite set, and ladies would have been somewhat out of place here. It was a grand success; that much I can vouch for, and the orchestra, oh! yes we had a select band of musicians; the orchestra, I add, comprised one of our members, well up in dance tunes, and could whistle famously, did his very best. He puckered his mouth, beat loud time on an empty soap box, with a stick in each hand, and the graceful forms began the whirl. Every dancer did his level best, many took it as a very serious matter, and with sober look, and graceful movement, tipped the light? fantastic toe. As I was no dancer, I contented myself with looking on. What a happy evening I spent. Away all care, I felt none, and when the whistle gave out, the orchestra yelled the tune, and the harder beat the time. Hands accross—Ladies Chain—how the rough faces glowed through the grizly beards; some good dancers were among them, and graceful movement, spite of the fluttering rags. Dick White excelled himself. Dick represented a lady; that is he was told off as one of the lady partners, then he became a gentleman, and choose a lady partner, a great six footer, hairy faced, and with a fist like a sledge hammer, pants tucked carelessly into his boots, which was covered with the mud of the river, while Dick, with eyeglass adjusted, held the huge hand gingerly, and by the tips of the fingers, then circling the waist of this delicate creature with the gentleness due to modesty and the fair sex, his lovely partner occasionally letting out a yell of hilarity, would roll the quid of Tobacco over to the other cheek of the sweet face, discharging the juice beneath the feet of the dancers.

The whole thing was so rediculous, I rolled with laughter, and this scene has impressed itself deep in my memory; it was one of the few enjoyable dots during this period of my life. The silvery moon shed light as bright as day—the figures were in dead ernest, and occasionally bumping against each other with a force that would have made dire confusion in a ball room, while they panted like high pressure engines. They were now in the last dance, and appeared to have gone mad, and when at last the orchestra stopped, and Dick White doffed his cap with the indispensible florish, and the moon shone on his bald scalp as he offered his arm to the fair one at his side, preparatory to leading her to a seat on a log, I fairly screamed with laughter; and then to see that modest young lady suddenly throw out one of her number eleven Boots, and sledge hammer arm, and place Dick in an instant on his back, and to observe the lady stamping a jig around him, yelling at the same time that made the distant hills echo, was glorious fun.

"The lamps in the garden gleam,
"The rooms are all alight;
"The sound of the viols stream,
"Through the windows 'oer the night.
"And the dancers, whirling past,
"At the windows two by two;
"The dew is on the grass,
"And the glow worm in the dew.

I believe it is Dean Swift who says that dancing is Voluntary Madness. I wonder how far he is right.

I remember reading somewhere of a Ball given at a Port in China years ago, by the officers of a Man of War Vessel, and a number of Chinese notables were invited. These latter knew nothing of dancing, and looked on quite amused at the performance; during one of the interludes between the dances, a Chinese Manderin in conversation with one of the dancers, quitely remarked, "Why do you sweat and toil so? Why don't you make your servants do all this work for you?"

Sept 30th

[1872]

Some whites and Indians left us today, reducing our party to its proposed winter strength. We also received a mail today, and I, I got 3 letters from my dear wife. The last dated was written by a Mrs Cunningham, being herself too ill to write, ending with an ernest appeal, "Oh! Bob, come home, I can't bear it"—

I did not make an entry of the dates of these letters; but they were the last I ever received from her dear hand; and the last sad dying appeal, those last wailing words were dictated to the pen of a neighbour. My eyes fill now while I write. May God keep her memory green.

Octr 1st.

72

The trains left to day, and the Expidition, now reduced in men and animals, once more sets its face toward the rugged chain of mountains through which it must pass to the work assigned to it. Since the Howes Pass has been abandoned by orders from head quarters, our way lies North East, and in order to reach the new starting point laid down, namely the Leatherhead, or as it is sometimes called the Yellow head Pass through the Rocky's, we have first of necessity to make our way through the Athabasca Pass.

It appears, but little obstruction is to be met between this point and the entrance to this last named pass. And for several miles the way is open, there has probably been some cutting through the thick brush of a mile or so, when the Valley lies an open gravelly plain before us, a narrow belt, the foothills rising precipitious on either side. At the further extremity of this Valley the foothills cease, and immediately in front is the foot of the pass proper; guarded on either hand by mighty giants, their sides scored by deep gorges, grim with the ages of time, gloomy with the firs, which wave their wierd boughs so long as their hardy existance can be norished, becoming dwarfed and stunted in upper air as that norishment decreases. And then the everlasting snow, where nothing vegetable can find life and sustain it. Range the eye upward still, as one stands right under these twin sister guardians, and the topmost peaks cut their way far up into the clear sky, their snowy outlines showing with delicate pencilling, and as one gases, clouds of feathery snow will be seen to occasionally obscure those outlines, whirled into mid air by the wind tempests of those giddy heights. As I first saw them on the one of very few clear days I dwelt, in their shadows, a very mite at their bases, the rays of the setting sun was playing upon their peaks, all in the Valley being in deep shadow, and the effect was most grand, the rays of red sunlight played upon the immense ice belts, flashing on their surface, and impressing one with an appearance of warmth where none existed. If anything can force to the mind of a sceptic the wonderful works of our great creator, methinks it must be found in such soul stirring scenes as these.

The Valley is quite level, with a river fed by the snow waters on either hand and in the pass; and as it serpentwise courses its way through the passage it has cut, first on one side then on the other, we had of necessity to cross and recross it many times, some little difficulty was experienced in finding easy fording places, but with one or two exceptions easy crossings were found; but the detention necessary was very galling to the loaded animals, for standing for any length of time becomes far more fatiguing than when on the move, and at times half an hour would be consumed in finding a proper fording place. I verily beleive we forded this tiresome stream twenty times.

As evening advanced, the rain set in; the trains leaving again early tomorrow for Boat Encampment are compelled to chew the cud of hungry disappointment tonight, there being nothing whatever eatable for them in the Valley; consequently, so long as they are bringing the supplies forward through this section, their treatment will be unavoidably hard. The constant plunging in and out of the ice cold water, and the long march either way, is of itself trying on them, but when we consider that two days fasting has to be experienced with each trip, it becomes very hard—no food, save at Boat Encampment compels the Packer to give one days rest after each trip, therefor making the bringing forward of the supplies slow work.

I somehow have great sympathy with dumb animals, and I often feel like sharing my meal with them, as I frequently give some especially forlorn looking object of charity a hunck of my bread.

But among our long eared, light heeled, four footed friends, I have singled out one pet, or was it that she singled out myself. Certain it is, since her advent (for she belongs to the Mexican train, and started with us from Fort Hope), certain it is we are, and always have been great friends. Jennie is a small mule, a pretty creature, spite of her flopping ears, eyes soft and beautiful as those of a gentle woman. Into whatever camp I may go, Jenny quickly knows it, and though she may not see me, she knows my tent, and as soon as her pack is off, she trots up and announces her arrival by a loud winnie. I always give her some Sugar or a little Flour, and she thrusts her nose at my face, rubs her head on my breast, demonstrates in every way her regard for me. Alas, poor Jennie! like all else we love, you are gone. She died in harness; hard work and hard usage broke her gentle heart, and although one of the best pack mules for her size in the train, she one day lay down under her cruel load, sighed a few times, and was dead.

Friend White remains in charge at Boat Encampment, while I presume I shall remain here and form a depot, being midway between feeding grounds; one portion of the trains pack from my present standpoint to the Party, a few miles in advance, and at the foot of the pass, where much work has to be performed in order to clear a passage for the animals, so for a few days the advance will be slow.

The day following ushered in with a heavy rainfall, such rainfalls as can only be experienced when one is in some valley in the mountains. The clouds gather on the mountain peaks overhead, and break, teeming their overcharged blackness down in a deluge. In a short time the dry seams in the sides of these everlasting hills are turned into foaming, bellowing torrents, and as I dart into my cotton tent, about as large as a good sized umbrella, I find none, or at least very little shelter there, and can only hurry out Blankets and Stationery Box to the cover of our thick cargo covers, and find what comfort I may in any hole I can squeeze my-self into.

Have had news from the front. The Party have succeeded in killing two large carriboo; these animals are of the Deer species, and will frequently reach 600 pounds when dressed. The meat is simply delicious. They had seen no less than seven Grizzly Bears in one group; these monsters attain a great size and weight. Although by no means as large as the Grizzly's of California or further South, nor yet I understand by any means as dangerous. They will dress hereaway nevertheless 600 pounds if full grown, while I am informed the California Grizzly's will drop the scale at 1000 pounds. The knowledge of the vicinity of this species and the Cinnamon have always claimed respect for me, and I often feel as though I should like companionship myself to keep up a sufficient amount of courage and freedom of action. The paw of the Grizzly is immense, and can easily be distinguished. I have observed their tracks on the sand in my locality, and am therefor fully alive to the necessity of precaution, both as regards my own safety, and that of the goods. Bear tracks are in fact thick everywhere, crossing and recrossing each other, and this would assuredly be a noble field for the Hunter and trapper. Bear are not only numerous, but Moose & Carriboo Tracks are likewise to be seen.

I go to bed tonight in a very ill humor: my Blankets are soaked, and I am little better. The rain still pours down; having consumed what food I was possessed of, and as my cooking gear cannot possibly arrive until tomorrow night with the incoming train, I fancy I shall fare slim until then, unless the weather moderates materially. To anyone used to life in the wilderness, it becomes easy to improvise the where-with to bake Bread and Bacon, always supposing the ingredients are at hand to make it of. It is a simple operation to mix up ones dough on a piece of canvas, or even a moderately clean pocket Handkerchief on a pinch, then pat it into cakes, and on an inclined plane, upon a peice of flat wood or thick bark, bake it before the fire, or else in hot embers, and while this portion of the meal is preparing, cut your rasher of Bacon or Venison, and hold it on the end of a sharp pointed stick until done to your satisfaction; but to try keep up a fire, and make all the necessary preparations, with the rain coming down in a solid sheet so to speak, is more than my limited amount of patience can submit to; so as long as my inwards can be kept in any decent kind of control, I conclude to dispense with so dire an operation and turn in cold, and grumbling. Nor is my situation rendered the less cheering with the thought that under the present lookout, our fording places will in all probability be no longer available. The river is hourly rising, and the chances are the train cannot cross, or if at all, to the great damage of much of the cargo.

On the following morning my determination to fast grew weaker, and as the morning advanced failed me altogether: I had to satisfy nature. Eating being about the only luxury attainable, I set to work, and kneeded me some slapjacks on one end of a cargo cover, and after much difficulty, succeeded in coaxing a flame; this, with some Bacon, and a drink of water, of which, thanks to providence, there was an unlimited supply (for the rain had not abated one jot), formed my repast. What remained, I devided between Nip and the cats.

What a dreary outlook to be sure; the flat was in many places a sheet of water the entire width, and I felt considerably like De'foes Robinson Crusoe, save that his domain was green and beautiful, mine green and desolate. I was fortunate in selecting the highest ground, as I always did, dumping the cargo's where I could insure a fall of water from it in all directions, and am content to beleive the water may surround me, but cannot drown me out.

Benson (the fellow who shot at the growse) quite unexpectedly rode into camp from the front in the afternoon, and asked for something to eat. Now, I never yet was able to do good for evil, that portion of Scripture which teaches us to "do good to those who despitefully use you," and "if a man smite thee on the one cheek, turn to him the other also," "if he take thy coat, also let him have the cloak," &c. are commands I have ever rebelled against. I had a grudge against this man for the way Reaume and he received me at the Placid River, and had inwardly made up my mind at that time to get even on the first opportunity. And now, I reasoned, with a grunt of satisfaction, my turn comes. I was mighty pleased to inform that fascinating? young gentleman, I had not a thing to eat in the larder, that I was not hungry, nor likely to be again that day; and I had just fared sumptuously, and given the residue to Nip and the cats. He remarked, he was satisfied he could not scare up a fire in such weather, and with no dry wood at hand. I told him I had done it to satisfy my hunger, and so could he, and I showed him the place where my fire had been, now of course cold and dank like the rest of nature, for what embers there were left, I had carefully extinguished, and stowed away, as dry kindling for my next meal, and which I did not think fit to produce. He said he was very hungry, but he would starve before he would make any useless attempt at getting up a meal, and in high dudgeon he left his orders, and started back to join his mates, my last shot at him recommending him to be more of a philosopher.

A poor wretch of a mule, having cut an artery on the way here, is under my charge, and stands near my tent, humped up, the very picture of woe, tied as he is to a tree, and shivering with cold. He has no alternative but to starve until the train arrives, when a quantity of grass will be brought for him. Out of pity for the poor brute, I have doled him out a little Flour, but we may not feed mules on so precious an article.

Two trains reached me late this evening, with cargo's, as I anticipated, badly damaged. As no fording places could be found, the packs had to be seperated, and a portion left behind, and the animals, lightly loaded, with cargo likely to receive the least injury, were swam accross the several fording places where bottom could not be reached. The rain still coming down, and the whole valley like a lake. Thus, under the present state of affairs I exist. My drenched clothing is taken off at night, wrung out, and I turn into my equally wet blankets. When resuming my clothing in the morning, I shiver all over, and the teeth chatter, as I dolefully reflect how difficult it will be to prepare a meal, and as the old saying goes "Misery loves company", I found my quandom friends, the packers reduced to the same straits as myself. And—yes, they swear harder about it than I have yet thought it necessary to do, although, I fear me, I am not much given to the admonitions of conscience. I presume though, he would be a very Job himself who could, whether necessarily or unnecessarily, submit without murmer to this unhappy state of things. Imagine men like these; hard worked, forever wet, and poorly lodged, rising early on such mornings as we are experiencing, and instead of a warm solid breakfast, stand shivering and swallow slapjacks half baked, larded over probably with bacon grease, or maybe a rasher of Bacon, the appetite for such viands stimulated by a muddy compound honored with the cognomen of Coffee, the beans probably placed in a piece of canvas, and bruised between two rocks, and when dished out having neither the aroma nor flavor of that refreshing beverage. All this may be borne, but when the men see their animals famished, every limb trembling, ears down, and to appearance half drowned, it will send the ill nature bubbling to the surface, and when he opens his safety valve, and vents his spleen, the oaths roll out in a volume. There is ever a rude sympathy between the Packer and his charges, and here they are compelled to secure them with lariets through the night to prevent them making back tracks to the feeding ground.

There is another source of trouble also—the feed is dying off, and we must hurry the goods forward, 'ere the animals become too weak; many of them are becoming considerably hogbacked, and their bones are more sharply outlined than is agreeable, nor is this all, the constant wet and chafing of the gear is producing nasty sores on some of them.

On the 5th I had to saddle a mule, and ride back to Boat Encampment to look after certain matters, before finally vacating that locality. My duties compelled me to remain longer than was agreeable, not having much spare time to go there, transact my business, and return in one day, and when yet 6 miles from my depot, it became so dark I could not see the mules ears, and she was well graced in that quarter; the darkness of night was as complete as it could be; and I therefor let the reins fall on the animals neck, and trust to her instinct; my only fear was she might turn back, and make for feed again; I could see nothing of the streams as she splashed into them, keeping a firm grip on the horn of the saddle as I felt her going deeper into the flood. It was a strange sensation, I felt the water first on my legs, then to my waist, as she commenced swimming and snorting, then I could feel her touch bottom, and walk over solid ground, and this aquatic travel continued as long as the ride lasted. But after what seemed to me half the night of this duck puddling, I found her quickening her pace, and finally with a loud neigh she put into a trot; listening, and hearing no response, I was satisfied she had kept on to my solitude, where nothing could be save the cats, if I exclude the wild animals. Nip I could not induce to remain, and I had little doubt he was somewhere at my heels. At last she stopped, and I got down, and stiff and sore groped my way to my tent, turned into my wet blankets, and slept soundly.

On the 6th a train came in from the front, and after loading, left again, the distance being but short; being short handed, I volunteered to accompany them a short distance, and render what help I could. I got back again just before dark, drenched as usual, the rain not having let up one iota. My mule suppered on slap jacks and Flour, before being tied up for the night. During the day I had a Bear adventure, although I did not figure very conspicuous, nor can I pat myself on the back for any bravery—if discretion be the better part of valour, I was discrete enough.

At an old camping ground of the party, and as we were tightening the ropes on the animals packs, before crossing a deep fording place, two of the Packers who were some distance from the others, I observed were shying stones into the bushes; the dog at my heels observing them likewise tore up to the spot barking furiously. Guessing it was some animal they were throwing at, I took no further notice; but presently one of the men shouted to me to bring up my Rifle. It so happened I had not my Rifle with me, only my Revolver; I went forward however, to satisfy my curiosity, and found a more than half grown Cinnamon Bear was in the old camp, and Master Nip skipping around him at a respectful distance. Bruin had his temper pretty well aroused was evident; and as the dog kept harassing him, darting at his heels, his time was pretty well occupied. Knowing full well my Pistol was about of as much use as a boys Pop Gun, I did not quite stomach the idea of going near him, but as mine appeared to be the only offensive weapon at hand, and fearing to be considered to have shown the white feather, I advanced, determined not to fire until close upon him, and inwardly praying he would turn and run, and I have no doubt such a move would have suited him, only for the dogs movements. After several attempts to strike Nip down, he turned his attention to me; I was now getting uncomfortably close. I encouraged Nip all I could to worry him, and that I beleive, and that alone, kept him from attacking me. Opening his cavernous mouth, he advanced a few steps, and reared; but Nip was upon him from behind, and he dropped, and made for the dog, then ran off a few paces and faced and reared again as I still kept advancing, and Nip was attacking at all points at once, the bearship likewise thought as I did, and took to his heels, crashing through the thicket, with Nip closely following.

Now, I am aware the Dog could do no harm to such an animal, beyond harassing him, but he did so most effectually, and I was glad when he came trotting back, with his tongue out, and highly delighted doubtless at his success. I can't understand why the packers were without arms; it is the first and only time I ever caught them so. As a general thing, they are not happy save with a revolver slung to them. I thought bear signs were thick enough at Placid river and along Kimbasket Lake, but here, one cant go a hundred yards scarcely without seeing signs, and their droppings are everywhere. This is to be accounted for in a measure, feed having become now scarce on the steep sides of the hills, they are forced into the valley. Moose and Elk for herbage, and the tender branches; and bear for the Skunk Cabbage and berries &c. My camp is I dare say a bonanza they covet, and I am satisfied there are always some lurkers in my neighbourhood, not only by the restless movements of the dog, but I can hear them, and not unfrequently smell them during the night. When upon Skunk Cabbage, their droppings can be smelt quite a distance. The Bacon, Sugar &c are delicacies Bear are extremely fond of. I hardly dare venture to think what might be the result had I to dispense with the bright light in my tent throughout the night, with so many ursine neighbours near, and so many toothsome dainties around me.

I had forgotten to mention that I endeavoured to make a sketch of some light foliage up a gulch not far from my camp, and during a respite the rain god had given us, fortunate for me probably, I was partially hidden by low shrubs in the valley, and seated as I was upon a piece of drift timber, only my head and shoulders were visible. I had made some progress with my sketch, and was about quitting the spot, when I heard a rustling amid the foliage I had been penciling down, and so waited patiently to see what came of it. I guessed it was a bear, as I knew it was a heavy body moving about. But I got

URSA MAJOR.

my Rifle ready, hoping it might proove to emerge an Elk or Moose. At length it did emerge, and shaped itself into the powerful form of a Grizzly—and such a monster I had never beheld, looking to me as large as an ox. He was evidently a patriarch among his savage bretheren, as grizzly an old rascal as could well be imagined. The hide appeared as though it laid in flaps or plaits over his shoulders, and as he stood irresolute, looking up and down the Valley, my heart went pit a pat, for I feared every moment he would observe me, and being on the open ground, I had no friendly tree I could take shelter in. The idea of conquering such an animal with my Winchester never occurred to me, and I dare not fire; luckily it did not take him long to decide his course, which was away from my camp, and up the Valley towards the foot of the pass. I watched him leasurely shambling off, and finally had the satisfaction of seeing him turn a bend in the foot hills and disappear, a veritable Sampson.

Octr 8th

1872

With my Blankets and a Stationery Box on one mule, and riding another, I left my depot by order, and pushed on to join the Party, leaving McNeal, who brought my marching orders, to take my place until the Packers arrived. At night I camped in the pass at the first likely place I could find, thankful the rain had somewhat moderated. The following day I waded through another Valley in the Pass, equally lake like, and in consequence, could not distinguish the tracks of the animals, so was at a loss where to find their fording places through the many crossings of this tortuous stream, and I was no end of time in trying point after point 'ere I succeeded in reaching the further end. It was none the less trying to my not very mild temper that I had to lead my pack mule, and I thought the stubborn brute would have pulled the arm out of my body, and on more than one occasion he came nigh unseating me while making bad crossings. I had the good luck though to do my fording without swimming, I got into my camping ground early, at the end of this Valley, where I found Hall waiting for me; The Mexican train having, he told me, left shortly before my arrival. Hall was therefor the only individual in camp, the party being further in advance. Being hungry, I made enquiries about something to eat; and was much chagrined to find Hall had stupidly let the Mexicans get away with every available cooking utensil; and even worse than this, he had secured nothing from their cook eatable 'ere they left. However we went at it, and improvised means as usual to furnish ourselves with Cakes and Bacon, and our appetites appeased, we enjoyed the balance of the day, at least I did.

On the following day I took the Pack animal and forged ahead (to use a nautical expression), Hall releiving me of my riding mule, on which he left for my old camp ground. The trail I found led up the steep backbone of a mountain. talk of Alpine climbing! there was no avoiding it, it was a breather, and no mistake. The trains had to struggle up this steep ascent very lightly loaded. The extent of this weary traveling was about five miles; three of which were exceedingly steep. It remains a puzzle to me to this day how the animals, in their weakened condition, succeeded in conveying the stores up this incline. But once I had reached the upper level, I was not long in experiencing how beneficial the change was; away from the lower Valleys and swollen streams; I stand to rest, and rest my blown dumb friend, and I see through an opening in the timber, heavy rolling clouds far beneath me, and which are doubtless discharging their apparant in-exaustable moisture over the lower lands, and while as for some time old sol has not shown his fiery face to me, I now feel his rays, and see them checkered through the waving pine boughs overhead. Well, thought I, it is well worth the climb, I can surely feel happier here than in the heavily charged atmosphere below, and I felt the air bracing as I drank deep of it; the rarified air had an invigorating effect. The ascent, during the last 3 miles was 2,040 feet.

Having rested, I started again, but had not proceeded far when I came upon a depot, with Reaume in charge. According to instructions, on my arrival, he left for the second summit, further on. My new depot is guarded on the right by the lofty hood of Mount Hooker, 15.700 ft. and on the left, further in advance, the still loftier Mount Brown, 15.890 feet above sea level.

Forward is the watch word, and everything is hurry in consequence. Men and animals are put to their best licks, our goods are away behind us for the main part, and where I now stand we are at an elevation of 6500 feet, in the heart of the Rockys, full 50 miles from where we may hope to winter, and winter may close his icy fingers upon us any day. It must be bourne in mind 50 miles is a long distance where no trail exists, nor ever has existed; in fact the section of country through which we are traveling wholly unexplored, and every mile to be contended with, swamps to be crossed, heavy timber to be hacked through, and dense undergrowth to be leveled for our animals. No place, so far as known, to winter our mules until the goal is reached, hence all energy must be put forth to reach the broad plateau in the mountains where the traders of the Hudsons Bay Company once had a fort or post,

MOUNT BROWN. 15.890. feet.

as also I believe the Great American North West Company, all long since abandoned.

Yesterday, I up stakes again, and moved on towards the summit of the pass: I had been told what a grand sketch it would make, and had decided to hurry and try my hand at the attempt, if ever so poor the attempt might be.

I would not have you run away with the idea I had any hopes of making even a presentable picture, I am not that conceited. I ought to know my own failings, and if I did not, I should richly deserve to be laughed at. The poor apology for a picture I try to possess myself of, is probably, as satisfactory to me as one of ever so much merit to a competent artist. I do as he does probably. I like to do my best, and am content if the picture pleases my fancy.

And as I was never taught drawing, surely it would be unfeeling to laugh at my efforts, be they ever so poor. I cannot embellish, but try to do the job as neatly as I know how, and

October 18th.

72

make as faithful picture as I know how. And if I succeed sufficiently to render it unnecessary for me to write on my
sketches "This is supposed to be water," or "This I mean for a
mountain"—or "You must suppose this is a forest"—if all this
becomes unnecessary, then you must rest as I do, contented.

I cannot conceive a more miserable day for my hoped for
view and sketch, even the packers had told me it was a beautiful sight at the summit, and they are not men likely to go into
raptures at a pretty picture of natures, but the sky looked
threatening 'ere we got started, although it had not yet commenced to rain. At the foot of a steep ascent I left the train,
and made what haste I could toward the summit; and as I
ascended, I caught glimpses of Mighty Glaciers through the
timber, and I believed the Packers, when they told me it beat
anything they had ever seen; and I was in a fever to gain the
summit. And after all I was to be disappointed. I was not to
see their description of the immense mountains on either side
of the summit rent and split asunder, and the crevises thus
formed burdened with glaciers hundreds of feet deep, blue
walls of cold ice, and the beautiful cascade like a horses tail
pouring from one of them, the summit of the pass proper
formed like a huge bowl, or the punch bowl as they called it. I
scarce felt fatigue as I hurried on, on foot, until, suddenly
turning a bluff of rock, I observed right before me, as if to bar
all further passage, a wall of ice, solid, and I should suppose
two hundred feet in depth, supported on either side by jagged
peaks of dark rock, their spiral peaks cutting upward, hoary
likewise with crowns and garlands of ice and snow. I had
heated myself in my haste, and now the close proximity of
this mass seemed to chill me to the marrow. I left the mule
path, and picking my way among huge fragments of the slippery substance, I passed on. Oh! how I wished I could transfer
even this beauty spot of Gods nature to paper, or that I could
draw a pen picture worthy of it. But pshaw—I am a poor
untaught mortal, I can only see and wonder. See sketch page
125 [in original journal; "Athabasca Pass"].

But the day was wearing on apace, and large flakes of snow warned me I must not delay. Soon the snow fell fast, and when I reached the summit, the wind was howling through the pass, unfelt until I reached the higher point. The hailstones which occasionally deversified the dismal state of affairs, cut like a knife, and during a lull in the snow storm, I could only see the bases of the mountains on either hand, the clouds overhead hanging low and pall like, black, threatening, and floating like huge wings, giving one a depressed feeling, spite of the cutting wind, all on earth visible being an unshapely mass of sterility, huge fragments of rock intersperced with the fast whitening ground on which I trod, fragments from those mighty Cathedrals of nature I knew were far over my head, with the storm king now whirling in mad career round their silent peaks. I caught a glimpse of the commencement of the descent of the eastern slope, wearing a bright look, and disappointed as I was, and wet and cold, with a sense of depression caused probably by the reaction, and the black canopy overhead of threatening clouds, yet the glimpse of brightness beyond, and towards which I was hastening, had its charm for me, and I laughed inwardly, and wondered if it was an omen, an omen for good, and if bright days were coming for me ever. Alas, I found a few days after, and while amid that patch of brightness, as seen from the summit, that not yet were the bright days for me. I had yet to hear of the death of my wife; and I had yet to suffer another loss, the pain of which did not leave me for many a day. And a gush of tender memories comes upon me now while I write, for a truer friend would be hard to find than poor dog Nip.

I did get a rude sketch under difficulties, and in a very hasty manner, the snow blurring the paper the while, and my fingers so numb I could scarce hold my pencil.

On this summit there are three small Lakes, scarce larger in fact than good sized Ponds, but about which there is something worth notice. The extent of the summit is probably two miles long by half a mile broad, therefore these three lakes cannot be very extensive, nor do they cover one half of this plateau, but what is worth recording of them, is, that the one nighest the point from which I advanced discharges itself down the west slopes of the Rocky's, thence into the Columbia River, whose waters are poured into the Pacific Ocean. The other two small Lakes start brawling and leaping down the eastern slopes of the Rocky's, gathering strength through a long course of travel, until reaching the McKenzie River in the Susquatchwan Country, they roll on mingled with the waters of that frozen river, and finally empty into the Arctic Ocean. These Lakes are not a stones throw from each other, yet how widely are they seperated when they lose themselves into the ocean. They were all frozen over when I passed along their margins.

I reached our newly formed Depot as darkness was stealing up from the Valleys below; the snow, which had been falling on this eastern slope for many hours I found 'ere I reached camp nigh two feet in depth: luckily for me, the formation of the ground was such that I experienced no great difficulty in finding my way; had it been otherwise, I should probably have perished: I was about beat out when I came suddenly upon life. I passed two of our men camped nigh the summit making a cache for storing supplies, with whom I left poor Nip completely tuckered out; they were anxious I should remain likewise, but I was anxious to reach the Depot some five miles further on.

I said I came upon life at the Depot, which I scarcely did; Dick White and Old Man Smith were there, and as they had a tent pitched, had betaken themselves to it, and had turned into their Blankets, not expecting me in such a storm. That I was hungry, wet and tired may be supposed, and that I felt mad as a hornet upon finding no fire after reckoning upon a cheerful blaze may also be imagined; and as these heroic individuals seemed to show no disposition to throw in one crumb of comfort, I had of necessity to try [to] build a fire myself, and it was with no little difficulty I did so, there being no material on hand save wet wood, and that I had to cut myself. White and Smith had actually lain in their tent since morning, and had preferred to go supperless to bed rather than bestir their latent energies; we all bestired ourselves though, when a hot fire had induced them to throw off their torpor, and all three did justice to a hastily cooked supper.

The train did not reach that night, nor could it be expected; I therefor concluded to share their Blankets, but not being sufficient covering for us all; in fact they were lightly supplied with covering anyhow, for we had come up suddenly from an autumn climate to midwinter; and as I could not take off my clothing, I lay as long as I was able to bear it, wet and shivering, then got upon my feet, determined to keep up a good fire for the night and dry off outside, the snow having entirely ceased.

Today was a very sad one for me. Today I received the first intimation of my poor wifes death. White and Smith had gone on, on the return of daylight, leaving me as usual to myself. In fact they were only there temporary, or until my arrival. I was busy setting my supplies in order, when an empty train drove in from the front, enroute to the first summit, Rheume being with them; he brought me instructions to move on at once, a train of twenty-six additional animals had reached the party ahead, and also some men. They were a portion of Mohons Surveyors, and had been surveying towards us through the Selkirk range and Eagle Pass. Mohon and his party were on their way to the lower country, having completed their section of work, and had sent on his spare supplies to us, also sufficient men to cut their way through. I had to go forward and receive over these supplies, and take up men and animals on our Books &c. Rheume also informed me several letters had arrived, letters which had been sent to Mohons party in error from time to time, but that there were none for me. I brooded over this for some time while preparing to leave, and finally asked Rheume again, "Are you quite sure there was not a letter for me." He said he was quite sure, he heard all the names called. Presently I said, "Rheume, this

Saturday
Octr 19.

72

117

is becoming unbearable. If I had left a healthy wife I should have felt bad enough, but I must do something. He then said, Jane has joined us, he knows you, and gave me a message for you. Jane was an old Sapper, and a fine straightforward man—John Jane being his full name. He was a Surveyor, an officer in Mohons Party, and in that capacity had joined us. Asking Rheume for his message, he handed me a slip of paper, upon which were the following words "Dear Rylatt, The papers state your wife has passed beyond the stream of time. Dont be too cut up, dear old fellow." It was a shock, yet I hardly felt it just then. Rheume told me he hated to give me the paper, knowing the contents. I told him I did not know just yet if it might not be good news, as I knew the worst, but later on, when again left alone, and when remembering the last loving wail in the last letter she ever dictated, "Oh! Bob! do come back, I cannot bear it"— the words cut like a knife, what misery for the next few days especially. I hardly remember how I got through my work, I have only a keen sense that a great trouble had come upon me, and a weight of sorrow that bowed me down. Oh: what would I not have given to have been transported to her grave, that I might there give full vent to my feelings; but here, how could I be otherwise than I was, left all alone, not one human being to speak to, only my dumb friend Nip as a companion.

Rheume had told me the party had known for several days of my wifes death, the informer being a Douglas Indian who had known her, and who had joined with the train. And this was all I could glean, no particulars whatever. Your wife is dead! no more, and this state of things only made it the harder to suffer under.

To return. I at once packed up my blankets, received that morning, putting in my Haversack such books as I could carry, and mounting a Cayoosh from the train, Rheume and I set out. Old Man Smith, who had gone on as before stated, was brought back, and assumed charge. I unfortunately got on to a bucking, walleyed animal, with as mean a disposition as it is possible for a horse to possess; in fact I paid no attention to him when saddled for me, being too full of trouble; the wretched animal started all right, and seemed gentle enough, until we came to a big mud hole, when he tried to dislodge me by drawing his legs together, humping his back, and making sudden and ugly jumps; finding this was not a success, he tried to get his head round to bite at my legs; he evidently wanted me in that mud hole; had he not been up to his knees in sticky mud, he would have succeeded better, but it prevented his jumping very high, although he tried hard enough. I pounded the brute over the head and ears with the butt of my Pistol, the only thing I had at hand to chastise him with. At the foot of a steep rise he made another attempt, and succeeded in pitching me into the midst of a thorn bush, badly shook up. But this evidently was not sufficient for him; he intended to repay me for the pummeling I had given him, and turning his heels towards me, he backed himself up, set his ears back, and let fly with all his might; at every kick he let out a squeal of rage. It was lucky for me the bush was very thick, and that the final hoist he gave me was sufficient to settle me all in a heap in the midst of it, and still more fortunate that Rheume was with me, or I fear the beast would have succeeded in reaching me, and kicking the life out of me. He was finally cooled down, and the Pack animal I had at the last moment concluded to take along, being unloaded, the pack was put upon him, which he took to quietly enough, having never before been ridden I fancy. Mounting the other nag, we reached the depot two hours after dark, when I turned in, and passed a wretched night.

And now, as though to verify the old proverb "Misfortunes never come singly", I had to bear another stroke of sorrow, and if it was only a dog, it was the loss of a very dear and tried friend nevertheless.

Three days after receiving knowledge of my wifes death, and while brooding alone in my tent, I was startled by a strange cry; and on rushing out, saw my faithful dog in the river, struggling to free himself, and get to shore. I hastened to the bank, and fancied I could see a gleam of pleasure in his eyes as I drew near calling to him, but at this place the water was deep and swift, and ice had formed along the shores on either side, but not sufficiently thick to bear my weight. Nip had ventured on it to get a drink I suppose, and it had broken at the extreme edge with his weight; he was therefor some thirty feet from me; his forepaws were on the ice, and he was vainly struggling to raise himself. I could see that his paws were cut and bleeding with his frantic struggles, and his tongue, hanging out of his mouth, was also bloody, having bitten it I suppose in his efforts. I was half beside myself, rushing hither and thither in the vain hope of finding something wherewith to reach him: to get a pole long enough was out of the question, but finally I secured a rope, and attempted to lasso him, but without success. I could see the poor brute becoming weaker with each effort (he must have been some time in the water), while his pitiful whines, and my inability to save him, made my heart swell, and cries of distress escaped me, almost as pitiful as his own. Not a soul was within many miles of us; every effort I made with the rope of no avail; and I could only see my only friend, whom I dearly loved, dying a painful death. Oh! God, I cried in my distress, must everything be taken from me? At last his struggles ceased; his paws gradually slipped from the ice; then one more weak effort, and with a cry that wrung in my ears many a day, and with his loving eyes full upon me, as if in sad reproach, the greedy waters covered him, and I was alone indeed. Ah! but it was hard. But I have done. Sketch. Page 129 [of the original journal; "Death of Nip"].

I have read somewhere, "Who can enter into the penetralia of the affections, weigh and estimate anguish, count the heart drops of sorrow, and say, here is so much misery, or, there is so much of resignation."

Thursday
Octr 30.

72

Made another start towards the party today. Hall has asked me to procure him, if possible, a suit of skin clothing from the Indians, and I am desirous of fitting myself out with a suit. I am told a few Indians have visited the party, and are disposed to be very friendly. They are Assignaboines, and are tall, well made men; Hall says their habits are extremely primitive, and although an agent of the Hudsons Bay Company visits them yearly at a place some 24 miles beyond where the party have now reached, yet these children of the Plains and forests had no idea what Flour was used for, looking upon it curiously, and tasting bread with suspicion. The food of these people consists mainly of Roots dug from the swamps, Berries, and game. The game being preserved as pemican.

I may as well state here that Pemican, as I found later on, is a very strengthening, and economical food, and is prepared in this way. The flesh of the Moose and Buffalo is freed from the bone, minced up fine, then placed in bags made of the hide of the animal, the hair of course outside, after which the fat and marrow is boiled down and poured over and through the meat, which, when set becomes a solid mass. No salt or other seasoning is used, your primitive Indian does not understand such luxuries. After partaking of this food a few times, I grew very fond of it, and it is astonishing how small a quantity will satisfy a man. I should desire nothing better than a limited supply of Pemican with me when traveling. Half a pound or so thrust into a mans pocket, and which he can nibble at when becoming hungry, returning the fatty lump from whence it came after breaking off a small mouthful, is not only convenient, but a want supplied. In the mountains, a grease spot or two more upon our not over clean garments dont matter; we are not apt to be fastidious, or turn up our noses at trifles; I have known men [to] carry a chunk of Pemican, a peice of Tobacco, a comb, and possibly a peice of soap in a rag in the one pocket, and with unclean hands fish out the Pemican, take a bite, pass it over to their chum, who also digs his teeth into it, said chum relishing the morsel immensely.

I have said men who have been long in the mountains are in general not over fastidious, not over nice with reference to eating and drinking, and such has been my observations and experience. You must not understand me to mean, a man will as soon take up a dirty platter as a clean one: by no means: he will pick up the clean platter all the time; he is not fond of dirt, but he becomes so used to taking his meals as he can catch them, frequently without any plate, and as frequently with nothing better at his disposal than a very dirty plate, that he is exceedingly cleanly if he snatches up a few leaves or a handful of grass and gives said plate a wipe off. He gets his meals anyhow, and is content anyhow so that he gets them.

Why, how often in a city do you see men who will take a chew of Tobacco from anyone who offers it: the giver in all probability taking it from his not over clean breeches pocket; and the other does not stay to examine it, or wipe it, but digs his teeth into the very spot where his neighbor has deposited some of the tartar from his teeth, and yet mister man, city man, lays it to his cheek, giving it an occasional squeeze and enjoys it. Where's the difference?

Jack Cox I believe, procured a Moose skin coat and Pants for a couple of worn out shirts, Benson a pair of Mocassins for a needle, some others of the party trading old clothing for Mocassins, Pants and coats of Buckskin, and whosoever was fortunate enough to have a Blanket to trade away, could get skins for the same worth at least $25. or $30. if taken to market.

On page 127 [of the original journal] will be found a sketch of Mount Hooker, before mentioned, with two trees, at probably an old camping place, and which had been done 45 years ago; but I have committed a blunder; I should have said, two trees bearing marks, which had been done 45 years before our advent, and before your hopeful son was introduced into this world of ups and downs. I surmise the marks spoken of to have been the work of some of the Hudsons Bay traders, or else that of explorers, decidedly not gold hunters, for the precious metal was not thought of hereaway at that period. Upon one of these trees, cut in with a knife, were the letters PNK, and upon the other, J.H. Octr 2nd 1827, thickly marked with a lead underline pencil, but not cut in. Prior to forming these initials and date, the axe had been employed to

ATHABASCA PASS. ROCKY MOUNTAINS.
Ice gorge. near first summit.

make an evan surface. There would be nothing worth mentioning in all this, if the knife had cut the whole of these characters into the wood; especially this wood, the mountain fir. Some of the softer varieties would have outgrown these marks, so as to render them illegible, the Alder and Birch, or the Cotton wood for instance; but these pencil marks were as fresh as the hour after the hand that traced them in an idle moment, put past his pencil, and thought no more of them. The resinous substance had oozed out from the wound made in cutting out a flat or tablet surface, and had covered completely the injured part, thereby not only healing by excluding the air, but preserving beneath a transparant glaze, the mutilaters handiwork.

On the 2d November (my birthday by the way), I reached the depot; but not the party, who were several miles ahead. This spot had been picked upon by our chief for our winters quarters; and glad I felt when I thought that at last a resting place had been found for the supplies moving ever onward, becoming beautifully lessoned by constant handling, the inroads made by the mules especially, and the action of the weather. The hot suns had fried out about all the grease from the bacon, leaving little beyond the leathery skin and rancid lean, and the gunnie bags containing the same, and which at starting were plump and well favored, were now soggy with grease, ragged with wear and tear, and dirtier than a squaws petticoat with dirt contamination.

I was delighted to find company here, McCord, with a few of the axemen, who were hard at work in this hitherto solitude, felling and hewing timber for the construction of the necessary houses; and I was made welcome and comfortable by them. Two famous storehouses were already completed, each having a fireplace; and I lost no time in selecting the one best adapted for my quarters, such being the instructions left by the chief, especially as my storehouse would contain the more important of the supplies, such as Clothing, Provisions &c. McCord, doubtless judging my choice, had fixed me up a bunk near our primitive fireplace, and I was soon comfortably settled, for with our nomad mode of existance, we soon settle down, and are perfectly at home.

Today I passed the site of what was called the "Henry house", and at a mile or two from this depot, but no sign remained of this once trading post of the Great Northwestern Company, save one solitary post, and the main feature for the eye to dwell upon, beyond the scenery of wood and plain and distant mountain top, being a lone grave (Indian I presume), a sad rag of something flaunting to the breeze from a pole, doubtless a ragged blanket, for which the occupant of that quite grave had hunted and packed peltries to the amount of two or more hundred dollars (market value) to obtain in trade from his white brother. "Sketch on Page 133" [of the original journal; "Meeting of the Athabasca and Leatherhead Passes"].

In the days when the Great North Western Company of Fur traders were in existance, great rivalry existed; the old

Sketched at an elevation of 7000 feet.

MOUNT HOOKER. 15.700 feet.
Initials found on trans. dated 1827.

established Hudsons Bay Company of England, who first obtained their Royal charter from King Charles 2d (I think), and who considered themselves the rightful claimants to all hunting grounds within certain paralells, the limits of which immence territory I don't know, and who, if all be true, did not confine themselves to any limits, but made war upon all who hunted and trapped in the dangerous solitudes of this vast northern country, whose servants were a hardy, though often a harassed and ill fed community, whose humbler staff were many of them kidnapped from their dear old homes in bonny Scotia, and got only the dogs bone when removed to these wilds; who from their better, or more fortunate brothers in exile, received often short rations, (meager at best,) stripes; nay, life and death were in the hands of the factor and chief traders; who if all be true, drove the common horde with, and fed them with the dogs of their sledges. Between this great company of traders, whose heads were in merry England, and were the stars of nobility, between these and the new sprung up Great North western Company, great rivalry existed, and many collisions, and as a natural consequence, where no law but the law of might was observed, much bloodshed. But the Great Northwestern Company has passed away, also The Charter of that Royal libertine is expending itself, for the steady tramp of the vast army of civilization is crowding West, North and South. The might of the great Hudsons Bay Company, whose sole object was to keep the Indian, and its own employees in ignorance, is succombing to the great army of advancement; and the day is coming, please God, when that stain shall be wiped out, and the surplus of civilization shall find new fields for industry, and the merry laugh of the white child shall take the place of the whoop of the savage, and the bark of the traders dog train.

We shall have about 40 men all told, to winter here.

This place, picked upon for our winters quarters, is in a Valley, not altogether open, but densely wooded in sections with black fir and alder, and portions of it is also swampy, though not bearing that impress to the eye. During heavy freshets, much of this Valley becomes flooded, as is plainly indicated, and the whirlpool river, flowing from its source at the summit of the Athabasca pass, winds through the Valley, and during the autumn, as seen in my sketch, with everything green (the grass starts late in the mountains) it is very pleasing to the eye, and the Meyette River, whose source is at the summit of the Leather head Pass, meanders through the limited extent of Valley through which it flows; and after a noisy whirling and swirling, as if loath to join its sister river, the combined forces of which push rapidly onward, gathering strength from innumerable mountain snows, finally emptying into the Athabasca River proper, and from thence into the great Slave lake, whose surplus waters, discharged into the McKenzie River, find their level at last in the Arctic Ocean.

On my arrival, I was informed the party had suspended work eastward, and had gone to the summit of the Leatherhead, from thence surveying back to this point, and onward

"DEATH OF NIP."

" Then one more weak effort, with a cry that wrung in my ears for many a day, and with his loving eyes full upon me, as if in sad reproach, the greedy waters covered him, and I was alone indeed."

as before. Fort Edmonton, a prominent Hudsons Bay Company Fort, about 300 miles distant, being our terminus.

McCord showed me some very fine dressed skins of the Moose and Bear, which Moberly and others had procured at some trifling compensation, and which, he alleged were to be cut up for making into Mocassins &c.

Of the Indian mode of dressing skins I pretend to no knowledge, but I beleive they are submerged in water to loosen the hair, which is then easily removed with a kind of chisel made of hard wood. All fatty substance adhering to the hide is also removed, then the brains of the animal is rubbed well in on both sides, making the hide soft and pliable; lastly, it is stretched to its utmost limit, and firmly pegged down, and left to dry.

All this is the labor of their women, in fact anything like labor or drudgery is done by them. A hard lot surely, the life of a squaw. Packed like beasts of burden (which by the way they are), their lords leading, or leasurely following with an old flint lock musket, and a knife, the bigger the better. Indians in their primitive condition, and very many who are not, think it degrading to toil; the noble red devil is many degrees above it, his partner (or partners) of the opposite sex must labor for him. He is much of a polygamist, and where the white mans pernicious laws do not restrain him, he has his slaves, male and female, to do his bidding; part in fact of his goods and chattels, to be pinned, or tied to a tree if he can afford the luxury, and made targets of for the arrows of his friends during their great feasts; to be sold or swapped from master to master, tribe to tribe; females especially, to be beaten unmercifully when fancy leads, or blame is attached, and all to be received patiently and unmurmuringly. To be fed with the remains of the feast, be it little or much: when their lord has sufficiently gorged himself. The life of an Indian woman is truly a hard one, and woe betide her if she looses favor; and if she is only sold or exchanged, 'tis merciful; but often more brutal measures are adopted, especially if she is old, or not strong to labor; 'tis then the troubles of the poor wretch are cut short by an exit some way to the happy hunting grounds, a favorite method with the nomads of the interior being, to club out their brains, or leaving them at some old camping place, if old, to starve to death.

This is the noble red man novelists tell us of, that Fennimore Cooper extols! The noble? red man is a savage every inch, and nobleness and savagery do not mix well: The word savage means wild, cruel, uncivilized; and I must confess, I have been cast in their midst, living in their Villages, and seen more of them and their habits than falls to the lot of most men, and I have yet to find any disinterested good in their natures. I recopy these memoirs in the midst of one of their Villages, the Quinaielt Reservation, where my boy Ernest first saw the light. I have been acting agent on two several agencies, have been clerk; taught their young; have seen nigh all the tribes west of the Rockys between the 46th

Sketched at an Elevation of 7000 feet.

ATHABASCA PASS. ROCKY. MTS.
Second Summit.

and 54th Parallels, and also some of the tribes east of those mountains, yet I can truthfully state I have seen nothing to recommend them, no trait of character, individually or collectively, worthy of the slightest notice, nothing disinterested, and I do not confine myself to their behaviour towards the whites. I allude equally to their bearing towards each other. The white mans teaching, be it ever so good, cannot destroy the devil in them as it would savages of almost any other country. Theirs is a stubborn nature: resisting, as strongly as they would voluntarily giving themselves up to death, habits that compelled them to totally abandon the ceremonies and pastimes of their fathers. I have had bright boys and girls leave school, and the brightest in intellect, have generally turned out the most degraded when becoming masters of their own actions. Our Philanthropists may tell you what they will, my knowledge of my red neighbour leads me to speak as I do. Morality they have none; nor can you teach them its blessings, gratitude is a virtue they do not positively possess. there is a stubborn subtle demon inherent in a North American Indian that cannot apparantly be overcome, nor driven out. The Papoose (or child) sucks it from the breast of its mother: and as it grows older, nothing forms so good a plaything, or so meets with the parants approval, as something to torture. A bird for instance, the parant shows the child the most approved plan of making it cry out and struggle, if a gull or a crow, one of the youthful delights being to pluck all the feathers, save those of the wings, and let the naked bird go. Putting out their eyes—pulling off legs, and all this is instilled into their young minds. Seldom a cat in an Indian Village but is minus ears or tail. And so 'tis, that when manhood (forgive the term), I should have said when they become old enough to take any active part in the doings of their tribe or nation, the brutal instinct of the savage "torture" is fully developed, and thus it is that the demons dance and yell, while the victim squirms in his great agony, while the women begrudge that torture has its limits and will kill, and will foam and work themselves into the fury of incarnate devils. I may be reminded of here and there a tribe, like the Iroquois in Canada; the Cherokees for instance; who sow and reap, and who have distinguished men among them, but these are a few peoples who have not been driven north and west by the tide of civilization, whose homes were dearer to them than the hated white mans presence could quench, and who besides saw their only chance was to side with the conquering, the white or ruling race: and as they became surrounded with industry, and had the alternative of work or starve set before them, and the right hand of fellowship given them by the country no longer theirs, and its laws, they could do no other than learn the white mans ways; but surely it must have been a hard lesson to learn. I dont pretend to know the history of these nations, and how very few they are compared with all of these very troublesome wards of Uncle Sam: but if you know anything of Indian character, if you read (not official reports, manufactured by officers whose duty it is to keep poor 'Lo, the Indian in leading strings as much as they are able; and render false reports to hoodwink the government, and retain their offices, as useful servants) but read,

"MEETING of the ATHABASCA and LEATHERHEAD PASSES." Site of the "Henry House": an old trading-post of the "Great North West Trading Company." —Indian grave.—

and east, west, north and south, the atrocious devils are rising, now here—now yonder, and the mangled and tortured remains of dear, innocent babies, little prattling children and their mothers, bronzed and toilworn men, gods own images, if man bears his image! all these are the achievements of the "Noble Red Man." Possibly he would be a goody, goody sort of a human, if thrown in the midst of us, and forced to struggle with the stream, or starve, this is one way in which the Indian could be deprived of his sting, if it were possible, but until they shall have become extinct, to which they are fast tending, he remains an untamable Hyena. And the accompanying sketch is as true today as it was a hundred years ago, with this difference only: the musket supersedes the Tomahawk; but let us be thankful their strength is waning fast; and the day is not far distant let us hope, when the happy hunting grounds shall have received the last of their race. I am much of the Missourian's belief, "dead Indians only, are good Indians."

It may be argued, there are not so many uprisings among the Indian Tribes as formerly; and especially in the Northern states and territories. It must be borne in mind the Indian of today is not the same power as when civilization was in its infancy in this country; when the tribes counted by the thousand, but now count by the hundred, and in some cases but a few score warriors remain to them. Tribes that were a power

His domestic relations to-day.   *As a warrior.*
"THE NOBLE RED MAN."

and a terror in the early days of the commonwealth, are now dead or scattered, so that their names are a matter of history only; in the northern states, for instance, the Indian is surrounded by the white population, whose strength is far the greater, and that, since the treaties of thirty years ago, agents, or supervisors are placed over the tribes, with a fixed residency, generally in the heart of their Villages; that said Indian agents have a corps of white employe's, and a corps of Indian Police; which last named, to use the old adage, of set a rogue to catch a rogue, are the best adapted for the position they fill. they are fed, clothed, and paid a regular monthly salary; they know all the tricks of their people, and are on the alert to gain information, and tattle every little passing event. The agent and his white associates become acquainted with the habits of the Indians they govern; and the Indian himself, who has a wholesome dread of the bluecoated soldiers, and the power of Pen, Ink and Paper, is kept in order by fear, and not as some would have us beleive, by improvement in himself, and the moral effects of education and example.

There is another power by which the Indian is kept in subjection, and a very effective power to boot. Each tribe, though recognizing a head chief, has several chiefs in reality; all alike ambitious, all pushing forward their claims; attaching to themselves, each his adherents. Hence, the tribes are broken into factions (encouraged by the agent) all anxious to rule, all wanting the supremacy, and jealous of each other, currying favor by reporting any real or fancied greivance, and thus, instead of unity, and a banding together in one common cause, they are distrustful of each other, as their treacherous natures would warrant.

Occasionally however, an outbreak occurs, and in thinly populated districts, and then the hostile Indians generally leave the agency in small bands, place their women and children in security, and meeting at some given point, commence an onslaught on all whites they can find, be it man, woman or child. The idea with the Indian, when going on the war path, is extermination of the whites. The death of the little infant is alike important with the braining of the adult, for "Nits make Lice" they say.

In the southern states, the Indian is ever on the war path; and outrages, as cruel as a hundred years back, show the red man has lost none of his ferocity. There, where the whites are more scattered, Uncle Sam has forts erected, and soldiers stationed. Yet the cruel Apache, and other tribes are ever harassing the sturdy white bread winner, burning homesteads; the war whoop ringing the death knell of the white settler, his wife and little ones.

But I have transgressed long enough, and will on with my little history. I found at the depot a couple of halfbreeds, big bony fellows, one of them with a little smattering of English, also French; these men have been in the employ of the Hudsons Bay Company on the plains, at Fort Edmonton, and also at Pembina. They are assisting McCord and Party to put up the buildings. Three squaws are in their company, and two or three children.

On my way here I passed the whitened skulls of many Buffalo, but the half-breeds tell me there have been none in this vicinity for some time; having been so hunted and killed by the Indians as to compel them to seek safer feeding grounds: There is much bunch grass and rich feeding here, but withered at this season.

I also came accross a Victoria Colonist Paper, containing the announcement of my wife's death; it bore date of July 31st 1872—and ran as follows.— "Mrs Rylatt, wife of Mr R. M. Rylatt, formerly of the Royal Engineers, and now engaged on the Canadian Pacific survey, died at New Westminster, on Wednesday morning last, after a lingering illness. The funeral took place on Thursday, Revd Russ officiating." The announcement did not appear in this paper until a week had expired; doubtless copied from the New Westminster Guardian.

On the first night of my arrival I was kept long awake by the howling of a pack of Kayottes (a small species of wolf, or wild dog), their number must have been considerable, by the fearful uproar.

On the 9th November the Thermometer was down to Zero, with the party and pack trains still out; thin cotton tents being but slight protection against such severe weather. As regards myself, I am at last well housed, and for once, have the advantage decidedly.

I give the latitude and longitude of this place
Lat: 53'.19" Long: [118]'.10"
      Magnetic Variation 26 -
also that of Fort Edmonton, 300 miles distant,
Lat: 53'.31".40'" N. Long: 113'.13".17'" W.

Novr 25th
[1872]

Wolves are plenty, large gaunt brutes; and the party ahead have their sentries placed to keep up the fires for warmth during the nights, and find it equally necessary to scare away these animals. The cold is increasing, last night being 14 below zero, and some eight or ten of our animals have succombed, four having been devoured by the wolves, the balance dying from exposure. Three of the animals have got badly sprained likewise, and are useless, and the remainder doing service have a hard time of it; not only by being compelled to carry extra loads, but the snow balls their feet, and the steep and slippery grades makes it a difficult matter to work them at all. Then they loose rest by cold and their terror of the famished and snarling wolf, so that work will have to be

"Handsome Harry."

suspended, the party returning to winter quarters; the animals going forward to a sheltered valley picked upon, where they will be cared for until the spring.

Herewith I copy a sketch of Harry Herbert, "Handsome Harry" a genial, good natured soul, whom we all liked. I wonder where he is now, and how all fares with him? I know but little of this mans history; but what little I know I will dot down.

"Handsome Harry" had been a Lieutenant in the British Navy, and attached to one of the Men of War stationed in the North Pacific, having got himself into serious disgrace somehow, through some wild prank; he hastily fled service, to save further disgrace by a Court Martial, but whether from advice, or from any decision of his own, he returned to his ship, was tried by a body of his fellow officers, and dismissed the service. It is generally understood by the party (though how obtained the knowledge is more than I can say), that his family are very wealthy in England, and that Harry, although ernestly solicited to return, and receive a prodigal's forgiveness, will not face his people.

Harry is very close upon his own history, and never disposed to be garrulous about himself; and resents at once any allusion to his family connections.

Upon one occasion, to illustrate the recklessness of the man, and his indifference to consequences, he was before the court for some breach of the peace, and being asked his name by "His Honor", replied, Men call me Handsome Harry, and yet there are some who call me a "bloody gut." And Harry was decidedly faulty, very faulty; he swore a good deal, and I fear where it was to be had, drank a good deal, but a man with a kinder heart would be hard to find: Light hearted, full of Jokes and briming with good humour. Yet there were despondent fits, and it was known to his fellow packers, that at times, while watching his face by the flare of the camp fire, he would be very saddened and thoughtful, and upon one occasion, when the other packers had turned into their blankets, and he probably deemed us all asleep; I heard him sigh heavily, and upon looking up, saw him staring into the fire; and I am certain there were tears on his face, and as he moved and sought his blankets, I heard him mutter—"cant be helped now, but its pretty rough."—

The sketch represents Harry as he came in from the pass.

Decr 10th

[1872]

I have been some days alone at the depot or winters quarters, with a vast amount of stores under my sole charge, and to tell truth I do not feel as secure as I have hitherto done, in a country where animals alone had to be guarded against. Here however, the case alters materially; we are now in a country where roving bands of Indians are to be met with, Indians who have known no restraint, and consequently know nothing of the white mans law of right of possession; and to whom plunder comes as natural as mothers milk. The restless spirit of the Blackfeet, Assigniboines and Crees make them more to be expected at any unlikely spot than would be looked for with many tribes, and the Blackfeet especially are no great lovers of the white man. I have a feeling that upon hearing of our vicinity some one or other of these tribes may have some of its members wander this way, and what would be easier than to plunder, from such a strong inducement, with but one man to fight against. I told Hall yesterday or the day before, I had too much respect for my scalp than to remain here alone, and that if I was not reinforced forthwith, I should leave the stores to take care of themselves, and strike out for the party in front, for not only did I consider my life unsafe, but the supplies of the party were in danger of being transported on the backs of Indian ponies. I am therefore tonight reinforced by one man, and Hall himself came along, so that there are three of us.

Last night, while we three were sat smoking in the cabin, quite a severe shock of earthquake was felt! the oscillation made us quite dizzy; and at first, each man looked at the other, thinking a feeling of dizziness had come over himself; but a low rumbling sound, not very distinct, nor very near apparantly, and the sight of the several pairs of new Boots hanging from the beams overhead, and gently swinging to and fro, convinced us of the fact. The shock was quite long, probably more than two minutes, and was from east to West; half an hour later, another shock was felt, but not so heavy, and accompanied by little or no rumbling. I fancy it gave us all a scare; I can answer for myself. There is a something so ominous, and unnatural; a threatened danger against which we feel ourselves so helpless.

Today I was strongly reinforced by the arrival from Fort Edmonton of seven Dog Sleds, or Tabogans, a Mr R. Logan, of the Hudsons Bay Company at Fort Edmonton accompanying the Dog train. This (to me), somewhat singular train have been ordered to assist in getting our stores forward, a large quantity being still in the Athabasca Pass.

This Mr Logan appears to be the trader of the Company destined to make his yearly visits to the Jasper house, about twenty one miles in advance of this depot, (a sketch of which will appear in its proper place [page 169 of original journal; "Jasper House"]) and releive the Indians of their peltries, who

Sunday
Decr 15.

1872.

Saturday
January 4th

1873.

Buckskin Suit.

congregate at that rendesvous from their distant hunting grounds, and receive in return Blankets, Beads, Gaudy Calico's, Powder and Ball, Muskets, and a variety of notions known to the Indian trade. He is now making his annual visit, and will not return I hear, until April. I suspect his stay has been prolonged until that date, in order to secure all the skins the Indians have to dispose of, and prevent as far as possible their falling into the hands of our party. Logan has already found out several pelts and mocassins have made their way into our camp, and does not hesitate to say, to the injury of the Company in more ways than one, no whites have knowingly been permitted to poach on the chartered rights of the Hudsons Bay Company, and he has intimated to Moberly the wishes of the Company's agents in this respect. Just how far he or the Company may succeed in inducing Moberly to issue an order forbidding the party to clothe themselves &c by trading with the red skin remains to be seen. The Indians make their clothing in a great measure from dressed Deer and Moose skins, and so long as one does not get wet, they are warm, elastic, and comfortable. I beleive every man Jack of us have set his heart upon having a suit, and why not? We all feel we have been long enough in the mountains and on the frontier, to be called such, and there is I believe a little vanity in the heart of most men to dress as such, if they have gone through the rough and tough life of frontiersmen, and with plenty who have not. There is a charm in the fringed and betasseled and jaunty air this suit gives one, that induces us more than any thing else to donn it, and beyond this, a few pairs of mocassins (skin shoes) and a buffalo robe, our purchases may not go; for certain we could not pack them out of this wilderness. The Hudsons Bay Company have the Indian at their mercy, and give him just so much for his wares; and the Indian has no alternative but to dispose of them; what else can he do with them? There is no opposition in this far away country; enough is allowed the red man to admit he receives some compensation for his valuable furs, enough simply to call it trading; and barely enough to justify the H.B.Co from denying they steal them. True they have large establishments to keep up, a vast army of paid dependents (poorly paid), ships, animals, Dogs, and a thousand other expenses; but the wares they dispense to the Indian in exchange for such valuables, is of the poorest, all Brummigam Cheap Jack.

Logan is very anxious that the eyes of the Indian shall not be opened too wide, nor his understanding enlarged; himself a half breed Scot, his mother an Indian woman, makes no manner of difference, he is a servant of the Company, and as such is bound to see to their interests. What! says he, a blanket for a Buffalo robe? By the way, a warm hairy covering twice the size of a blanket, and beautifully tanned; soft, and must have cost the squaws infinite labor. A blanket was far too much to give them; a colored silk Handkerchief purchased from one Indian, half a doz. pairs of Mocassins and three or four Martin Skins, the market value of which was not less than $8.—that of the handkerchief probably .50 cents—a complete Buckskin suit, sewn neatly with the sinew of the animal for a tin match box and three needles, all these were ruinous prices to pay, and the Indian would be apt to reflect upon the matter, and give this powerful but very disinterested and unselfish company serious annoyance by coming the "Oliver Twist" on them, and asking for *more*.

Each sled, or Tobogan more properly, is drawn by four or six powerful dogs, with a half-breed driver, and not unfrequently the owner of his charges. When not loaded, they will travel from forty to fifty miles a day over moderately good country, and each sled can be freighted with about 450 pounds.

These dogs are very large and muscular, formidable looking brutes; evidently crossed with wolf; and having, though to a less degree, that animals grizzled and mangy appearance. They are very quarrelsome among themselves, but are kept so cowed down by their brutal masters, that their ferocity ends at that, will show no hostile signs even toward a stranger. Their dispositions differ materially, one when spoken to will wag a friendly tail, come forward and show a desire to be noticed, another will drop his tail, sneak off, and lie down, desirous of being let alone, while yet another will turn his head in another direction, and treat you with utmost indifference. In this they are very unlike the Indian dog; who is all one way; whose hostility is strong towards all whites, and whose only acknowledgement to notice taken, is to double his mangy tail between his legs, show his teeth, and sneak off.

As I pick my way back and forth through this formidable looking pack, they appear not to observe me; but a hint from their masters has given me to understand they are great thieves, and while apparantly indifferent, are watching an opportunity to purloin anything edible. They are fed once only each day, and that is in the evening when work is done. Each animal receiving one and one half pounds of Pemican. I saw them fed today; and as I had somehow gotten in the midst of them, I felt anything but brave. I felt a cold chill creep down my marrow, as their great white fangs were snapped together with a clash, as they snarled and quarreled over their meal, and although it was decidly new to me, and I had looked forward to an exhibition and a treat, I felt it anything but that, being afread to move a muscle, and spite the presence of the drivers, who used their cruel whips freely, I felt, in the midst of those thirty odd monsters, tall and gaunt, with hair erect, and coarse as bristles, that I was in the centre of a pack of hungered wolves, and that some invisible power alone kept them from rending me peice meal. I was heartily

FEEDING TIME.

glad when the show was over, and I could extricate myself.
The Pemican was as hard as a rock, and had to be broken up
with an axe; the impatience of the dogs was sufficiently manifest by their temper towards each other, and I expected every
moment they would break through all restraint, and attack
their keepers, rations, and poor me simultaneously. The
uproar was pandemonium. The younger dogs, upon receiving their share, were quicker with their sharp fangs in disposing of the dainty morsel, and would fain render assistance to
the older dogs, whose teeth were none of the best, and then
came the play of the whips, the fighting, snapping, snarling
and yelping.

When the dogs get footsore, their feet are put into shoes
made of buckskin or stout canvas, and tied round the leg
immediately above the foot with a peice of leather thong. The
brutes, knowing the advantage of these shoes, never try to rid
themselves of them, as might be supposed.

I found out the pay of these sledmen was to be, as agreed
upon, one dollar per diem, and one dollar for Sled and Dogs
and Rations. The Canadian Government, paying the same
so long as their services were required.

The dogs made the run from the Jasper house to the depot in five hours; the distance, as I before remarked, about 21 miles, the trail I am told being of the roughest kind; the usual pace is a steady run; and frequently over levels, a loup. The driver has no easy time of it, and none other than tough, longwinded fellows could endure the fatigue. Now riding over levels, yelling and cursing a blue streak, at the same time using his long lashed whip unsparingly; when a steep grade occurs (and by the way there are more grades than levels), the animals go as hard as they can run, and the Tobogan comes tearing after them with a velocity threatening to overtake them any minute, then as it strikes some impediment, or shoots off at an angle, it checks the poor brutes so suddenly, as to roll them over; while the driver, with his hold upon a rope fastened to the hinder end, tears after it, steering as well as he is able, it is cruel work at best, and one can but pity the poor dumb, wretched curs.

I noticed that many of them had bad sores under the throat, and that these sores bled very freely; upon questioning the Drivers, they gave me to understand they were subject to it, and is not caused by the galling of the collar; I suppose they ought to know better than I, yet I cannot but imagine the unsightly tumourous sores are caused mainly by galling, and the choking sensation the poor brutes must suffer, spite of the drivers assertions to the contrary.

It will be understood these dog trains are only used in the winter, and over the snow.

There exists some six miles beyond this depot a Mountain Stream of considerable size, in fact a good sized river it may be called, and a very difficult crossing for our animals: The Indians in their language give it the name of Snake River; but whether from its being infested with this reptile, or owing to its serpentine course, I cannot say. These half breeds inform me that some years back quite a large tribe of Indians made this river and the vicinity their home; and that buffalo used to herd in the Valley we are wintering upon in vast numbers. I can well beleive this from the many bones and bleached skulls of Buffalo I saw through the Valley, and that it must have been a sheltered spot to yard in during the winter. My sketch on page 133 [of the original journal; "Meeting of the Athabasca and Leatherhead Passes"] shows a small stretch of the upper end of this Valley, and will give some idea of what it is throughout its extent of twenty odd miles. These Indians I have mentioned were called the "Snare tribe" by the Hudsons Bay Company, in consequence of the favorite method of taking their game being by the Snare. I allude more particularly to the smaller kinds of game; fur-bearing animals for instance; the halfbreeds say this section of country is still a favorite summer hunting ground, being well stocked with Mountain Sheep, Rabbits, Grouse, Bear, and Moose, also some Carriboo.

Owing to this fact, the Snare Indians were kept constantly in hot water by other tribes intruding themselves upon their hunting grounds, and frequent fights occurred. Cheif among those who most annoyed them, were the Assignaboines, a powerful and warlike people, who finally made war upon the Snare's, and in a battle so desasterous to the latter, that but a remnent of them remained; these betook themselves to the mountains close at hand, and only came down to the Valley to hunt. The Assignaboines were not content however, they wanted the last scalp of their enemy, and secured it. Taking the Snares unawares, they fell upon them in their weak numbers, killed every man and child, and took such of their women as were worth the trouble into Slavery, the old and sickly were likewise butchered. With true Indian ferocity, as many as were taken alive were put to the torture; and some few of the most noted were skinned alive; or slowly burned by hot coals being placed upon the stomach of their victims.

It was a victory, or a massacre complete; not one of the hated Snares remained. And triumphant they betook themselves to their own country, passing in the way the trading post of the Hudsons Bay Company, where they not only florished the scalps of their dead enemies, but flaunted before the eyes of the whites the skins of those they had flayed alive, with hands and feet attached, at the same time jeeringly telling their hearers they were skins they had for sale.

January 12th

1873

The Dog sleds came in with their first load tonight quite late, but as there was a bright moon, no difficulty existed on the score of light. Some of the animals are foot sore to commence with, after their hurried march from Edmonton, and doubtless they have been at work previous to joining us. I may mention, the amount of stores they are engaged to haul is 23.000 pounds; this being the balance left back in the pass by the trains; in fact, had the season permitted, the mules were in too weak a condition to be kept longer in the field. The distance to the depots where these stores are concentrated is about 29 miles, and the sleds will make the round trip in two days, and there being seven sleds hauling, we may look for all to be safely housed here in about 3 weeks, unless exceedingly bad weather interferes. It may seem a long way to bring these sleds, a matter of 300 miles, and for so short a period; but 300 miles of travel is soon covered by these quick travelers, and it was not only more profitable than building sheds stout enough to cache the supplies, and where damp would have destroyed a considerable portion; but these supplies could not have been considered safe without a sufficient guard in such close proximity to an Indian country, and our party were not strong enough to admit of its members being scattered. Moreover, it would be late in the spring 'ere these stores could have been transported by the trains, and it would not have been wise to have them handling stores away in the rear, when their services were required at the front. Dick White and a couple of men are left in charge of these stores.

I estimate the whole amount of our supplies, including Tools, Provisions, Clothing &c. to be about 40 tons, no inconsiderable amount to be transported into the very heart of such a wilderness, over mountains and through rushing streams, swamps and thickly matted forests for hundreds of miles.

THE BIG HORN, or MOUNTAIN SHEEP.

One sled is kept here for general chores, such as hauling in a good supply of wood &c.

It was the work of but a few minutes to discover, after ascertaining the number of mouths we had to feed, that our supply of Pemican was far short of the ration required for the period; those mouths would have to be fed, and a change of diet will be a necessity, much to the dissatisfaction of the sledmen. 2 pounds of Flour and 1 pound of Pemican will be the daily ration, and I do not blame the drivers for grumbling, as they declare a full meat ration is necessary to keep the dogs at their work. Flour they have never known, and they are satisfied it will cause half the animals to be down sick. Now this being on the sick list means a great deal to the dog; it does not mean rest, it means hunger. A sled dog placed upon the sick list no longer receives his rations, and is turned loose to scramble for himself; how he does it, God only knows, but he does exist; if their owners are questioned upon the subject, they are unable to explain. They shrug their shoulders, and tell you they hunt it up some how.

Our chief, seriously alive to the necessity of keeping the dogs in condition, and having them complete their work, has promised the drivers he will send a party into the hills to hunt Mutton. Mountain Sheep are occasionally to be seen high above us in bands of from ten to twenty, and although they appear to be on heights almost, if not altogether inaccessible to the human foot, some of our intrepid fellows are anxious to try a little Alpine climbing; the mountain Sheep during the winter months confine themselves to the higher altitudes, far above the everlasting snow line, and without the aid of the field glass, they appear but little specks, when at all visible. Should success crown the efforts of the hunters, the flesh will become food for both men and dogs.

January 17th.

[1873]

The first party of hunters went out at an early hour yesterday, and returned at nightfall with two fine specimens of these Sheep, or as they are more generally termed "Big horns." As this animal was entirely new to many of us, I took a sketch of them, quite pleased the men had brought them into camp entire; they said they had imagined I should want to see them, otherwise they should have cut off the head. The specimens before me were male and female. Moberly and I weighed the head of the ram, and found it to be 23 1/2 pounds, horns included. The horns of the male are immense; the carcase, when dressed, and without heart and liver, was 108 pounds.

After this success, the boys were all anxious to become nimrods, and we soon became well supplied with meat; dogs and men fared sumptuously so far as fresh meat was concerned. So far as to the Mutton itself, it is very coarse grained, dark in color, and tasteless, is entirely devoid of any gamey flavor, nor has it the taste of Mutton. Instead of wool, the big horn is covered with coarse, short hair like the deer, the color of the animal is a tawny brown, not a reddish brown like the deer, except at the buttucks, which is a dingy white. The tail is short.

The boys state they saw two or three goats, their bodies covered with long fleecy wool, and wholly white. Thus it would seem nature reverses herself in the mountains. These goats were very shy, and could not be approached.

Logan, the Hudson Bay Company trader, has been spending a day or two with us. He is a great talker, and has greatly amused us by his stories.

Although Logan is a halfbreed, the son of a Scotch father and an Indian mother, he is nevertheless very fairly educated I should judge, and very smart and shrewd as a trader. His days have been spent away from the great world of civilized mankind; born far away at an isolated trading post, he has gone through life with only a very few white men as associates, and the main part of those as ignorant almost as the redskins, who were assuredly the most numerous of his own species. How, or in what manner he received so fair an education I do not know, but someone evidently was instructor; it may have been his own father, or it may not, most certainly not his Indian mother. He is content with his world he says, and the half wild life of a trader pleases him well; he has known no other life, hence he declares all he hears and reads of cities, nations, big ships, telegraph, Railroads and stranger countries has no interest for him beyond the amusement they afford in reading of them, as they have failed to awaken any desire to become more intimately acquainted with them. News of any kind must be very meager, and very stale when coming within the reach of these buried alive little communities, nigh upon two thousand miles from cities, with no other means of locomotion than by accompanying mule or dog trains, for man may not travel alone; it is seldom that more than one, or possibly two mails a year reach them.

Logan is as full of superstition as an egg is full of meat, and equally susceptible of hocus-pocus and jug-glery as the Indian himself, and I must say I was astounded at some of the yarns he spun us, either vouching for their truth, or fully beleiving

147

what he related. A couple of them will be sufficient to demon-
strate the man; to me it clearly shows how much of his mothers blood flows through his veins. In examining his features,
one can scarcely find a trace of the Indian in him. He would
pass with 99 out of every 100 for a full blooded white, see him
where one would, and it was while examining him critically,
as so much nonesense emanated from his lips, that added to
my surprise. At the same time there was an envelope of
Scotch utterence to still further mystify or perplex me, as well
as others of his hearers, and we had drawn each other out of
all that could interest us, so that a stranger coming among us,
a stranger with a glib tongue, and a good story teller, was like
to claim all our attention. There is nothing like a camp fire,
and a knowledge that we are dependent on our own little
resources for our little amusements, and the wileing away of
long and dreary evenings, to make us good listeners, and
thoughtfully regardful to every little detail; we drink it in, not
maybe as knowledge, we may not beleive a word of the tale
teller, but everything new to us, let it be absurd, we take it
with a relish; and we become little children again, with
mother reading us wonderful stories of Puss in Boots, Jack the
Giant Killer, Bluebeard, or Cyndarella, as the nature of the
story warrants. But to return to Logan and his yarns.

We had been speaking of running, and running races,
when Logan assured us it was very dangerous to run races
with these Indians; upon being asked why, he remarked,
There are some among them who possess a power known
only to themselves, and which power no white man, or any
with white blood in their veins has ever possessed, although a
few have experienced the effects produced. Let us suppose an
instance, he continued, one of your party shall be a remarkable runner, and let it come to the knowledge of the Indians,
he would not be long, if they were on friendly terms, 'ere he
would receive a challange (for the Indians are fleet runners),
and he would accept; then the redskin and his friends come
trooping to the contest ground, and among them would be
one or more of those gifted with supernatural powers; for the

white man may not be permitted to outrun the Indian at all hazards. The race is run, and the redskin outstrips his white brother, and all is well, with many "Ughs" and disdainful gestures their white brother is made to understand he is the lesser man, and all ends amicably; but let the reverse be the case, and the white bid fair to outstrip the Indian, and win the race, in that case he will probably not reach the goal; instantly, as quick as the lightenings flash, he will stop, waver for a moment, then fall like a log; this has been the doings of one of the gifted redskins. If however, two of them should work their spell at the same moment, the victim would go into convulsions, and perhaps die; and where are these big medicine men when they perform this miracle? was asked. Why, with the crowd of spectators, and not even the Indians can tell who it is, it may have been a buck, or it may have been a squaw, for both sexes have the gift; and what asks another of his listeners becomes of the poor devil? Why, those who laid him under the spell can at leisure restore him.

Again (and Logan asserts he can produce living proofs, were we near Edmonton), there are squaws (women) who possess the wonderful power of throwing a spell over any of the male sex, and of making him their slave at will. Again he supposed a case, yourself for instance; let one of these squaws who have the gift take a fancy to you, be you white or redskin, or be she ever so comely or ever so ugly; woman she is if she is an ignorant savage; and in more ways than one she will show a preference for you; you, becoming alive to the fact, turn the cold side of you towards her; may be she is not your style of girl, or may be she is old enough to be your mother, and as forbidding as one of the furies, no matter, she has some little tenderness, and it is centered on you, hence she tries her wiles, she does not care to use harsh measures where her heart or passions (as the case may be) is fixed, but she will possess you, and tiring at length of resorting to fair means, or jealous perhaps of your court to another, she works her spell, and you draw gradually towards her, your regard increases, becomes love, passion, a madness to possess her, and her only, you despise all others for her dear sake, and if your charmer be old, she will wag her old jaws, show her toothless gums and grin as you lavish upon her embraces which in your blind and bewitched infatuation you cannot resist if you tried. She may be vindictive, and may be jealous of your proceedings should she take her spell off you, you are ready to do her bidding. Any act, however criminal you will commit for her dear sake, and you are ready to steal or kill as your witch wife dictates, for the possession of this particular power is only given to those who are hungering for a certain one of the opposite sex, and but very few receive the power. She may leave you to go on a journey, but seperation does not break the spell, and so supreme is her power, she can make you find her by instinct as it were, no matter if she be closely hidden in some spot of which you had no previous knowledge. You are ready to imperil life and limb to possess her. And Logan says some of the ill favored ones resort to this practice to seduce unfortunate males, and that he knows of two or three cases at the present time; that he has always a fear of these gifted squaws, one of them might take a notion to wean him from his wife and little ones. He evidently considered it very serious.

He was asked, suppose two of these beauties should fancy the same unfortunate devil at the same time, and both should throw their spells over him? In that case, he replied, I don't know, but I suppose the strongest would secure him, and should she know she had a rival, she would probably work upon the man to destroy her; and so we were, if not convinced, silent, thinking however, that this was reversing the order of things with a vengence.

I may as well give one more, and I judge that will be sufficient of such nonsense.

Logan holds that through spite, or jealously, there are both male and female Indians existing who possess the power to deform their enemy in a frightful manner. He himself has seen, or knows (I forget which) a woman whose mouth is (or was) by the vindictive spirit of another woman turned athwart her face, so that it became located where one of her ears should be; but where the enchantress placed the dislodged ear we did not learn; it may have been in the place previously occupied by the mouth; most certainly, unless it was removed altogether, the one would be in front and the other at the back of her head. Hey-day, fancy being in love with a girl, and have to peep round the side of her face to see her smile, and to hear her converse out of her ear as it were, or to go round to the back of her head to whisper sweet nothings to her. We were releived to hear this woman had been mercifully restored to her original beauty(?) again;— Let us be thankful—

Horses, Dogs, and other animals can be served in like manner, but the power of working upon other animals is given to very few.

Logan was asked if he had ever seen cases of paralysis? I have known of cases he replied; but none of these cases were paralysis, they were powers possessed by Indians of which we whites (for I consider myself a white man) are ignorant. Upon one or two of his hearers commenting somewhat severely, telling him in plain words, in fact, he was either very foolish for holding such tenets, or else that his hearers were very empty headed, and expected to swallow such an overdose; or that he must have imagined he was uttering such absurdities to men equally superstitious with the Indian, or that— but here the Scotch in his nature got the better of him, and he was mad as a hornet.

Do I really beleive the man was in ernest? Assuredly I do, in dead ernest; impossible, you say; such statements coming from an Indian might be in keeping; and pray, what may not be possible with a man whose companions through life have been Indians? Cradled among Indians, who has probably heard from his Indian mother stories equally improbable, recounted to him as facts; and Mother is Mother, though she be Indian. What child will grow up and doubt his mother.

Well but education say you! Yes, education will do much; but we require to be surrounded by an atmosphere which breaks through and drives away the clouds of superstition. How long is it ago that our brightest scholars beleived in witchcraft? How long ago since innocent godfearing women were arraigned before learned judges, and witnesses testified that she had been seen riding in the air on a broom, or in the form of a black cat had sucked the life blood of infants, and a hundred other lies equally absurd, yet enough to the consience of these learned lawyers to burn her at the stake, and at which a superstitious people approved, and made it a holiday to witness the tortures suffered by such damnable practices. Even the wise of the land not a hundred years agone would cry— "put her in the witches chair, duck her, duck her—if she is innocent she will live under water, if a witch she will drown"; so that something beyond education is necessary to drive out even the grossest and most impossible of superstitions. What could have been more impossible than an old woman in the seventeenth and eighteenth centuries transforming herself into a cat? Or riding on a broom handle in the air? And yet had you or I lived in those days, there is little doubt but we should have beleived it: No; the great purifier, and disperser of darkness is light, the light of the gospel; that is what has driven out from us those terrible blots of a comparatively late day; we no longer beleive them, because Christianity has taught us better; it has entered our schools, and instead of an old mans tale, it teaches our children its first and fundamental principles, that everything is subservient to God, who is all goodness and mercy; and that no portion of the creation is the devils, to warp and twist into uncouth shapes, making men and women into cats and furies. We know now, let a man be ever so under the influence of Satan by his evil doings, he has no power granted him by that blackhearted potentate (if the term be not wrong) to change his form, nor work spells and sorcery.

As we are speaking of the Hudsons Bay Company, I may as well give you some idea of their trading posts, and I cannot do better than insert an article I cut from an old paper, and which is a very truthful pen picture; and it will give you a much clearer insight than I could render you.

"Hudsons Bay Trading Posts"

The trading and interior depot posts of the Company are strange, quaint looking places, built according to a general type. They stand generally upon the second or lower bank of some navigable river or lake, so as to be easily accessible to the boats which annually visit them with supplies. A trading post is invariably a square, inclosed by immense trees or pickets, one end sunk deeply in the ground, and placed close together. A platform about the height of an ordinary man is carried along the inner side of the square, so as to enable anyone to peer over without danger from arrows or bullets. At the four corners are bastions, octagonal in shape, pierced with embrasures, to lead the Indian to beleive the existance of cannon, and intended to strike terror to any redskinned rebel bold enough to dispute the supremacy of the Company. The entrance to the stockade is closed by two massive gates, an inner one and an outer one. In the center of the square stands the residence of the factor or trader in charge, and of the upper class of employe's, while about its four sides, close to the stockade, are ranged the trading store, the fur room, the warehouses, servants quarters &c.

Besides the larger dwelling arises a tall flagstaff, bearing the flag of the Company, with its strange device—"Pro pelle cutem"—skin for skin,—and near by a bell tower, the tones from which mark the hours of labor and rest.

In front of the gate lounge a few half-breeds or Indians in tasseled caps and dirty white capote (coat), or tattered blanket. A band of horses graze in a distant meadow, while nearer by a few feather tepees, or bark lodges, from the frilled poles of which the smoke curls lazily, indicate the home of the original hanger on. At one side of the palisade a few rude crosses or wooden railings, stained by snow and snow drift, and blown over by the tempest, mark the resting places of the dead.

The trade rooms at all the posts are arranged with strict reference to the wants of the peculiar custom which they attract. From the heavy joist in the ceiling depend twine, steel-traps, tin kettles, frying pans &c. On various shelves are piled bales of cloth, of all colors, capotes, blankets and caps, and in smaller divisions are placed files, scalping knives, gun screws, flints, balls of twine, fire-steels, canoe awls, and glass beads of all colors and sizes. Drawers in the counter contain needles, pins, scissors, fish-hooks, thimbles, and vermillion for painting canoes and faces. On the floor is strewn a variety of copper kettles, from half a pint to a gallon, and in one corner of the room stands a dozen trading guns, and beside them a keg of powder and a bag of shot.

In some of the trade rooms a small space is railed off by the counter near the door, behind which the Indian stands to trade. Sometimes they are confined to a seperate appartment, called the Indian trade-room, adjoining that occupied by the traders, and business is carried on through a loophole communicating between the two. In many of the posts in the plain country the trade room is cleverly contrived so as to prevent a sudden rush of the Indians, the approach from outside the pickets being through a long narrow passage, only of sufficient width to admit of one Indian at a time, and bent at an acute angle near the window at which the trader stands. This precaution is rendered necessary by the frantic desire which sometimes seizes upon the Indian to shoot the clerk, which he might easily do if the passage were straight.

At most of the interior posts time moves slowly, and change is almost unknown. Today is the same as a hundred years ago. The list of goods ordered from England for this year has exactly the same items as that of 1773. Strands, cotton, beads and trading guns are still wanted by the Indians, and are still traded for musquash and beaver.

The system of trade at the Company's post is entirely one of barter. Until very recent years money values were unknown; but this medium of exchange has gradually become familiar to the Indians nearer civilization; and the almighty dollar is rapidly asserting its supremacy in savagedom.

If the statements of many of the Company's servants be true (I allude to the underclass of white helps), the life of these people is a hard one at these interior posts; only half fed, often completely isolated, made to drag sleds over the ice and snow for hundreds of weary miles during the severity of winter, a scant allowance of dried fish, weighed out to them, being their chief subsistance, I cannot but think there is much truth in all this, I have heard so many tell the same tale. Often some brutal wretch is in charge of a Post who will whip them like dogs; and some member who having been unfortunate enough to incur his displeasure is dispatched to a distant post with a message or letter, in some cases the same being a sure death warrant; all this may not be so today, except at very isolated posts, for the vast wilderness over which the Company claims control is becoming more known and visited; the march of the sturdy minor and husbandman are gradually limiting this Companys hunting grounds, and although the time may not be yet, so vast are their possessions by charter, yet eventually, like the red man, they must make room for the teeming millions of other nations.

One thing appears certain, great and unnecessary have been the hardships heaped upon the green young highlandmen in past years, reflecting no credit on the aristocratic shareholders and directors in England. It is no secret that these trading posts were hard places to be stationed at during General Simpsons regime as head of the H.B.Co affairs on this continent, and that many brand him as a harsh and partial despot, spite of his cleverness in administering the affairs of the Company.

There are some strange characters among our boys; and I find as I glean from my diary something from my friend "Handsome Harry", who, stationed some twenty miles away with the pack animals, became the recipient of a note from

Winters Quarters. Athabasca Depot. Leather-head Pass.

me, requesting to know why he had employed a certain Indian, who had put in a claim for work performed for the Packers.

His reply is as follows.

"Dear Sir,

As regards the Indians, and the work performed by that industrial individual, you appear to be better informed than we are out in the suburbs. I mentioned in my last note to pay the above named gentleman the sum of $3. in ikta's (goods) and charge the same to my individual account. Any further demands my dear red skin brother may have against me I will settle on our next meeting with the toe of my boot. —My love to him.—

I may state, in answer to your enquiry, our Commissariat is in a healthy condition, if I except the following articles, to wit. Flour, Bacon, Yeast Powders, Syrup, Oatmeal and Groceries, and I would suggest the expediency of sending down a small supply of these luxuries until camp breaks up, &c—&c—&c—"

On the next page [of the original journal, page 161] I finnish a Sketch of our winter quarters, with sled and dogs in the fore-ground.

While the party were out in the field last December, they were visited by a small party of Crees, who hung around camp several days, and during which time much had been done by the boys to create a friendly feeling, and their women, which were kept away, were gradually permitted to draw near, and indulge the curiosity natural with their sex. The boys were on their good behaviour, for it was quite well understood that any liberties taken with the squaws would be likely to call down vengence from the Indians, and should any member of the party so misconduct himself, a pretty rough handling would have ensued from his comrades; we had some pretty tough customers among us, and anything in the shape of a petticoat was likely to become insulted if some stringent measures were not adopted. The Indians, seeing therefore how matters stood, became very friendly, especially as many odd scraps from the table fell in their way, and they hovered around us like so many crows. Strict watch had to be observed however, that nothing was stolen, the women especially are great thieves.

One morning, the boys were somewhat surprised to see Bucks and squaws kissing each other all round, apparantly each Buck kissed every squaw, and each squaw kissed every Buck. Now the kissing performance of an Indian would not be judged quite the thing with us, and I have a notion if the same was our mode, there would be less of the desire to indulge in this thrilling embrace. The Indians when they kiss, are not content with the usual smack on the touch of the lips, but the squaw sticks her tongue into the bucks mouth, and he receives it, gives it a hearty suck, and then protrudes his

February 20th

1873

157

Fun for de' boys . yum! yum!

tongue into the lady's mouth to receive a like complement, and if they are devotedly attached to each other, the game goes on probably for some seconds.

It was fun for the boys to watch these proceedings; but judge of their surprise when the squaws, by a universal move- ment, drew near and fastening on to the numbers of our party, there were four of these women, all well advenced in years, which means, all exceedingly repulsive. The first man encountered was a Frenchman, and an old Hudsons Bay man by name "Dupois," for him they had no repugnancy. There was little choice between them and him so far as cleanliness was concerned: he grinned, drew his sleeve accross his chops, to wipe some of the Tobacco juice from his beard, and went through the ordeal bravely. The next they tackled was our nigger cook, who in fact pushed himself forward for the embrace of the fair ones, but unlike the Frenchman, he did not approve of the tongue business, which was thrust against his black lips in vain; and I am told, such is the power of woman over man, that nigh the whole party consented to their embrace, and the vermin infested heads of the ladies mingled for a moment with the locks of their white brother. As they yielded to the fair sex, so had they to yield to the bucks, who each in turn slobbered over them to their hearts content. Yet I have reason to beleive most of the boys were foully wronged, and but three of four stood their ground, the others taking to their heels.

But I am neglecting the best part of it. Prior to the kissing, Bucks and squaws blacked their faces with grease and charcoal mixed, which gave them a yet more hideous appearance. One old hag being especially marked by a grinning cavern of a mouth, toothless, and with lines of gums almost white. She was the leader of the lady band, and left on each mans face a patch of defilement. I was told the Indians did not seem well pleased that many of their white friends refused this singular love offering.

It would seem this ceremony is performed by them at certain periods, but why, and to celebrate what, I did not ascertain, and doubtless they thought it a condescension and an honor they were conferring upon their white brother.

An amusing incident occurred with my assistant, Dick White to day. One of the Douglas Indians of our outfit has become possessed of a very fine Moose skin coat; fringed and tasseled, and altogether a gay garment, envied I fear by not a few of us. We would all like to trade with Johny for it, but Johny is not on the barter. I know of no one so anxious to possess it however, as Dick White; it is a nightmare to him, he talks to me of it, he dreams of it, he swears he will have it if he has to steal it. He made a last effort today: deliberating upon what he could tempt Johny with, for money he was not possessed of, and his personal effects were light, finally he brought out a white linen blouse, carefully smoothed out the wrinkles, of which there were many; then a sheepskin coat, a Souwester hat, and after contemplating them complaisantly and reflectively, again thrust an arm into the canvass bag, and unearthed two pairs of half worn out shoes, all of which he carefully stowed away out of sight; his next proceeding was to coax Johnny in, for Johnny was growing tired of being bored to death to part with a garment he was desirous of

March 6th
1873

retaining in his own possession, and moreover, like the girl all the boys were paying addresses to, thought herself no small potatoe, so likewise Johnny thought his coat, which everybody envied, to be a mine of wealth, and worth ten times its actual value. But Dick, with his Irish blarney and adroitness took Johnny from his duties as dishwasher to the nigger cook, and started upon his business offer. First came to the front the two coats; White launching out in his chinook upon their probable value, quality of the material &c, looking all the while as though he was making a terrible sacrifice, and furtively eyeing Johnny, who remained stolidly indifferent; with the usual wave of his hand, and a graceful gesture he then produced a pair of Shoes: but Johnny shook his head, and Dick produced the other pair Shoes; and was exasperated beyond measure to think he had nigh reached the end of his pile, with no signs of success. He haggled and coaxed, he dwelt on the value of each article seperately, and then summed up the total value, sticking on a dollar or two in the amount, knowing Johnny and arithmetic were strangers, but to no purpose; worse than that; the Indian was grinning, Dick was getting white; I expected to see a boot whiz through the air; but White had yet one more chance, and in desperation he produced the Sou-wester hat. One glance at Johnny however, was sufficient, the wretch had his tongue protruding from his mouth to its full extent. Not only his magnificent offer, but himself treated with contempt. This was the last straw; dropping the everlasting glass from his eye, he rushed upon Johnny, and was only prevented from giving the redskin a severe mauling by two or three of the boys who had been watching the fun.

Suffice it, Dick never possessed the coat.

By the end of March the party were again in the field, and on the 12th day of April I left our winters quarters, and pushed on to Fiddle River, a stream of no magnitude; in fact almost dry during summer. Here a depot had been built comprising three log houses, as it was intended to advance and store considerable of our supplies throughout the summer,

"DICK WHITE NEVER POSSESSED THAT COAT."

rendered necessary in consequence of the Athabasca river being unfordable at certain seasons of the year, said river lying between this and the winter quarters.

While at wild horse creek, by the aid of my friend Jim Normansell, I had collected quite a library of miscellaneous reading matter; both Religious, Historical, Scientific and Romance . . . they did the boys great service during the long winter, and I was well repaid, they were grateful for my thoughtfulness. They are left behind at the winter quarters with Brown, who has relieved me.

Fiddle River Depot is situated near the end of the pass proper; in fact, on either side tower the last snow capped giants, the guardians of the Pass from the Eastern side. In front of us lies for probably one hundred miles, rolling hills thickly covered with forest. For sketch of Fiddle depot see page 169 [of the original journal].

The Packmaster, Johnny Ahern accompanied me as far as the Jasper house on my way to Fiddle river, which lies a couple of miles off our route, and by which means I was enabled to get a sketch of it, Johnny holding our two horses and insisting upon being included in said sketch. It was on a beautiful Saturday morning we left our winter quarters behind us, having a train of 37 Pack Animals in our wake; we made about half the journey and encamped, still in the Valley: The night was very cold, and the wind moaned its music through the bushes behind which we had sheltered ourselves with deep and heavy sighs, each sigh an icy blast.

The Valley of the Jasper, as this end might be named, shows a good feeding ground in the summer, and the whole Valley is, I should suppose, about 40 miles in length, by 2 1/2 miles in width; the buffalo grass, coarse and nutritious, being plenty, and might well be a favorite feeding ground for this animal. Several small Lakes are scattered through the Valley, some formed by the widening of the Athabasca; resting as it were; though swiftly and silently rolling on, to by and bye become again a roaring, grand and mighty cascade. On either side of the river grow the Alder, Cotton wood and black fir, blending in a delightful contrast, while in our line of travel there is a freedom from underbrush, making traveling easy. Heavy fires have at some period devastated the Valley, leaving the standing timber in places bare and scathed, bleached white by the winds and rain since their bark has fallen off, and as twilight creeps through the silent scene, it wears a ghastly aspect; indeed far up the sides of the mountains on either hand, even to the snow line has these raging fires devoured their way, stopping only at the line of everlasting Snows. It is a beautiful Valley during the summer months, grand, sublime in its surroundings; an earthly paradise, that can only be reached after toil and danger. A valley not for every eye, this Valley of the Jasper, but the time I trust is not far distant when it may be within reach of all who can afford

"JASPER VALLEY. ROCKY MOUNTAINS."
OUTLET. EAST END.

to travel by rail, should this route be adopted. Yet but little can be realized or felt from a train of cars. No! to see it and enjoy it, we must meander through it, rest in it, after a long and troubled march; this is to truly enjoy such a scene.

Yet why is this beautiful Valley so rich, and yet so empty? Why is the devastation by scathing fire? Where are the Buffalo herds that should be grazing here? For their whitened sculls lie thickly around. Certain it is they come here no more, and why? Ask the redman; he can answer it. But he does not seem to make his home here now. No; he has driven the herds from this place, and as they depart, so does he, he goes after the meat. He it is who has lighted the fires that has devastated spots in the Valley; that have robbed the mountains on either hand of a portion of their forest garment, and the cause is clear, the cunning savage year after year crept past the herds as they fed, and attained the upper end, then fired the long grass during the heated term, driving a thundering living mass in terror to the only Outlet at the end of the Valley, where the main body of their enemy waited to destroy as many as the opportunity offered. If this mode of warfare against them was the only means of securing or lessening their numbers, the buffalo would be in their ancient haunts in bands of many thousands, where today not a single head can be found. Civilization drives them further north, where they become an easy prey during the deep snows of the winter; and 'tis then the redskin, nay, whiteman likewise, tripping lightly over the snows crust on his snow shoes, comes upon a floundering, half starved herd of hundreds, half burried in the drift, and unable to fly or defend themselves; they are shot, with gun and arrow, or slain with spears; and their slayers, after stripping them of their hides, leaves the huge carcasses to the wolf and decomposition. The Indian usually appropriates the tongues likewise. They reap a rich harvest assuredly, the large hides are dressed by them, and sold, after reserving sufficient for tent and clothing outfit.

I presume that so long as there is an Indian to hunt, or a buffalo to be hunted, this state of things will go on to the end; not many years will elapse 'ere the American Bison will be an animal of history only, like the Mammoth, and other extinct animals, their bones alone can be seen to represent them. But an all-wise providence seems to be diminishing the hunter and the hunted alike; as the Buffalo herd become lessened, so do the Indian herd, somewhat more slowly, perhaps, but not the less surely. The white race are inheriting their territories instead of their children, and they are being driven into yet more and more limited regions of country; the Souix, gradually edging north, by the wedge of civilization, crowd the Blackfeet, causing bloody and stubborn fights, aiding the ravages of increasing maladies to wipe them from off the face of the earth. The civilized wedge still enters deeper, surely and steadily, and the savage moves on and crowds the Crees, who encroach upon the Assignaboines, and are all kept in a state of ferment; now more projected Railroads, more wedges of civilization are being inserted through their very midst, and the end may not be just yet, but it will assuredly soon be,— "Enter the ranks of progress or die," and if I am any judge of

'JASPER HOUSE.' outlying trading huts of the Hud- -son Bay Comp'y. — near foot of Leatherhead Pass. — Rocky's. — Graves of Company's Servants. murdered by Indians.

Indian character, the latter will be the choice with nine-tenths of the red race.

The Indian is a wasteful hunter, where game is plenty. He has no thought for the morrow. With many tribes, semi-starvation through all the preceeding winters fails to convince him of the necessity to lay in a sufficiency for the coming one, and as now, his game fields are becoming more limited, and his buffalo herds more scarce and scattered, he fails yet more to provide, and his peltries are not as many as in the years gone by; so that his chances of procuring necessary comforts and what not from the white trader are not so good. Many a proud tribe of the red men, who half a century gone carried proudly his Eagles plume, is now content to squat him down by the side of some stream, and fish for food; his game is scarce worth the hunting; his tribe is dwindling to a handful, from a nation of warriors; and his death song has commenced long ago; it has taken the place of his whoop of defiance and

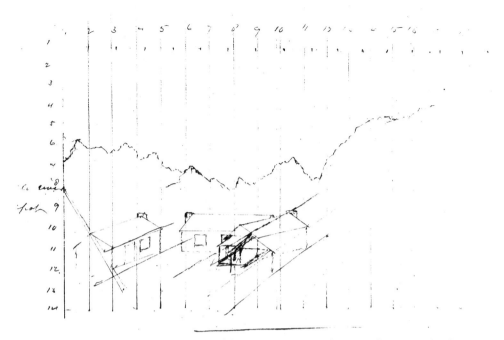

war; the scalps of his enemy's no longer float in the breeze before his wigwam of buffaloe robes, but his home is some smoke dried ranch, that scarce shelters him, and a few dried fish hang at his door, out of the reach of his half famished dogs.

April 15th

1873

I am suffering somewhat from Scurvy; my mouth is in a dreadful state, the gums being black, the teeth loose, and when pressed against any substance, they prick at the roots like needles; at times the gums swell, almost covering the teeth; to chew food is out of the question, and so have to bolt it without mastication. My legs are also becoming black below the knee, altho they appear to give me no uneasiness beyond the knowledge their symptoms bear. My breath likewise is somewhat offensive, and I am troubled with a dry cough. In fact I feel like an old man, and have a disinclination for anything like exertion. The quantity of blood discharged somewhat alarms me, while the eyes are dull, and the cheeks hollow. I am by no means a brave man under ailments, and sometimes fancy I should be a poor subject to fight against final results if the king of terrors should poke his nose in at the door.

As a remedy, I am digging roots in the swamp near, and feel that [they] produce a check, if nothing more, but they are poor substitutes for a vegetable diet, which we all need, and is I guess the primary, if not the sole cause of the desease, for I am not alone, by any means.

I am in hopes of leaving the party next month, I have been planning to that effect, and if I can induce our chief to see with my eyes, and releive me, I shall make a break for the lower country once more, and for home; and yet not home, home to me means wife and my own fire side,— No, let me leave out the word, home. I am aware it is too early to make the attempt, but I feel as though I must be away, even the bracing air of these higher regions has a stifling effect when I get in my impatient moods.

As I am upon Sickness, I will state that the Indians of British Columbia are great beleivers in the Sweat-house remedy for Sickness. Some tribes have one method, some another, some apply the remedy in a mild form if I may term it so, although their mildest form would cause a Physician to stand aghast; I will however give an example of the severe method.

I remember being located at an Indian Village on one occasion, and some 10 years prior to this history, and saw the remedy applied. The subject to be operated upon was a decidedly sick redskin, and looked as though the happy hunting grounds were to be his very soon; this was especially apparant when the dirty blanket was discarded, and he stood as nature formed him. He looked a skeleton with a skin drawn over the rattling bones. But first let me explain a little. The sweat house was a cone in shape, though somewhat rounded at top; and made of a wickerwork of willows, thickly plastered on the outside with mud. It was not capable of holding, or rather accommodating more than one patient at a time, and as the opening was very small, said patient must creep in on all fours, and squat doubled up, knees and chin together.

A rousing fire had been made, and a number of good sized rocks heated red hot, which had then been rolled into the house and allowed to remain there until the mud walls had become warmed up; in fact as sufficating as an oven I should judge, when the rocks were withdrawn; a very small hole at top of the house let the gas escape, and in order to proove the proper temperature for the patient, an Indian (doctor I fancy) put his head into the entrance hole a few times. Finally, all being in readiness, the patient was produced, and in he crawled, the door was then partially closed by a squaw holding an old mat over it, one having been previously laid inside for the sick man to squat on. He remained in quite a little while, sufficiently long to have roasted me I beleive, his friends on the outside holding converse with him meanwhile. At length the interesting subject had had enough of this baking process, and the mat being removed, he came out, streaming with sweat at every pore, and without a moments hesitation, and still in this heated condition, he made for the river close by, and plunged headlong in.

Now, had I an enemy, and he undertook to try this sweathouse business, I should console myself with the idea that in ten minutes he would be sufficiently frizzled to leave me one enemy the less, or if that failed, let him come out, and at once plunge into a cold stream of water, that would fix him sure,— What was the effect in this case I cannot say, or I forget. I left at once, with a kind of feeling I was an aider and abetter in a fellow creature taking his own life. I doubt not this kind of treatment decides the matter, and very frequently adds one more to the vast army of good Indians.

The Cree tribe of Indians on the plains likewise use the sweathouse, but on the patient crawling out, he or she is wrapt in warm blankets or skins, to prevent a chill, whereas the other invites a chill with a vengence. A sweat is good, but such a drain upon an exhausted system must be very trying.

Now, it has ever been my aim through life to never exhibit myself before ladies unless fully costumed; but I have to admit I was sorely tried on the night of the 16th April. I carefully noted the date, as an occurrence that does not often effect us, nor even come within our knowledge. On this night it was quite dark, though the stars were shining overhead, for the depot lay deep in the shade of the tall pines. I had a comfortable fire on the hearth, the cold been severe, and was busy patching some of my old clothing, when without previous warning of any presence save my own for many miles, my rude door was opened, and an Indian glided in, and gave me to understand he had some friends outside, and would I let them have a place in the hut that night, that they had no blankets, and the night was cold. He spoke chinook kind of mixed with french, but I understood him pretty well; he was in fact excessively polite, and said they would not laugh and talk, meaning I suppose they would not break my rest.

It is needless to say I bade them welcome, in fact I was glad of any company to break the dullness of solitude; I had no fear from his manner of anything unpleasant transpiring, such as pillage for instance, and they behaved admirably, save for one little instance. Out from my presence my red brother went, and presently returned accompanied by a boy and three squaws. I was somewhat surprised they should ask this favor, Indians of the plains prefer the open air, seldem sleeping under a roof. I was more surprised when I saw him introduce the woman. I suppose however, they were quite aware I was here and alone, and that a snug house and blazing fire were preferable to the open air and no blankets.

I produced some Cold Beans and Slapjacks, frizzled some bacon and gave them a meal, and we were soon on a good footing with each other. I supplied the Tobacco, and the buck having his own pipe, we smoked, we all smoked, save the boy, the buck graciously passing his pipe to one of his lady friends, and she to her companions, so we all took comfort. Nay, I went further, for they were the first lady guests I had had the honor of receiving for many a day; so I produced blankets, even made them a comfortable bed on the floor of the hut, and as it was now getting late, became somewhat impatient for them to retire. I knew it was not necessary for me to hide my face, or leave the hut for awhile for that purpose, as these people dont usually undress to go to bed when at home. But evidently they had no intention of retiring. The beggers sleep through the day, and like the Owl, are exceedingly wakeful at night. As to myself, in my present half sick state, I was determined not to lie in my clothes, and taking the opportunity when the fire was burnt low, to slip into the darkest corner and undress. I was just ready to make a move for my bed, when one of the women, sitting close to the fireplace, suddenly poked the embers into a bright blaze. I had previously put out the candle, but now this was a brighter light than half a dozen candles could give. They all saw my fix and laughed heartily. I had to come close to them in order to get to bed, and I could not sit up longer. My bed besides was some five feet from the floor, and in order to reach it, I had to make use of a rude stool I had to sit upon. One of the ladies had taken possession of the stool while I was disrobing, and was now grinning at me from said stool, but at my request, she got up, and I clambered as quickly as I could into my bunk, and covered myself with my blankets, a loud peal of laughter ringing in my ears meanwhile. Confound them, they enjoyed the joke immensely, and were laughing and talking of it as I fell asleep. In the morning, when I woke, they had disappeared.

[space left for drawing of wolf attack]

April 19th
1873

This morning, not expecting any train, and assuredly no other visitors, I took it into my head I would go back some six miles, and sketch a singular looking rock, somewhat cathedral shaped, the same being the bluff like terminus (see in the sketch of the Jasper house) of a chain of mountains. So shouldering my rifle and with sketch block in my wallet, I set out.

I had never paid much attention to wolves, and whenever I had observed their tracks, passed them unheeding, in fact, I had never anticipated danger from them, as I knew they did not pack well, but generally were either single, or in two's or three's save where animals were congregated, when they became somewhat numerous and troublesome. I had never taken to mind that the huge timber wolf was a formidable and savage beast, but as they had never attacked any of our men, but had confined themselves to the animals, I grew careless, but when the unmistakably long footprint of the Grizzly Bear was observed, I used every caution. I was satisfied danger lurked somewhere, and watchful care was necessary. Although, to be honest, I must say, I have seen Bear many times, and have had their footprints thick in my vicinity, but never was attacked by them; very frequently they will run, at times walk leasurely away, turning to look at you wonderingly, but always wishing to avoid man. In fact, I had never met a bear when his fits of rage were upon him, or a mother bear with cubs to protect, or the case I fancy might be entirely different.

But to return to my wolf adventure, I had followed up the trail to the desired point of observation, and was sitting on a fallen tree preparing for my sketch, when I heard a crackling of dried twigs, and quickly turning, beheld three large timber wolves; they observed me at the same moment, and came to a momentary halt; their great jaws were open, their tongues hanging out, and their cruel teeth fairly gleamed as it were; at least so it seemed to me, as we stood for half a minute watching each other. I can tell you my heart thumped pretty loudly, when quick as a flash I stooped for my winchester; the move was their signal likewise; with savage snarls they bounded towards me, leaving me no time for an aim; I pulled the trigger, and as might be expected, missed, but the loud report made them pause when within twenty paces, and they commenced circling round me, the strange and loud noise of my gun evidently causing them to change their tactics, and attack their enemy with caution. I kept my eye on them, and could see they were gradually narrowing in upon me; not wishing them to get too close before I delivered my fire, I took good aim at the formost wolf, and gave him the ball, but I did not succeed so well as I had hoped I should, being half sick, my nerves were some what unstrung I suppose. I simply broke one of his hind legs, prooving how wild my shot had been while aiming for his shoulders. With a loud yell, and a savage snarl he rolled over, but regaining his feet again in an instant he bounded off for cover, followed by the others, and I fired again just as I had the satisfaction of seeing them disappear behind some huge fragments of rock; and I saw no more of them. I hastily finished my sketch, and made tracks for my depot, not wishing for any more such close shaves.

Such specimens of wolves as I have seen with caravans could convey no idea of these monsters; they are but wolves in miniture compared with these mountain species, standing as high as an ordinary sized mule, tall and gaunt, with immense muscular powers; their cruel jaws could crush in a mans skull, as easy as cracking a nut. They had a look about them to make one shudder. Ever after when I came upon wolf tracks, I prepared for fight, and so long as I was alone in the mountains, I kept my winchester in a pretty close embrace. These animals I suppose, had crossed my trail, scented me, and followed me up, and but for the noise of the breaking of dried twigs, would probably have been upon me before I had had time to arm myself, in which case a few bones would have been bleaching yonder at the foot of the "Rocha Mayette" as the Indians named this bluff, and my tale would have remained untold.

Unlike the western slope of the Rocky's, small game of any kind are scarce on this side, in fact the only game is large; Moose, Cariboo and Mountain Sheep principally; of course I speak of this latitude, and with such game, whose numbers do not appear to be vast, the wolf of the plains would have but little chance. On said plains, Buffalo and the jumping deer are plenty, especially the latter; the former are yearly becoming less. The little distance we have traveled on the eastern side has made the absence of game very noticeable; here there are bands of Indian hunters, on the western slope there are none, the beasts of prey alone hunt them, mans footprint is never seen, nor the crack of the rifle ever heard.

The Bear family are numerous on this side, but as I neither consider them game, nor beasts of prey (being vegetarian in diet) I have not named them with the large game. The Grizzly especially are numerous, and these large gaunt wolves are oftener seen on this colder slope, a single one of which will attack man when famished.

There are no wolves in the higher altitudes that run in packs, and it is only when we reach the plains that they congregate in large numbers, where they hover on the skirts of the Buffalo herds, picking up the stray old and sick, or occasionally a calf. But woe betide the poor hunter who may come within their circuit; like the wolves of Norway and Russia, their charge is terrible, and although by no means as ferocious, their great numbers make them bold and irresistable, their howling throats death, and the body of a victim, be it ever so large, is picked clean in a few minutes.

On the 22d April I received a visit from Moberlys half breed guide "Karraquenta" who presented me with a letter, in reply to one I had penned asking to be allowed to resign as soon as it was practicable to reach the lower country. He wrote me very flatteringly, but requests I will remain at my post some few weeks longer, or until he can reach the Macleod River, and make tracings to that point; as he wants to forward them by me to the authorities at Victoria B.C. He also reasons, the delay will facilitate my travel, as it is impossible to start before June and get through, that I cannot travel alone, and that the animals I shall take will be in better condition for the journey, the young grass having now fairly started into life. The scores of mountain Streams to be crossed will be so swollen that nothing short of a large party could travel, the snows still deep in the thick timber, and I dont know how many other hindrances, that while I felt he was quite right, and was far better posted than I, I nevertheless felt greatly put out at my compulsory delay, and blamed him not a little for not granting my request last fall. And so I fear my reply would not be just what he had expected of me, as upon maturer thought I know he was advising for my good, and took all pains to try convince me.

April 23d

[1873]

The day bitter cold, with a strong N.E. wind.

One of our horses, a roan, and Halls favorite riding animal, which had been left in my care, came tearing into camp today in a sorry plight; he had received an ugly gash on one of his haunches, the flesh being torn and partly detached, to the size of a dinner plate; at first I thought he had snagged himself, but his actions, snorting and trembling, and the shape of the wound told very plainly the paw of a grizzly had done the mischief. Bruin fell a little short of his mark, or the horse was a little too quick for him. As luck would have it, Hall was with me at the time.

[April] 26th

[1873]

It has been snowing heavily all day; and would seem to verify Moberly's letter of advice to me, of don't be in a hurry. I am however, making my preparations for as early a start as possible, overhauling my slender wardrobe, patching shirts, sewing a buckskin seat into my pants for riding &c.

And now I am in receipt of another line from the chief, who informs me that if I am determined to proceed at all hazards, he will release me; particularly as I will not be advised. His few lines have made me a little ashamed of myself I must admit, but I have made up my mind, and would not now turn back if again asked to do so.

Dick White comes tomorrow, and we at once commence the transfer of all properties. Thank God, at last I am to leave, and set my face towards the one little spot left to me, a desolate home, and a year old grave.

Saturday
May 3d

1873

Having completed the turning over process here, and supplied White with a detailed list of the properties, stores and animals at our winters quarters, I started down towards the party to-day, made 16 miles, and encamped on a good sized prairie: It must be a delightful spot during the short summer months. A sluggish stream winds through it, swarming with land Otter, Beaver and Muskrat. I am entering the long stretch of foothills, and have startled a few willow Grouse. The land appears as good as any lying out of doors, but the summer being so short, renders it valueless for agricultural purposes I should imagine; in fact frosty nights are experienced the entire year, and the land never becomes thoroughly thawed out.

I am on my way to make final arrangements for my departure, and the day has been full of happiness to me. It has been cold but pleasant, and although I am alone, I have had much to occupy my mind. I remain here tomorrow, to give my animal the benefit of the sweet grass, and myself revel in this delightful open; to me a little earthly paradise.

[space left for drawing of prairie near foot of pass]

Reached the party about 3 P.M. after a ride of another 16 miles. The trail has been very trying to me, and although a great deal improved in health, I find any unusual exertion tires me. The roots I have been taking has checked the scurvy, in fact greatly reduced it, but has left me weak; at one time I had great difficulty in getting the animal I rode out of a mud hole, and again for miles with the greatest difficulty making our way through the Muskegs as they are called; literally, a thick moss some three feet in depth, and as full of water as a wet sponge. There is no escaping these muskegs. Take the highest points attainable, it is the same, the animal belly deep in this wet yielding substance. For miles the party have had to thickly coat the trail cut, with branches of trees and underbrush; for miles the moss was so deep that an animal would be buried overhead in it and become suffocated, hence progress through this section of country was slow; slow in making a narrow mule trail, and likewise slow in packing the goods through it. The Fiddle river depot was constructed on the outskirts of this singular Morass, and it required a packer to

May 5th
[1873]

every two or three animals; the animals haltered each to the other, to prevent any of them breaking out of single file, and going down to suffocation and loss of the supplies with which it was packed. The poor brutes had a hard time of it; though very lightly laden, one or other would be constantly breaking through the thick coating of boughs, and rolling over on its side, would have to be unloaded before it could gain its feet again. An animal traveling through this sponge like substance comes out of it slick and clean, and for all the world as though it had emerged from a river.

I dont know from what the name Muskeg is derived, but suppose it to be a tecnical French Canadian term.

From where the party are now hacking away, the Macleod River is distant about 19 miles. All appear to be working with a will, being tired of the Mountains, and anxious to be out of them, and above all, to be through this extensive Morass.

The Hudsons Bay Company nor the Indians ever travel through this section of country save when the ground is frozen, during which time, this muskeg section becomes firm enough to admit of loaded Dog sleds passing over it, but I am informed it never freezes to any depth, never in fact considered safe for horses.

Since the boys started in the field again, they have been considerably reinforced from Edmonton, and what a motley lot they seem. We have English, Canadian, Scotch, French Canadian, Greek, Half breeds, and Indian hangers on.

One of our Packers, by the name of Church, "Doc" Church more generally called, has been very anxious to leave the party, and join me in my trip down; and we have talked the matter over and over, and I had congratulated myself on having a chum ready at hand, but behold, at the final moment he backs out, to my disgust; and gives as an excuse he does not think the animals can stand it, as he came up that way with Jane and party, and that no two men can make the crossings at some of the rivers. I put him down for a coward, and must look around me for a chum somewhere, nor have I long to wait.

With the party lately arrived from Edmonton came a big, dark-bearded, pleasant faced Scotchman by the name of "Henry Baird", a man of superior intelligence as I should judge, who asked me if I thought I could manage it to have him as a companion. He told me he had traveled accross the entire contenant, and was making for British Columbia and the Pacific, to take passage to Australia, having a brother in that colony, or rather in New Zealand.

[space left for drawing of foot of pass, east slope]

I liked the burly Scot's appearance; he was young, evidently not more than six and twenty, and it is needless to add I was delighted at his offer. I thought it a decided improvement on talkative, bragging Doc Church, who by the way, afterwards twisted weathercock-wise, and said he would'nt mind as there were to be three of us.

But Moberley does not relish the idea of loosing any of his white hands, and would have me take "Tim" one of our Douglas Indians as a companion. This I stoutly protest against.

With reference to this Indian "Tim", he is a lithe active young fellow enough, but as lazy as Indians generally are, who have learned to labor a little. Now Master Tim has considerable back pay due him; and this fact having become known to a party of "Crees" who have been hanging on to our skirts, they have conceived a great liking for him, so much so, in fact, that they would adopt him into their tribe, nay, more, a chief with them tells him he has two daughters, handsome girls, whose mother was a half breed, so that white blood intermingles with the Indian, that they are Fort Edmonton way; and that if he joins their people, he will sell him one of his girls for a wife. Tim has drank all this in, until now he is almost desperate to get his pay, quit the expidition, and leave with his quandum friends for their wigwams and a bride. But Moberly, has informed Master Tim he shall have neither discharge nor money, and as regards money; he did

not carry any. He could only give him an order on Fort Edmonton; and this he would not do. You fool— he continued, are you so blind you don't see their move. As regards your joining their people, and securing a wife from them; they are cramming you in order to induce you to go with them to a distance, when they would club you to death, and get your money without the bride. But as Tim could not be convinced, he has become an ugly Indian; so much so that our chief would dispense with him, but will not let him depart with his new found Indian friends, knowing well what the result would be. And thus it turns out, with many thanks to our chief for his magnanimity, and his return for all my faithful services, he must needs at the end, and in sheer selfishness, try to have me content myself with a dissatisfied Indian, whose will does not turn in my direction, but in the opposite one, and would have me entrust myself with him as my only help and solace through a long and dangerous journey. Not if I know myself, I had surely not dreamed of so much perfidy in our chief. What a world to be sure.

Let it be understood the chief referred to above was not wholly Indian, and had been about the Fort at Edmonton a great deal, and knew the value of the almighty dollar.

The half breeds of the party told Tim that they would kill him if he refused to be made a slave of, and if he submitted, they would sell him to the first band of Indians who would purchase him. I may state, Tim never became their dupe, but returned to the lower country with the party.

It has been discovered my friend Rheaume has the gift of using the soldering iron better than any other of the boys, and I was greatly amused while observing him mending kettles the other day.

Henry Baird informed me he had crossed the Continent in a somewhat unique manner, that he had worked his passage along the great lakes, and then fortunately had fallen in with a train with supplies for the Red River settlement, midway accross the plains, that he had been a help to the trains for his support and their company, that on reaching Red River he had, (being a brother Scotchman), received kind treatment at the hands of the Hudsons Bay officials, and had finally joined a strong party of miners to proceed to the Susquatuan [Saskatchewan?] River, where it was said gold had been discovered, that he tried his luck there, but failing to strike it, he had, with others, made for Fort Edmonton; was there also kindly befriended; and as Moberly had written to the chief factor at that place, to send him additional help, he had come along, the only white man among the number, the rest being half breeds.

Fires had to be kept going the entire night, as the wolves are congregating somewhat thicker than is agreeable, and have attacked the pack animals during the nights.

May 8th
———
1873

At last, having gained Moberly over to my ernest entreaties to let Baird accompany me, we are all ready for a start

May 13th
———
1873

home; home to me at least, and when our chief did give in, he did it handsomely, so far as myself is concerned, being in fact exceedingly generous. First, he allowed me one months salary from date, and $44. traveling expenses as soon as I strike civilization. Secondly, he has permitted me to take two horses, one as a riding animal, the other for my baggage, and provisions, but he is so vexed with my poor chum, he will allow him nothing beyond his pay up to date, which is right enough, considering he has but lately joined, but he will allow him no horse. He is a strange man, our chief. He knows full well it will be out of the question his traveling without a horse, but it is not unlikely he knows what is floating through my mind while he states as much. There are animals at our winters quarters which are grazing idly, and must be fresh now, and he has given me permission to change my animals if they do not suit me, and take others, and although he has given no written order to this effect, I am content it should be so, for I know, and probably he knows, I shall appropriate a third animal without his leave, as I am certain Brown would not question my veracity when I tell him the chief has so ordered it, and as I impart this in strict confidence to Harry Baird, he smiles approval and satisfaction. I have observed my new friend Harry pretty closely, and find him a man of very few words, not much given to talk of himself and his affairs, and I apprehend no fear that between this and morning he will devulge our little arrangement. Harry grinned, and stated his determination to steal an animal if Brown refused short of a written order; he would do it he said if half a dozen Brown's said him nay.

And now, as we are to start with the first peep of day, our good-byes were said tonight. Every man in camp has given us a warm shake of the hand, and a god speed, for surely I have been a favorite with them all! And after we had turned towards our tents and blankets, the cook appears, and with a broad grin, lays before me a nice loaf of Bread, a couple of Dried Apple tarts, peice of boiled Bacon, and a great pile of dough-nuts. There is nothing flippant nor trifling in such good-byes. We had been connected for nigh two years, and although it had been my lot to be seperated from them the greater portion of the time, yet they felt my presence in their midst, for every endeavour had been made by me that their wants should be supplied; in all this time I had no complaints of short supplies while in the field. The task was a difficult one, but I was ably seconded by my packers, who were men well up to their duties, and as I turned into the Blankets between Jane and Reaume, who would have me sleep with them this last night, we were like school boys I felt: I felt regret at having to turn my back upon such comrades, but I wanted to be away, and I should only feel freedom now when we were plodding on toward the summit of the Leatherhead Pass, for after leaving the Winter quarters, our route was to be a totally unknown one to us. And now good night all, the sentry awakes us at an early hour, so let us haste to dream the short night away.

We were up before daylight, to find Hall and the Dog sleds, whose services were no longer needed, preparing for their journey to Edmonton. Hall was to hire more halfbreeds to

Wednesday
May 14th

1873

181

labor, as Moberly was pushing the work to the utmost. Not long after every tent was emptied of its occupants, for pandamonium was again let loose, Dogs clamouring for a morning meal, which they had been ordered, and which the sledmen were getting ready for them with many a blessing reversed. Five or six of the party were likewise proceeding to Edmonton sick with scurvy. Roots and Tea, made from the bark of the spruce tree having hitherto being the only remedy. Hall comes forward, and is all smiles and attention to our little party of two: he gives me his own Packsaddle, and even assists me to saddle up, and as the Dog trains with some fifteen men en 'suite set their faces to the east, two men face to the westward, and we commence our marches as a wild cheer cleaves the raw mountain air, and echo's among the hills.

During the day we pass a Pack train coming in with supplies, and one of the men hands me his small brass kettle; as a gift, Rylatt, you will find it handy, so it is transferred to our pack train of one animal, and again the hand shake, and forward.

I wondered how many of these old comrades would ever cross my path again. Ten years hence, how widely will all be scattered.

We reached the Fiddle River depot in due time, and my friend White gave us a larger share than common of his blarney at parting, and that is saying a good deal. We found the Fiddle river much swollen from the melting snows above, and whereas, on my downgrade I had difficulty in finding a place deep enough to wet my ancles, we now had some little trouble in finding a fording place; the bottom being composed of large boulders, which were moving with a muffled mumbling sound, by the swift current, and as apt to trip an animal while fording as not.

On our way here we started a large moose out of a swampy peice of chaparel, which went snorting and charging up the hill, hastened by the report of my revolver. This fellow was as large and heavy as a good sized ox, somewhat longer in the legs in fact.

I sold my Rifle before starting down, being convinced I could not pack it without damage, and depended upon my revolver, if need was had to firearms at all; I had found that during my sojourn in the mountains, although I had looked upon it as a friend in need, and felt some degree of safety when having it within reach, I had but twice had occasion for its service, once against my own species, and once when attacked by the wolves, and after all the last named was by far the least of the two dangers, for the human wolves were likewise armed. It was therefore expedient I should encumber myself with nothing I could dispense with. My sketches and diary I had safe slung to me in a tin case, soldered and perfectly water tight, as also sundry drawings and writing from our chief to the authorities in Victoria.

Upon reaching the Athabasca, we found this river overflowing its banks; at all times both rapid and dangerous, it was doubly so now; we tried in several places to ford it; especially about the old ford, now some quarter of a mile wide; but the animal was taken off his feet at every attempt, and nothing remained to us but to raft it, as we had not calculated upon meeting any serious obstruction before reaching our winter quarters, where we were to supply ourselves with ropes; we were delayed until Harry rode back to Fiddle river for a supply. During the absense of my chum, with the remaining animal, and by forcing a passage through the thick underbrush, I examined the river higher up, but found no place where a crossing could be made. While thus engaged, I came upon some bear droppings yet warm, and the largest footprint of a Grizzly I had ever seen. The knowledge that he had but now passed this spot, that he was a monster, and was somewhere close at hand, that I was virtually defenseless, possessing only a revolver, caused me to retire, and again seek the open spot, and patiently await Harry's return, when we at once set to work in the construction of a raft. It was our misfortune however, to find nothing better suited to our purpose than drift timber, which, being watersoaked, was not very buoyant; however, we tied six or seven logs together, having cross peices at either end. It was a clumsy affair owing to the material we had, and we were doubtful if we could manage to force it through so swift a current, but resolved to sleep upon it, and try our luck at daylight. We therefore secured our noble craft, and being now dead tired, and quite dark withal, we eschewed cooking supper, but turned into our blankets at once.

We were up at dawn, ate a hearty breakfast, and was much chagrined to find our raft was too small to carry ourselves and baggage. It was not without some forebodings we commenced the construction of a larger one, and after considerable delay in scouring the bank for material, we finally proclaimed all ready, and after lashing all our worldly goods securely to the raft in case of accident (a precaution we always took after this our first experience), and after forcing the animals into the stream, and seeing them heading for the opposite shore, we cast off, and paddled vigerously. Alas, we had not left the shore a dozen yards, when I became fearful for the issue. Harry had told me he understood something of the water, and the use of the paddle, but he soon convinced me he knew nothing of either. I took the steering end, and the unweildy affair claimed all my powers to keep her up stream;

as we got out of the eddy, the water became rough, and washed clean over the watersoaked raft. Harry at this became excited, confused and frightened, and suddenly turning round on his knees, began paddling with all his might against me, and wanting to go back. I yelled at him it was too late, told him to turn again, and paddle with all his might for the other shore, and we should fetch up somewhere. In his excitement he caused the raft to keel over, but fortunately on the lee side, and then in sheer desperation, gave way with a will. All this time we had been loosing our chances, and we were being bourne swiftly with the stream, and past the eddy on the opposite side I had calculated upon entering. Our case was becoming a little desperate. We were close upon some rapids; not very formidable it is true, but with such a contrivance as this upon which we had embarked, forced upon me the great uncertainty as to whether our ropes would stand the strain, and the raft, parting from under us, leaving us but a small chance of escape, and in any event, with the certain loss of all of which we were possessed. No such ill luck befel us however; we shot the rapid swiftly but smoothly, and labored like trojons for the shore we were fast closing upon. Our next difficulty was to effect a landing; there were so many projecting snags I dare not run her in, but spying ahead a good chance, I turned her head to meet it, and striking the bank and a sunken snag at the same instant, Harry was rather thrown than clambered on to the bank, head line in hand, and we had effected a landing. Our first lesson in rafting a large mountain river was over, a risky business certainly; and with but little experience myself, and a chum who had none whatever, we concluded we had been favored, and felt correspondingly thankful; it was a rough lesson for Harry, but it taught him wisdom, as was clearly prooved at our next venture, but of all this in its proper place. After a breathing spell, during which we listened to the roar of more formidable rapids probably a mile below us; and after I had enjoyed my comforting smoke, we began to devise means to get back upstream to the fording place and the trail. With axe and hatchet we cut our way to where the Horses had made their landing, and which was nigh a half mile below where we started them in, and as they had made a bee line for the shore, it will give you some idea of the strength of the current. As to ourselves, we had been carried down some three miles before effecting our landing. We were moveover fearful our horses should find the trail of the pack trains, and leave us in the lurch, so it spurred us on to work with a will.

Late in the afternoon, having cut past the animals, we came upon the trail; then returning without loss of time, we were mortified to find the brutes had not reached the shore proper, but were on an island, and in order to reach them, a deep slough had to be crossed. As it was but sluggish water, Harry divested himself of his unmentionables, and straddling a log, paddled accross, and we soon had them secured. We were by this time precious hungry, but deciding to make the most of the daylight left us, we pushed on to our landing spot, over our newly made trail, packed the animals, struck out again, and reaching the trail of the pack-trains, encamped for the night. On the night of the 18th May we reached the Athabasca depot (winter quarters), where we secured a horse from friend Brown, securing him by handing him a receipt for the animal. Possibly he thought it somewhat strange Moberly did not send him an order in writing to the effect, but he could hardly doubt my veracity, as until now all such matters had rested mainly with me; however, for once said veracity was not reliable, and it behooved me to lie to him, it being impossible to proceed without a third animal, and Moberly's refusal to supply us with one.

On the following morning we started merrily on our way in a pouring rain, and we soon found that it was only a difference of gradually becoming wet, and a sudden transition to that state, for, on reaching the Myette river (which takes its rise at the summit of the Leatherhead pass), we had to take the first crossing swimming, baggage and all. The river was not wide, but swift and deep, and I may add, our supply of Provisions were not improved any by being soused under water. We had to cross this abominable stream no less than nine times, and in some places the animals had all they could do to keep their feet, although after the first ford, we could find bottom; and the higher we got, the more shallow the fords became. At our third crossing, though, by some unlucky accident Harry's horse struck with his feet a sunken snag, when over he went: Harry made for shore, but the animal, not being able to regain his footing, he was rolled over and over by the swift current, until striking a shallow lower down, finally made land. Here was a delay, the dense undergrowth necessitating a rude trail in order to get him to the trail proper. We managed to make some 20 miles however, and encamped on a Prairie, some four miles from the summit of the Leatherhead; it was necessary here to tie the animals to trees, giving them rope enough to permit their feeding nicely, and making doubly sure, we hobbled them likewise. These were pack animals, regular old stagers, and adept at slipping a halter, or failing in the exploit, backing with all their might to break the rope. They were too near their old feeding ground; hence the unusual precautions.

The accompanying Sketch of the route from our winters quarters to Kamloops, showing our camping places, distances, rivers and mountain streams we had to contend with, feed grounds &c will do much to explain matters.

My friend, John Jane, came the route we proposed taking some two years previous, with a force of men and a pack train, and as many hands make light work, they experienced little difficulty comparatively, but in presenting me with this mapped out plan, he warned me it was a terror of a route. I have ever been thankful to him, for his thoughtfulness, or heaven only knows how we should have reached the settlements.

Although we had been up until quite late, drying out Blankets and provisions, we were astir bright and early, and after a hearty breakfast of Slapjacks and Bacon, we moved on soon after daylight. [At the top of page 195 of the original journal, before the words "a hearty breakfast," Rylatt had penciled in "plan of route attached here," but he left the space blank.] On reaching the summit of the pass, we found it a level plateau of moderate demensions, the soil soggy in places, in others difficult of travel through masses of broken rock; and, in fact, we were not aware we had turned the summit, until we perceived the water running in the opposite direction, or with us, so slight had been the incline during the last few miles. We were red-hot to push ahead, and accomplished 24 miles; which will make it needless to say more than that the trail was a very good one. Once or twice we were detained for awhile, to cut away fallen timber, but so slight in fact, as to be barely worth the record. I dont think we acted wisely in this matter, we were putting our animals to their utmost at the commencement, instead of norishing their strength for the severe trial we knew lay before them.

We had expected to find difficulty in crossing the Mountain Streams 'twixt the summit and Moose Lake, but were agreeably disappointed. Moose river, at which point we were led to beleive we should have difficulty, we took swimming, there was no fording such a stream, and as its width was not very great, we dispensed with the services of a raft; moreover there were several eddys strong enough to be called small whirlpools, and so we passed over, each taking a firm grip of the tail of his riding animal with one hand, swimming with the other. This method of crossing we were compelled to exercise on occasions, where the current was unusually strong; for instance, by taking the animals mane, and swimming on the upper side, the current would have driven us close upon him, and we should have been in danger of being struck by his forefeet. Again, of on the lower side, the force of the rushing water would have swept us from the animal, and have had a tendency to pull him over on his side, where he would loose his power, and probably end in the drowning of both man and horse. The tail business therefore is far the safest, man and horse being both driven down stream equally; and as a horse, when swimming, always strikes out with his hind feet well down, there is no risk of his hitting you, especially if you keep a good distance. We generally stripped to swim these dangerous streams, tying our clothes securely on the back of the animal, and the icy cold of these rivers, just emerged from the ice and snow fields above, were anything but pleasent. Most of the streams where this method had to be adopted were not very wide, so that we were not in the water long enough to become cramped: nevertheless to me, suffering from scurvy, it is a marvel I came through it as well as I did.

We camped at the head of Moose Lake. Experiencing a bitter cold night, and a strong wind howling down the pass, disturbed the surface of the water, and made music by grinding the broken masses of floating ice with which the lake was covered.

On the following day we made about 24 miles, and while skirting the lake shore, it was in many places unsafe, being slippery rock, and very steep, in other places it was a network of roots, where the earth had been washed out, and great care had to be observed to keep the animals from becoming crippled.

Moose Lake is some nine miles long, its average width one mile, and is the head of one of the forks of the mighty Frazor River.

The river called the grand forks was also laid down as difficult, but we found none.

Came upon our first cedars today, which we looked upon as good signs; for we were leaving the higher levels, and we might expect less severe nights. There are no cedars on the east slope of the rocky's, at least none on our route. Misquito's very troublesome. At about noon on the 23d May we reached Tete Juan, our fording place on the Fraser River. At this point a small hut had been built of logs by Jane's party two years previous, as a cache, to protect Provisions from the Bear and smaller, but equally destructive animals. These stores were so cached until their return trip, and here we found an old cottonwood canoe they had made, or dug-out, a peice of log hacked out roughly with the axe, but now so rotton, it was with feelings of great doubt we took advantage of it. Cottonwood is a soft and unservicable wood, spongy almost when green, and in fact until recently thought to have no marketable value whatever. As fuel, it is worthless, unless thoroughly dry, and decay sets in quickly after cutting down, if left exposed to the elements, but is becoming somewhat extensively in demand now, and is excellent for Barrels for dry material, such as Flour, Sugar, Pilot Bread, and a thousand commodities of commerce, where tight barrels are not required.

To return, this river, one of the largest in the great northwest, is at Tete Juan quite wide, consequently less rapid than above and below this place; it is of considerable depth though, but has a counter eddy, making it a safe crossing place by raft or dug out canoe. At this spot, and as the river winds, we were something like 1300 miles from its mouth, some nine miles below New-westminster, where it looses itself in the Gulf of Georgia.

Deciding to risk the dug-out, rather than delay by building a raft, we set to work fixing her up, and by dint of scraps of rags, moss and the pitch from the pine trees we calked the gaping slits or cracks, made rude paddles, swam the animals, and very gingerly placing our traps aboard, and as gingerly entering ourselves, we made for the opposite landing. The water trickled in, in the most unpleasant manner, and it was nip and tuck, for down she went when within a couple of yards of the bank, and a general scramble took place to throw our traps on shore as nimbly as possible, but if wet, we were at least on the right side of the river, which was some comfort. The day was fine and sunny; so calling a halt, we dried our Blankets & Grub as well as we could, the Horses meanwhile nibbling the sweet grass, of which there was plenty; our matches was always carefully looked after; wrapped in fold upon fold of waterproof cloth, and when crossing streams, divided, and carried on our persons.

After being well rested, we pushed on, but encamped early, to attend to Kitty's back; Kitty is our pack mare, and a most faithful old animal, but the abominable Pack saddle, and the wettings she has had to endure, has given her some nasty looking sores, on her withers and sides, so I washed them well with Castile soap and warm water, and afterwards applied powdered alum; having provided myself with some for such an emergency. It is not pleasant to reflect though, that she may become so sore, she may become useless to us.

We passed some grand scenery today, and if we except the Hope Mountain, the grandest my eye ever dwelt upon. One immense giant towered high above his fellows, his spiral peaks shooting heavenward, and bristling in the clear sky, a cold, rigid sight amid the solitude, while the suns rays scintilated his pinnacles and gorges pale blue, as they played among his glaciers. Robsons peak as it is called is a beautiful sight, an awful scene of beauty, made more so as we stand gazing upward, an isolated pair of humans, in the midst of a wilderness, with dangers past, and more to meet 'ere we can reach our kind, with dead silence all around, and a mighty chain of Snow Capped mountains on our right hand, and on our left, which, spite of their white heads, looked frowning and threatening. How forcibly do such scenes tell us of the great creators works. I am sure Harry felt as I felt, very lonely, something more than—"a long way from home"—feeling. Halting in an open space, and where the foot hills hid all save the peaks of Mount Robson, we swallowed our Cold Lunch; and after a little conversation, relapsed into silence, and drank in the scene before us. I give a very faint idea of the scene in the accompanying sketch.

[space left for drawing of Robson's Peak]

But of a sudden, the spell was broken, as a shrill scream overhead cut the stillness. A hawks nest, we had not observed, was above our heads, on top of a tree, or rather a portion of a tree, for the top had been wrenched off by one of the many fierce storms which it was plain to be seen swept this valley, and here dwelt a loving couple, and the voices of their brood could be heard as the old birds flying angrily overhead passed and repassed the nest. It was very early in the season we thought for young birds, but there could be no mistake about it. It had a funny impression upon us both. We had been moralizing until we had worked ourselves into the blues evidently, and in an instant the spell was broken, and we were no longer isolated; but all nature brightened under the power of a hawks scream of anger. We were strange looking animals no doubt; and unwelcome. So we moved on, and left them to rear their young in peace under the shadow of the great mountain, and his lofty peaks.

Our travel since leaving Tete Juan has been excellent; a dry sandy soil with open timber. Today it has been very warm, and our old enemies, the misquito's are very troublesome tonight.

On the 23d we reached within two miles of Albreda Lake, having had a hard days travel to reach this point, and it was quite dark when we halted.

Before reaching Canoe river, the trail became so indistinct, it was impossible to follow it, and we were undecided as to our whereabouts. Seperating therefore to recognoitre, Harry made down the hill on the left hand, while I took to a narrow beaten track to the right. After following my path for nigh two miles I should suppose, sometimes on hands and knees, at other times over fallen timber, and blazing in order not to loose myself completely, I came to a dead halt in a swamp. I knew the trail I had been following was animals trail, for both bear and elk tracks were plenty, and the claw marks on the logs told plainly of bruin, but I had hoped to cross our trail proper; I was disappointed however, and nothing remained but to retrace my steps, and follow Harry, who was fortunately in the right direction. In due time we reached Canoe River, a broad swift stream. After trying to ford it in several places without effect, although Jane told us a good fording place did exist, we gave it up, and made a raft; we did not anticipate any difficulty, as the banks were low, and together with the water, apparantly free from snags or other obstructions. And now when we were quite ready, our animals gave us some trouble. Twice we got them to the edge of the bank, when they broke and ran, and, the country being open in the vicinity of the river hereabout, they led us a merry old dance each time before we could secure them. I presume one could scarce blame the poor brutes; they were evidently getting very tired of the water. Finally however, we had the satisfaction of seeing them start accross, but judge of our mortification, on seeing them ford it the entire distance; what we had searched for in vain, they had found, the ford, with water scarce 3 feet deep. We lost no time now, but took to the raft, and followed them, finding no difficulty.

The night is very cold, with a cutting wind.

And the Queens birthday. As heavy a days travel as I have ever experienced. Man and beast thoroughly exhausted; our appearances anything but prepossessing, being mud from head to foot. Several times the horses mired deep, and it has been the result of great labor to extricate them. Poor beasts! How hungry they must be! No feed yesterday, and there is none here, and they have to be tied, to stand, cold and hungered until daylight forces them to another days toil, faint and unrefreshed. For some six miles today it was necessary to go ahead of the animals in places, and break a trail through the snow, which lay some two feet deep, with a frozen crust on top that would have cut like a knife. Our hearts are sorely misgiving us, for our animals show signs of breaking down altogether, and we are but entering the country (according to friend Jane) where we must expect no feed. They were poor at the start; they look dreadful lank tonight as they stand with drooping heads, their backs hogged up, and feet all in a heap. We have cooked our supper, and are partaking of it, when the pityful whinneying of our dumb comrades we can resist no longer. With troubled looks we eye our scant supply of Flour, and as our eyes meet, there is a womans softness in those of my burly chum, as he says, shall we, Bob?— A nod, and he

Saturday
May 24th

1873

takes the sack, and laying each his saddle cloth, he doles out to the starving brutes a little flour, not much certainly, but probably enough to stay hungers pangs a little while.

[space left for drawing of night on bank of Thompson River]

We have reached, and are camped on the bank of the forks of the Thompson river, and as we look at the troubled stream, we know that no childs play awaits us tomorrow, —and the animals! But sufficient for the day is the evil thereof, so we seek our blankets, and are soon lost in the land of forgetfulness.

Sunday
May 25th

1873

Had an unusually close call for our checks today. We constructed our raft of cedar logs, and seeing the fierce current we had to contend with, and the uncertainty of making a good landing, we made it as strong as our supply of ropes could make it.

It was an ugly sight, this river, tearing along with race horse speed, the shore line beyond bristling with snags and projecting fallen timber, the thickly matted undergrowth projecting far out into the stream, the black sullen clouds, and pouring rain, and our stiffened limbs as we rose from our wet blankets, the starved, shivering, unrested brutes hoping for a breakfast we could not supply to them, for even the thick brush was of a variety they could not nibble. It was about as blue an outlook as I had ever experienced; and as we set to work we tried to shake it off with all the effort we were capable of. To make matters still worse, and so leave us in greater uncertainty, the river took a sudden bend below us, hiding whatever obsticles there might be from view. Imagine if you please, the situation for a moment, and dont think us quite chicken hearted, glance at our dumb friends, certain they were indispensable to us; now reduced to skin and bone, poor as crows when we started on the trip, pushed through day after day over the roughest country, from 20 to 24 miles daily, hungered half the time, and scoured by their only food, young grass, swimming streams icy cold, tied nightly, or hobbled, and suffering cold.

I can tell you, as we eyed them this dismal morning, it was doubtful if they would endure until night, and no feed, none whatever for many miles, none surely to day, nor tomorrow, if Jane spoke truly. Then our drenched garments, this rushing swollen river, the bristling banks opposite, with no observ-able landing place, huge trees rolling along with the flood, sunken snags at intervals showing out of the stream, black and ugly; which the hurrying waters struck, and throwing up a white circlet, as they hissed and bubbled onward to where? —there we were at a loss, round the bend, and where the Albreda mingled with them, beyond we could not say, a cum-bersome raft, unmanagable I may say in such a current; if rapids or snags were below, we could not evade them, and if we struck them, —well, our chances would be mighty slim anyhow. Then I was no raftsman, my chum worse than nobody if we got into a fix; the Athabasca crossing told me too plainly how easily he became bewildered. I don't think the outlook was an enviable one, and anyone with our expe-rience, who would pooh-pooh us, and call us faint hearted, is either a gaspipe, to use a vulgar phrase, or a fool. We were in a trap as it were. Above us the bank rose steep, I may say precip-ituous; below, the swollen Albreda river emptied its contents into the Thompson, so that we were cut off on either hand; I had forgotten to observe this was not the fording place we were now about to cross; upon reaching this point, we were instructed to ford the Albreda, strike lower down, and then ford about a mile below, but although we tried and tried again last night to find a ford in the Albreda, we were con-vinced raft, horse nor man could live long enough to cross such a current; it was the recipient of many Mountain Streams, the rain had been a deluge, and it was over its banks, and hourly rising, drift was coming down thick and fast, and we considered by taking the larger stream, we were lessoning the danger.

Our first care had been, after turning out, and before pre-paring our morning meal, to exercise the horses on the few yards of beach at our command, and after a time their hogged up backs gradually assumed a more natural appearance, their stiffened joints became more supple, then doling them out a little more of our precious stock of Flour, we ate our own breakfast, and prepared for crossing. Counting our chances, we concluded they were about even, but if anything, the odds were against us. But our greatest trouble was the horses; for as soon as they rounded the bend (which they would do long before they reached the other shore), there was no certainty where they would fetch up; or, if they failed to make a landing, they might, and would in all probability, make for the shore they had left again. Their brute instinct told them there was danger ahead, for when led to the water, they trembled violently, and stood stubbornly receiving the blows showered upon them, in our efforts to compel them to cross. At length Kitty could bear no more, and plunged in, to be immediately followed by the others. I need not say we anxiously watched them (Kitty keeping the lead), their heads slightly up stream, and making bravely over, until the bend in the river hid them from sight. They were all good swimmers, Kitty in particular, swam very high out of the water. And now for ourselves. Everything securely lashed, and with nothing on but our drawers, we took our places, and Harry was about to cast off the head line, when we were both startled by the wailing cry of a child, and on the opposite shore, so natural the cry, we stared at each other for a moment 'ere we found speech. Here, amid a dreary solitude, with nothing heard save the pelting rain, and the rushing flood, it came out clear and pitiful. Yes, no mistake; for again it cut through the murky atmosphere, and under the impulse of the moment we both shouted, at the moment imagining an Indian Camp must be near, but what I have first stated was but the mistake of a minute, the delusion as quickly vanished; and both ejaculated the word "Panther," and a moment after we saw the tawny brute spring on to a fallen tree, glare over at us, and disappear. The panthers cry was not new to us, and in fact, once heard, it is hard to mistake it, but this was more human than I had ever heard it.

As usual, I undertook the steering, and had the hatchet in my hand. As soon, therefore, as Harry had slipped the head line (her head being up stream), she swung round with the current, and telling him to give way, I severed the small line at the stem end (not the stem line proper), when she shot out into the stream, and just clearing a sandbar below us, commenced hurrying down stream at a great rate. We were very naturally concerned as to what difficulties might await us round the bend; this matter of going it blind was somewhat more than unpleasant, the rush of the Albreda, and the noise as it dashed against obsticles in its course drowned all other sounds, and left us to conjecture; we fancied rapids, and formidable snags where none might exist, we felt doubtful if our cumbersome craft could be propelled beyond midcurrent, so swift was it, and that we might be carried down in spite of every effort to the contrary. Had it not been for sake of reaching feed for the animals, we would have sought the higher ground, and have awaited the going down of the flood; the downpour was as the bursting of a waterspout, only that it was continuous. Our camping spot of last night, which had been three or more feet above water mark was now nigh covered, but we had not long to remain in suspense; we were quickly round the bend, and one keen glance releived us. We bent to our paddles with a will now; the water was quite rough in places, and whirled in eddies, prooving a very uneven bottom. Several snags were passed, but providentially out of our line, or, I had not been sitting quitely perusing this little history; our craft could not be handled in time to avoid them, therefore we did not try. With all our might we struggled for our shore, but for some minutes we made no progress in the desired direction, but as we shot past, we had the satisfaction of seeing our animals safe, and standing on the bank, and just ahead, the river widened considerable, while lower down the banks again narrowed, checking in a measure the rush of waters, and here we gradually crept shoreward, and out of the midcurrent. Every moment made our landing more certain, and we crept in as near shore as was advisable, drifting, and on the look out for a chance to run in. Presently we were running past an immense tree, which, held by its roots no doubt, and lying lengthwise with the stream. As we were rapidly passing this, and before I had time to caution him, Harry, headline in hand, threw himself upon it; he had first doubled the line by a throw, over the stump end of a branch, and following, braced himself to check the raft, but powerful as he was, he lacked the power for such a feat; besides the tree had lain long in the water, and nothing remained but the short sharp stumps of the branches, the

[space left for drawing of rafting Thompson]

whole being covered by a thick coat of slimy mud. Harry, finding he had no power to check the raft, the only effect being to cause her head to dip more deeply, thereby gaining instead of loosing force, in desperation threw himself upon the log, and was in this position drawn along to the stump of the branch over which he had made a turn. The water at the time was making a clean breach over the raft; when with a yell my chum was compelled to loose his hold, and as the line flew from his hand, the raft lifted, and bore me onward, sole tenant.

But now comes the most singular part of this little history; was it providence? Were I ever so set against the decrees of providence, the following fact would shake such a belief out of me. Assuredly it was a most providential deliverence for us. It was Gods will it should not be here we should pass in our checks. I should say I might have drifted seven or eight hundred yards, and using my paddle to no purpose, when I felt a sudden shock, the raft was checked, the water swept over her, and I was thrown into the stream at the same instant. On starting I had loosely tied the stem line round my body, partly to prevent its being washed off the raft, and thus becoming out of reach in case of immediate need, and partly, I admit, that if we struck any obstacle, and the raft parted, I should be at least attached to one or more of her timbers, whereby I could keep myself afloat probably, and now this same line did actually come into play, for I was no sooner in the water, and beneath the surface, than I felt myself checked with a grip round my waist. I was too bewildered I remember to compre-

hend my situation; I felt myself choking, when I struck something, and with a drowning grip, I clasped it, somehow
worked myself upward; I soon comprehended matters more
fully. I had been thrown in by a swirl of the current, had
struck against the stout limb of a recently fallen tree, clutched
it, and instinct had brought me to the surface. The tree was a
huge cedar, overhanging the stream several yards, and this
branch with others were sunk beneath the surface of the
water; to struggle from branch to branch was the work of a
moment, and I had gained the shore. With a fervent, "thank
God," I sank on the scarcely less soaked ground; but was on
my feet again in an instant; for there was the raft, tugging and
straining to free herself. Harry, Harry! I yelled, and a not distant reply caused me to again ejaculate "Thank God."— In a
few minutes he broke through the underbrush, and was
beside me, but poor fellow, he was in a sad plight; the large
tree upon which he had thrown himself, and along which he
had been dragged, had lain in the water so long, that the
branches were all gone, leaving only the short jagged ends or
stumps. Over these poor Harry had been hauled, as he
clutched desperately the headline, and they had cut him like
knives. His breast and legs were bleeding, from some ugly
gashes he had received. He said he had become bewildered
somehow, had slipped off the log, fortunately on the shore-
side, and where the force of the current was broken, and had
managed his way ashore without much difficulty, but 'ere all
this was asked, and in fact, before exchanging a dozen words,
we both set to with a will to get our raft nearer shore. The
stem rope was still fast to my waist, and taking a couple of
turns round a tree, we commenced hauling in on all that
stood between us and starvation. We were soon lightening
our craft of our precious stores, wet and half spoiled; but
thankful they were not beyond our reach.

By some fortunate accident, forever to remain a mystery as
to exactly how the headline, after leaving Harry's hand, had,
through the swirl of the current probably, caught in some
object beneath the surface, and spite of the strain, had held
the raft firmly, while dipping and pulling like a live thing to

free itself; it was lucky the headline was very stout, and in fact almost new. Our puny efforts had been in vain to save ourselves, but God, in his mercy, and by means which will forever be a puzzle to me, had mercifully taken us in the hollow of his hand.

Here let me digress a little, and relate that it was in this section of country, that, a few years 'ere this, six men (I beleive) were lost; they were gold hunters, had wandered in these gloomy and sunless forests, until everything edible had been consumed, and at last, with starvation staring them in the face, three of them, yet strong enough to travel, had left their companions in misery, and wandered on, keeping the Thompson for a guide, in search of settlements, food for themselves, and releif for their comrades. In a pitiable condition, one at least did reach, but it was never clearly known how he subsisted, and his tale sent kind hearted trappers packed with provisions from the Kamloops country, and following the blazings made by this miserable surviver and his dead mates, came upon the camping place, found there the remains of two of the unfortunate men; the third had left, taking with him portions of the limbs of one of his dead companions, for what purpose can be easily guessed. He was never heard of.

Two Englishmen, Lord Milton (a son of Earl Fitzwilliam I think) and a Doctor Cheadle, with guides and a working party crossed the Contenant in the year 1863, and on their return to England, the Doctor published a work, profusely illustrated, of their travels and adventures. As their line of route is through this section, in fact the one we shall take from this on (further reference to which hereafter), a great deal is devoted to it, and a perusal of the work will confirm how dreary a wilderness it is.

But all this is keeping Harry and I before the blazing fire we have succeeded in lighting, where we are busying ourselves trying to dry out ourselves and our provisions in the pouring rain, which has not abated one bit, and conscious that our troubles are not yet over. Harrys sores have been dressed with balsalm from the spruce tree. The horses have been recovered, and are hard by, but we may not remain an hour longer, so rapid is the advance of the flood, that the island upon which we stand will be covered 'ere another twenty four hours has elapsed, and if we do not wish to be drowned like rats submerged in a trap, we must be up and doing. A low flat island this, originally a bar probably, now densely wooded, but low and flat, so after a hasty meal, we leave our animals and traps, and strike out seperately to explore the next branch or fork of this river, a difficult task owing to the dense undergrowth. We finally met on the bank, to find this fork more rapid than the one we had but now crossed, though by no means as wide; I should judge not more than ninety yards in fact. We were at once convinced no raft could live in it, and even were it possible, we could not control it. A way was before us, nevertheless. A giant tree, whose diameter might be five feet at the butt, had fallen, and spanned the flood, its roots embedded in the mud on the one bank, its top on the opposite shore, but the rushing, boiling current was already half over it in the centre, and the pressure causing it to bend like a whip. To hasten back was our first move, cutting a rough trail for the animals as we went; then, as quickly packing our traps, we hurried the poor brutes forward, only to find our means of escape gone. The strain had been too much, and the huge tree had snapped asunder, and was probably a mile down stream 'ere we again reached the spot. Again we had to cut our way, this time towards the head of the island. The lower end of our island was already under water, and every minute increased our danger, and lessoned our chances of escape. Our case was becoming desperate, and we were fully alive to the fact. To our tired bodies no breathing time could be allowed, and so rapid was the rise of the flood, it really seemed we were to loose our lives here. After cutting our way some distance, another large tree was before us, but recently lodged to all appearance, it had been some time in the water, was slimy, and divested of all its branches. The rising waters had dislodged it from somewhere above, and in its course down stream, it had evidently come in contact with some obsticle, had swung round, and got jammed.

Hurrying forward the animals, we eased them of their loads, and finding them dead set against taking the stream, in sheer desperation, goaded them with the points of our knives, so that they plunged forward to escape such cruel punishment. They were soon carried beyond our view, but heading bravely for the proper shore, and we lost no time in preparing to follow. Our frail bridge was oscelating in a warning manner, telling plainly it was but a matter of a very short time 'ere it would be gone, and each with a load, started upon our perilous trip accross. I must admit I was becoming somewhat shaky, and following Harry, who had taken the lead, had not gone two yards, when my foot slipped on the slimy log, and letting go the pack I carried, I saved myself from being carried away. The roar of the water over a drift just above us, and the patter of the rain, prevented my chum from hearing the splash of my load, and when he had reached the other side safely, and turned for a return, he saw me creeping along the tree, for I was past standing upon its slippery surface; my nerves were now completely unstrung, and the pack I had started out with was lost. I never could walk a log; or any narrow surface, when there was danger beneath, and to do it now, and in my present state, was impossible. My dear old chum only said a cheery word, and shouldering another load, was off again, nimble as a cat. I fairly cried with chagrin at my entire helplessness, and watched him in wonder. What would I not have given to be so sure of foot. Soon this powerful fellow had all over unaided, and proffering to take me on his back, and I have no hesitation in saying I beleive he could have done it as easily as he carried our traps, but I could not be persuaded. It must be remembered I was sick with scurvy, still I could not account for the terror I felt, and had I been alone, I should have drowned here I beleive rather than have tried that log again. Are there periods in our lives when we are assailed with this sinking of heart? I have found it so in my case; I found it so in the Crimea, and again now. To resume, —Every moment lost was lessoning our chances, and go I must. Even Harry, always so even tempered, was becoming out of temper. And so this brave fellow actually walked accross with me immediately in his rear, my hands grasping each of his shoulders. I call such an act true courage, nay, it was rash. Had I slipped and fallen, in my present state, the supposition is, I should have dragged him in with me, and both would have been lost.

What a strange mixture we are. Here have I, more than once, hinted my chum was easily scared, and so I still contend he was, and so he confessed, but see him now, how much he towers above the ordinary brave man, as he expressed it. I dont have any fears so long as I can feel my feet, but this idea of sitting quietly down, and having only a pair of arms to depend upon, seems like a poor devil minus his lower limbs. This is poor logic you will say, and worse expressed, but the words tumbled from his mouth haphazard as I was loud in my praises of him. It is possible some may think—no great thing to do after all; to such I should hate to depend if the case were theirs, as I am certain they would back out. I was trembling like a leaf, and I fear in such a state, nothing could have loosed my hold, and the water was actually lipping over the log, which was bent and trembling through the great force, augmented by several pieces of drift timber that had been stayed against it. When I put the question to him afterwards, "Did you have no fears I might slip, and drag you after me?" he replied, —"I did, but what was the use, I dont think I could reach the settlements alone."

[space left for drawing of crossing fork of Thompson]

It was now late in the afternoon, and our poor beasts had to be sought for; after an hour or so scrambling and climbing logs we came upon them, and were pleased to see them picking off the young shoots of the salmon berry bushes, or shrubs greatly resembling the salmonberry. No other feed could we see anywhere, so returning, we cached our grub, and returned to their vicinity, determined to let them have the benefit of this poor apology for a feed. The rain still poured down, nor had it ceased one instant during the whole of this exciting day; spreading therefore over our heads the tattered sailcloth, and by dint of perseverence, making up a rousing fire, we prepared our supper, of which we so much stood in need, and passed the gloomy night amid the equally gloomy cedars, dank with festoons of wet moss, the wet spongy moss under us for our beds, in fact moss everywhere, and over everything, the heavy cedars, matting their branches overhead, making all beneath them evening at mid-day, through which but few slanting gleams from the sun could penetrate. Ah! but it was a dismal night, black as ink, save where the light from our well fed fire penetrated, a drenching night, and very cold. Up again by the dawn, Harry went forward to recognoitre the one more fork we had to cross, while I prepared our breakfast. This second island was considerably higher than the first, and we were in no danger of being drowned out, wherein at least was one comfort. Supposing Harry on his return should give an unfavorable report, our island of yesterday was under water, save in a few spots; and as for the log over which we had crossed, it was gone when we returned from hunting the horses last evening; it may have been in an hour or so after we had crossed.

In a short time Harry reappeared, and in reply to my anxious "what luck," he informed me there would be no difficulty, that the distance accross the island was not great, and that he found a jam had formed, stretching clear across the stream, over which we could clamber dry-shod; hundreds of trees, and rubbish had so choked the stream, that upon its forcing a passage through, was smooth, and in fact but little water any way. The supposition being, this stream had become choked by a jam at its head, and the main body of water forced to seek a passage through the other channels, but by what means we were thus favored, concerned us not, and we felt no curiosity to ascertain. To get once more on terra firma was our aim, and it was with thankful hearts we ate our meal, doled out a handful of Flour to each animal, then cutting the necessary trail, we proceeded; moreover the storm was nigh spent, or we hoped so. The clouds were breaking, and scudding along in heavy black masses, and our hearts felt lighter.

As Harry had observed, a jam had formed, and of no recent date, and we were out of the difficulty at last. The Thompson was crossed. Our next move was to cut our way down stream until we struck the choked up trail proper, and once more resume our march. Pressing forward therefore as fast as our weakened animals would permit us, in hopes of striking feed, though with slight expectations, we experienced great difficulty; the long unused trail choked in places with fallen timber, where it was necessary to cut away round, and the trail itself, which had not been used since Jane's party had traversed it, was barely to be made out. The underbrush had grown to its original hight again where it had been cut down, and hid the blazings, our sole guide, if we except the river, which at times was near, at other times out of sight and sound, according to the windings of our narrow pathway, if I may so call it. We encamped early, and as I jot down in my memos this days travel, I can see the animals at the edge of a cranberry swamp, nibbling the tops of the low scrubby bushes, for there is no other feed.

Severe work today to force the animals along, and had to flog them unmercifully. We must push on, we must strike feed, or the animals must be left to perish. We must push forward, or we too shall be starving 'ere we can reach the wished for settlements. Unfortunately, the pack I lost in crossing the second fork of the Thompson, included our Bacon, and save a dozen or so, our matches also. We dared not give the animals any more Flour, we have so little left to us, but we gave them what sugar we had, concluding it was a luxury we could dispense with, and we would drink our Tea without. We look dolefully at our last fast failing sack of Flour, that and the Tea being all that is left to us. It is impossible to tell how long we may yet be in reaching the settlements. Yes, the settlements, the settlements; we are thinking of nothing else now, but the distance between us and the settlements, it is our topic at Breakfast, on the march, and over the camp fire at night. Under the most favorable circumstances, it could not be done under seven days, but with the present swollen

Wednesday.
May 28th

1873

state of the streams, it is all a dead uncertainty. Our matches failing us is our greatest trouble, for while we have the horses, we need not starve, but fire would be essential for the purpose.

The trail, if possible, worse than yesterday, and the animals very weak. Trees uprooted, sloughs belly deep to be crossed, through which the animals could not get through without assistance, and at the crossing of Styx river we found great trouble, the bottom being composed of boulders. At every steep rise, we were compelled to join hands, and placing them under the thighs of the horses, assist them up. One of them "Scotty we called him," delayed us nigh an hour in a small

[space left for drawing of horse Scotty in slough]

slough, the brute lay down, and it was the hardest work I think I ever experienced getting him on firm ground again. We encamped at a spot where was a little coarse feed, barely sufficient for one night; yet withal a bellyful for our poor friends, and thankful we were for it. Being dead tired, and plentifully plastered with mud, we made shift without a fire; the night too, was moderately warm, and after regaling on a couple of cold slapjacks, we betook ourselves to our blankets, and slept soundly. Encountered some patches of snow today, for no sunlight breaks through these dreary everlasting cedars, gloomy at midday. We conclude the distance still untraveled to be one hundred and eighty miles. We are nearing good feed though, and were it not that we have grave doubts hourly now for our animals, we should feel more easy. Kitty's back is a mass of running sores, yet she is the only animal we can pack a pound upon, the others have all they can do to pack their empty saddles.

Thursday.
May 29th

−73.

Started early this A.M. and (God bless John Jane for his chart) we came upon abundance of feed on a small prairie, the poor beasts are belly deep in the sweet herbage; halting for the day, we gave them the benefit of the night here, which was all we could spare to them; and making an early start, we reached Blue river, where Jane had informed me we should have trouble, but it was a pleasant surprise to experience no difficulty; Jane told me it was the most dangerous crossing of all; we crossed without rafting, the water not above our arm-pits, and the horses not swimming. We had been dreading Blue river, thinking we were to have a repetition of the Forks of the Thompson, in which case we concluded to shoot one of the animals, and carry away some meat, when the other animals would no doubt return to the prairie we had left in the early morning. I have grave doubts the government would hold me responsible for the horses in that event, which you will say, scarcely possible, but which I was by no means as sanguine about, but it would have been impossible they could have undertaken another such a bout, and have succeeded in the attempt.

Over this river, and we rested an hour, letting the animals feed, for there was abundance of coarse grass at this spot; then on again, all going merry as a marriage bell, until we reached Goose flat, a large swamp, and here we lost the trail; the river was somewhere on our left, but at what distance we could not say. For a good three hours we searched the edge of the swamp up and down, at times knee deep in water, when at length we found it. A stagnant lake spread itself out in this dismal hollow, and a few wild birds were swimming idly upon it, out of shooting distance, and consequently out of eating distance. These were the first thing living, edable, we had been favored with a sight of during the journey. Our shooting irons moreover, being confined to my revolver, and as the hammer would not stand at full cock, our armory was a very light one. I may state here, that we had no compass, in case of loosing the trail and the river. Bear tracks are plenty enough, but as Kitty has a bell on her neck, Bruin has fair warning of our vicinity, and scenting danger, keep out of sight.

At length, fortune having favored us, and the trail again found, we made a fire, and indulged in a cup of Tea straight, and a hot cake baked in the frypan. The days of slapjacks are over, for no bacon left us, consequently no grease. Did I let you into the mystery of making a good slapjack? You old country people should try it; get good and hungry, and take my receipt. Thus it is: The chef-de-cuisine mixes a thin batter, in the which a pinch of Salt and spoonful of baking powder is needed, but as frequently they are made of flour simple. Have a little hot fat in the pan, pour in a little batter, work it so that it shall cover the whole bottom of the pan, and when sufficiently done on the one side, the dexterous hand of the chef: gives the pan a sudden hoist, and a quick jerk, the slapjack leaps some three feet in the air, turns over before coming down, and falls back in the pan—slap—and if it was only a cake half done before, that—slap—as it strikes the pan, baptizes it a slapjack. While drying our clothing, and letting the animals browse (by the way, Harry has burned his mocassins by putting them too near the fire), we fell to cogitating on the possibilities and probabilities of the Canadian Pacific Railroad. And in the minds eye we pictured a train of cars sweeping along over this flat; over the fierce streams we had passed; puffing and snorting up the mountain sides in gentle curves and windings, shrieking wildly as some denison of the forest, scared at the strange monster of fire and smoke, and only anxious to put distance between itself and this strange monster, is hurrying off at greater speed as the shrill whistle reaches it, at the wearied looks in the eyes of the passengers, longing for the end of the route, yet rallying for a few brief minutes at sound of the whistle, and sight of the frightened animal, and we see them again settle back in their corners, yawn, complain of fatigue, and try to doze away the terrible hours of idleness; even the dinner bell, the imagined sight and smell of the spread which makes our mouths water, as we enumerate hot joints, mealy Potatoes, pies, cheese, &c and the wine to be had for the paying for. We pause here, and take a retrospect. Leaving these good folks to their enjoyment of dinner, and wild grandeur of scene, if they have not become surfeited with the one, and weary of the other, leaving the grumbler to roll himself up in his wraps, drop his discontented carcase in a corner, and vow for the life of him he cannot see where the luxury of travel comes in, that there would be more novelty in a slower and less cramped way of proceeding &c. We take our eyes from the nigger waiter, for he has not responded to our call for roast, and we are again here, by the side of the stagnant water, by the warmth of our camp fire, and our eyes rest on our famished looking dumb friends, and at our empty meal sack, and our retrospect begins.

But why should I weary you with the same? Suffice it the panorama passed vividly before us, the train of cars rolled on, clear to our mental Vision, and if any of the inmates of the train, with vacant stare over the scene, should see us, and nod towards our whereabouts, should drawl out, with a yawn of ennui, "Those two fellows yonder seem to have it pretty much to themselves, as they toast their shins over yonder fire, and are doubtless happier and more at freedom than we," to which his neighbor makes answer "Wonder what they are doing, hunting or trapping I fancy; but let's go to the dining car, I hear the dinner bell, we must eat I suppose, though eating's a bore," —or should our grumbling friend from out his wraps as he glowers from his corner, snort out in ill used tones on the slowness of the travel, and wonders why the engineer does not open her out and increase the speed, or the nigger waiter, passing round the juicy morsels, deign to find time to turn his wooly head our way,

"and thank his stars, he is in the cars,

"and reflect as on he's rolling;

That—but there, I am no hand at poetry, as these two lines will clearly show. And I can only conclude by stating that if we have relieved the ennui of our friend who called us, or thought us picturesque and fitted to the scene: we beg to tell him he is welcome to his imaginings, but must differ as to our being fitted to the scene. We did not feel particularly buoyant, and nothing seemed to fit comfortably, for that matter, but perhaps we were ungrateful, and only think so. Perhaps it is all a mistake or a dream, our meal sack is full, if we could only bring ourselves to think so, and the animals, standing yonder, are somewhat tired, that is all. And we have the audacity to grumble at the grumbler, fretting in his Cozy Corner, his wraps contrasting with our rags, and contrasting his "speed away" with our own, sigh for a change of places. And my ebony friend, the viends steaming under his nostrils, the wooly head with no idea, and no interest save in his monthly stipend, but why continue, we drew the picture, it has made us discontented, we count our Matches, requiring no arithmetical problem, we dive still deeper into our meal sack, for we must treasure our fire, we must henceforth only light it when necessity compels, therefor, lay in a supply of Cakes, eschew tea, and what seems still harder to me, my usual smoke, pack again, and one, speed away, iron horse, doze away grumbler, clear away the debris and the dishes, waiter, we prefer to dine on unlevened bread, thanks, and "get along Kitty, rattle the old camp kettles, exercise will warm up and supple your stiffened limbs," and—yes, we follow the cars. Still the picture we have conjured up frets us, and we resume the topic. Some seem to find enjoyment in irritibility, like "Tam O Shanters" wife, watching that reprobates coming by the midnight fire, and "nursing her wrath to keep it warm"— Some chew the cud of discontent, why may not we, so while we are chewing our cud (having little else to chew), we are toiling on our weary way, and loosing no time, that's at least a comfort. We address ourselves therefore to our vanished friends, and bid them be comforted; we have nothing else to offer. We bid them admire Gods handyworks in the grandeur of yon scene, nor think yon swamp dismal as they clatter on over its trestled surface, your iron horse feels no fatigue, ne'er gets a sore back, nor too exhausted to travel on. Dont turn up your noses because you feel no desire for the good things set before you. You are not reduced to a handful of Flour per diem. Your feet are not blistered, nor your cruse of oil spent. You are helped by the colored gentleman standing at your back, whose one eye is on your plate, the other admiring the bald spot on top of your head probably, and we have a waiter, too, and he stands ready at our backs, his name is hungar. We need not turn to assure ourselves, we are quite alive to the fact, and if we do not speed, and as speeds your train, he will stand before us, and hold out a skinny hand for settlement. The river you glide so easily over is to us fraught with danger, our bed, unlike yours, is on the wet earth; and we dont quibble about the sheets being well aired either. Lagoons and swamps you dont wish to notice perhaps; we must perforce, must enter them, and may be come out a horse short, ourselves half smothered in filth, and if I have not inserted a dose of the unwholesome, and tried your patience with gloomy ponderings, then you are as grouty as I, for I cannot have another darling pipe until our stock of cakes are eaten, and nature bids us light another fire, and shake out the last contents of our meal bag. Brooding is unwholesome, and destroys the appetite. We were better if appetite had less to do with our case.

We intend to stick to the river as closely as may be, and so prepare to enter the cañon.

On the mountain we have left behind us after leaving Goose flat, lie the bones of one hundred and twenty five animals, being a pack train 'enroute from the H party, to whom they had been with provisions, when encamped near Goose flat. While crossing this mountain a storm set in, so long and so fierce, that the snow fairly buried them, and they miserably perished, not an animal escaped. The packers had provisions, wintered here, and sought the settlements in spring. They had started out with the supplies late, but had to push through, or the H party (Mohons) would have had to leave the field.

Doctor Cheedle, in his work before mentioned, devotes a page to Lord Milton and himself finding, while enroute down the Thompson, the body of a headless Indian, also giving a full page illustration of the scene; this, it will be remembered was in the year 1863. John Jane and party on their way up came accross the skeleton of a human, minus the skull, being in all else complete, and further, that the skull was afterwards found some five miles from the skeleton; that they interred the bones, and placed a rough headboard over the spot. But Jane was a great joker, and spite his affirming to the contrary, I never beleived him, but as we were leaving Goose flat, sure enough we came accross the old headboard, a neat enough affair, hewn out with the axe, and could trace the lines, which had been heavily inscribed with a lead pencil, "Here lies the body of the headless Indian, found by Doctor Cheedle and Lord Milton—son of Earl Fitzwilliam—in the year 1863." Then below had been added more, evidently by a lighter hand, but which we could not well make out. Jane told me the bones were not complete to the best of his beleif. An old kettle, and what had once been a fishing line of grass was also found.

[space left for drawing of grave of headless Indian, Goose flat]

We camped early, having found a little feed, and fearing if we went further, we might fare worse, gave the animals the benefit of it.

We also came upon some young ferns at our camping place; and lighting a fire, we filled our pot with the tender shoots. They were the first Vegetables I had tasted for seventeen months: And, Oh! how sweet they were. Since we have entered the Valley of the Thompson, commencing at Canoe River, we have traveled through forest so dense, as to be in semi darkness—moss covering everything, dank and sumbre, moss covering everything, the trees, the rocks, and the soddened earth.

Only five matches left. How precious they are to us; and what economy we must exercise. Two matches gone today; but this evenings extravagence would not have occurred could we have resisted the fern tops.

Monday
June 2nd

-73

The trail during the last three days has been a dangerous one in many places, and exceedingly rough, rocky points, steep hillsides, and certain destruction in case of a mishap.

Passed through a portion of the bellowing cañon, called Murchisons rapids today; I hardly know what distance we traveled, but camped of necessity when the animals gave out. As for my horse, he is used up entirely, and no amount of whipping can make him budge when exhausted. Not a vestage of feed here; our hope is to reach a swamp ahead, and which we trust we shall fetch tomorrow, and what has harassed us not a little, is having had to submit to a constant downpour all day, making the soapy rocks more slippery and unsafe, our usual luck when in any unusual difficulty.

Started stiff and sore this morning, having slept in wet blankets, and wet clothes, and without the cheering influences of a fire. Plodding on we passed through the Hell Gate Cañon. What an awful sight it offers to the spectator, though but few see it, and it howls and rages with no other audience than the frowning cliffs on either hand. The immense volume of water, dashing and lashing itself in a quick descent through the monster boulders and chaos of broken cliffs, which have been hurled from the heights above through the preceeding ages, and by a mightier hand than Jupiters; the boiling volume curling in great whirlpools, and anon sending upwards its masses of fleecy spray, leaping, struggling with the huge rocks, and with a noise, deafening, and drowning your voice so that you cannot make yourself heard at a yards space, finally, as it reaches the vicinity of two towering points of Granite, pushing forward their ugly fronts on either side, it subsides, exhausted it would seem with its frantic efforts, and there not being ample passage for it, it rises, its surface dark, deep and sullen; it finds release however with contracted force, and dashes ahead again with lightening speed, so to speak, striking, whirling, and bellowing, until we are glad to turn a point in our perch like trail, and leave the scene and sounds, for the dismal, mossy, dark, yet silent woods again. This is Hell Gate so called, the passage between these two promontorys, a fit name, for thunder claps might roll among

June 3d

–73

the cliffs frowning overhead, yet not be heard in this awful chasm.

Finding but little feed upon camping, we make an early start in the morning; but so weak are the animals, we make but three quarters of a mile. Immediately upon starting, my horse, Charley, being unable, spite of every exertion on his own and our part, to face a steep incline, we were compelled to leave him to his fate. A choking sensation attacked my throat in spite of me; and it seemed hard to leave him here, so near feed, which we knew we must soon reach; we had chummed it together, and it was like leaving one of my own kind to perish. We become singularly attached to even the humblest of Gods creatures when thrown together as we were. Neither Harry nor I could find in our heart to shoot our unfortunate friend, so we turned our backs upon him, and toiling upward, turned at the top of the incline for a last look at him; we saw him lying on his side, trying vainly to get upon his feet, and as we stood thus irresolute, he lifted his head, and looking towards us, gave vent to such a pityful winny, I had to choke down a sob, and turn my back upon him. Yet so bad did we feel, that after going a short distance we encamped, and finding sparse feed, we turned the horses loose, and returned to our dumb comrade. We might have saved ourselves the trouble however, Charleys race was run, half dead when left, our leaving him to his fate had doubtless broken his heart; and the thought of how cruel we had been in urging him to exertion when his strength had failed, saddened both.

[space left for drawing of death of Charley]

We are still 140 miles from civilization, and have struck our last match. Fire can be gotten by the Indian by friction from two peices of partially rotten wood; we have both tried that, worked until our arms ached, but failed, so that all that remains to us is a little Flour and Tea, beyond these articles, not a pinch of salt even.

Traveling through a heavy rain all day, the only thought
uppermost with us now, is, "how long shall we be in reaching
Kamloops by the easy stages we are compelled to take". Progress may not now be quite so slow since Charley is gone; yet
we resume the topic, one or other of us, continually; we know
nothing of the obsticles yet to be encountered, or how far the
rivers may hinder us; we have the Thompson to cross again;
but we think it possible we may make our goal in ten or eleven
days, with moderate success. We had calculated upon killing
Charley for a meat supply, but our matches failing us, we gave
up the idea. The horse Scotty is our next anxiety; we have
serious doubts he will not hold out much longer, but Kitty,
dear old Kitty, though more emaciated, has wonderful pluck,
and pricks her ears as when first we started. She jogs along,
packing our blankets (about all she has to pack now),
refreshed with every march.

The trail continues bad, and very humpy, the roar of the
troubled Thompson is ever with us, and some of the rocky
points is very hazardous.

Dame fortune has not treated us lately to many agreeable
surprises, but the jade gave us one today. According to friend
Jane's map we should have been thirteen miles from our
camping spot of tonight, when we reached it in three miles.
There could be no mistake; we are upon the prairie mentioned, and our animals standing now, filled with sweet grass,
oblivious doubtless to the past, and the future no concern of
theirs, not quite as contented we, we have likewise swallowed
our supper, a little raw flour mixed with water in our tin cups
to stave off hungar.

Starting early, we encountered some difficulty in crossing
one of the many gulches on our route. Kitty got so badly
mired, we had a lively time in getting her out, on the same
side she went in. However, by cutting a trail higher up we
managed to make a crossing. We are on what Jane calls
"Round Prairie" tonight, and find the misquitoes very trou-

blesome neighbours, especially as we have no fire to smoke them out.

We left the Cañon this morning, and the view the Thompson afforded us as we meandered along its banks was a delightful contrast to the dreary scenes through which we had passed, one broad belt of silvery sheen running swiftly but placidly along, to join its forces with the turbulent Frazer. What a contrast from Hell Gate and the Cañon; there the sides were glowering walls of rock; here the banks are clothed with the cotton wood, Birch, and dark spiral Firs, mingling their shades admirably, and the mountains, as seen from the opposite shore clothed with the darkest of green to their summits. Here and there can be discerned silvery threads, whose sound is lost by distance, yet they tell us of rushing Cascades.

We camped amid abundance of feed, and as the sun had at last cheered our jaded spirits with his presence, laughing through the waving arms of the monster trees, we felt glad of rest such as this in the open glade, and lying prone on our backs, we listened to the soft wind sighing through the branches, and whispering through the tall grass as it played with our cheeks, fanning gentle as a mothers touch, creeping through the rents in our clothing, and cooling us as with a refreshing bath. Old Sol seemed to bid us an affectionate good night as he sank to cheer with his presence the other hemisphere, and with a wink and a blink, telling us he would see us again tomorrow.

Harry Baird is a wretched baker of bread, and if it could be helped, he was never permitted to handle the dough, but tonight I should have enjoyed bread of his making, were it the worst attempt he ever made. Harry swallows the concrete mess of flour and cold water, and makes it stick to his ostrich stomach without a reminder, but I, I have a sensation of sickness after swallowing it; but as there is no help for it, "dernier resort's" the word.

[space left for drawing of valley of the Thompson]

And possitively no incident to record, no little hitch to
mortify; absolutely nothing, if we except the state of our
stomachs. We crossed Mad river, a roaring, rushing, rollicking
mountain stream of considerable size, and which could not
be crossed other than by a bridge, and a bridge had been built
for the pack trains at this spot, which upon trial, we found
quite staunch, and crossed safely. We had entertained fears of
this stream, and were but too glad they were groundless.
More than this, the sight of so much labor bestowed, which
looked stupendous to our contracted views, after the rough
and tumble bout we had experienced through as dense and
dark a wilderness as can be found, gave us the delightful feeling of nearing our own species again, the long depressing feeling of isolation cleared away like a chilling mist dispelled, and
our spirits rose in consequence. Excellent duck practice was
afforded us during the afternoon, the water lying on the trail
in places to our waists. We were used to this practice however,
and if much longer prolonged, might have some fears of
becoming webfooted. We simply did the best under the circumstances, by following our noses, which led us through in
each case. It would have been waste of time trying to avoid
such small discomforts; nevertheless, in our hungry state,
and with no means of drying ourselves, when the chills of
night set in, was not healthy to say the least of it. The Thompson has again resumed its angry lashings, and noisily forges
along on our left.

We were glad to know by Janes map that Mad river is only
107 miles from Kamloops.

We have had a most delightful day, and the surroundings
have borne the most cheering aspect. Open timber, letting in
upon us the suns warm rays; good feed; all nature dressed in
her brightest colors; lovely wild flowers of white, yellow and
fiery red, the tall Lupin lifting his stately blue head amid the
maze; the branches of the smaller trees the brightest green,
and even the dead trunks of trees were covered with the deli-

cate white blossoms of the trailing bramble. Nothing could be more cheering; add to which numbers of humming birds darting like a flash from point to point, or poising for an instant, as it inserted its long slender bill into the honey cup of some pretty flower, robbing it of its sweets with[out] marring its beauty. Then there followed these busy humming beauties, with their marvellous plumage of shining gold, fiery red, and delicate bronze, the bass hum of the bumble bee, decidedly clumsy in comparison, his legs thick and clumsy too, with the coatings of colored matter robbed from the bright flowers, in his clumsy efforts to get his unweildy body within their treasure cups. He was assisted by the Yellow Jacket, more silent in his movements, with his slender waist, and body of striped yellow and black. Jolly dog he may be, yet quick to revenge an insult. The humming Songs of these could not be the same ditty surely, delivered in different keys. The humming bird might be

"Fairies dancing in the light"

The Yellow Jacket,

"Quick to anger, quick to fight"

The bumble bee,

"A burly Yeoman, a doughty wight,"

and my chum, he is singing merrily "Alls well—Good night," the limping gait proclaiming all anything but well, for Harry has no longer mocassins, the pair he had the misfortune to burn at Goose flat being his last pair. The greater goose he, however, it being impossible to travel barefoot, he is deminishing the size of his blankets, transfering a portion from Kitty's back to his number eleven trotters, which look like two somethings tied up in bundles. Let us be thankful, for although we do not feel quite as we should after a hearty dinner, we have had a gala day nevertheless. I do not cherp as merrily as my chum, I am not quite moulded after his temper, He sings to drive dull care away, and is more happy therefore, for Harry is a cheerful chum, and I shall ever feel warm towards him. Kitty too, dear old Kitty pricks up her ears, and I actually saw her making a lame attempt at arching her scraggy neck, or was it fancy merely. Scotty gives tone likewise to the surroundings and general gaiety, by shambling along more easily over the even and open country.

Our line of travel today is over a glorious prairie, sweet with the breath of a pure atmosphere, and our feet carpeted with, and crushing at every step the wild flowers in our path. Every foot increasing our backward track brings us nearer our goal. We know it to be so, Kitty and Scotty feel it to be so. We are all heartily tired of this solitude. Hitherto (as Mark Twain has it), we have moved along like a funeral train without the necessary corpse, and halt—here we are at a guide stake, another proof that we are drawing nearer, even did it not proclaim us but 96 1/2 miles from Kamloops. Harry throws up his cap as another indicator is passed, and we look upon it complaisently, and bless the kind hand of the Surveyor who, traveling here before us, planted this tree, so to speak.

The misquitoes are very annoying tonight, and are apparantly very hungry, like ourselves. Harry pulls a face at his gruel now, so I am not alone in this matter. The tables are turned, and the poor horses are having the best of it. It becomes our turn to do a little starving. Yet the buzzing, humming humbugs surround us, drive home their insinuating snouts, and gorge themselves, 'till we are blistered and sore all over.

We crossed Raft river today, here again a very shaky old bridge befriended us, and although it was a ticklish matter leading the horses over, owing to several of the planks being gone, as well as the supports, we got accross in a very gingerly manner, and proceeded.

Feed not quite so plenty tonight, but abundant compared with the banks of the Thompson higher up.

Had some difficulty in getting water, owing to the Thompson being so far below us, some 80 or 90 feet, the sides rocky and nigh perpendicular, and whereas we had hitherto suffered with to much of the element, we had to trudge some two miles to avoid suffering for want of it, dry flour being out of the question.

We crossed the Thompson again today, and no mishap. The clouds, which had been gathering their forces during the night, made things as miserable as possible during the early part of the day, by dropping their fatness. Eventually however, it cleared up, and by the time we were all ready to make the attempt, the sun had dispersed the heavy rain clouds, which were scurrying accross the sky as though to be out of his scorching rays, for old Sol came strong, and licked up the rain drops in quick order.

[space left for drawing of crossing Thompson]

Of coarse we had to raft it, as was usual with all the larger rivers. After vainly trying to swim the animals, we lost all patience, and barking a tree on the bank, I wrote upon it in pencil that we were compelled to abandon the animals here, owing to their being too weak, and dead set against crossing. Turning them loose therefore, and leaving their saddles and Blankets under the tree indicated, we submitted ourselves once more to the swift but in this case smooth current. The river was very wide, and the opposite bank appeared very dense with undergrowth, from out which were thrust out the ends of the down timber; it was therefore altogether uncertain where we should fetch up for landing, but we had no great cause for anxiety, the river being swift but placid as far as we could see below; we therefore made the best use of our paddles until we were near the other shore, when, not forgetting our experience on the Athabasca, I turned her head up stream, letting her drift down with the current. She was gliding rapidly along, while I was watching with all my eyes for a favorable counter current, or clear spot to work her in at, when suddenly she lurched over, and there was Master Harry, becoming excited again, and had nigh upset us in a frantic effort to grasp the branches of an overhanging alder. It was just as well he did not succeed in his attempt, or, our raft being of the lightest kind, would have Kel-le-pied (to use an Indian expression) and we should have been victims to foolhardiness again, for we had not divested ourselves of clothing on this occasion, considering all safe. Harry was becoming excited, could'nt feel his feet I fancy, and tried to work the raft shoreward with his paddle, but I had the whip hand of him, and persistantly kept her out, until below I saw a favorable chance, headed her in if that is the right expression when going stem on, struck a counter current, and landed safely.

Our outfit now being a very light one, and with nothing eatable save a handful of meal at the bottom of the bag, we determined to tie up our blankets, and proceed at once. Our kettles we concluded to leave, as we had nothing to put into them, and moreover, we were becoming weak on our diet; and if we did not make forced marches, we should feel hungars pangs proove too much for us. Shouldering each his blankets therefore, we were starting up the bank to cut our way back to the trail, when the whoop of an Indian rang out clear and startling through the silence. A second later, an answering whoop convinced us there could be no mistake, and that more than one human was in our vicinity. They were the first human notes we had heard since starting on our weary trip; we dropped our blankets, and bent our gaze to the opposite bank, we had left so short a time before; in a short time we saw a small canoe dart out from shore, and make rapidly towards us; the occupants were two redskins; when a short distance from us, they opened conversation, and kept aloof, paddling against the current. Feeling satisfied they must have been acquainted with the previous survey parties, and having no fear but that they were friendly Indians, we soon gave them an idea of who we were, and how we came in the vicinity, when they seemed satisfied and came boldly towards us.

After profuse shaking of hands, mainly on our part I admit, and a general Chinook introduction, wherein we learned our savage friends were named Saah and P'pleep, of the Clearwater tribe of Indians, we came to what was of more consequence to us than their genealogy, i.e. something to eat. But alas, they had not a mouthful; —yes, they had a small dead Bear in the bottom of the canoe, but as they protested they had no matches, nor means of procuring fire, we were bound to beleive them, for we wished to use them to our purpose in another matter. They appeared anxious to be gone, as they wished to gain their village that night, and although we would have gladly accompanied them for sake of something to stave off the hungar knawing at us unpleasently, their craft would scarce have carried us, nor would they have been so hospital, where nothing was to be given in return. So we asked them very civilly if they would bring over our two horses, and their traps, which I knew they could do, as they are well practiced in such matters, all Indians being very fond of owning horses, even though they have not a place big enough to turn them round in. We were to experience some difficulty however; they were determined, if there was a drop of juice in us, to squeeze it out. Heaven only knows we were dry enough; and as hard up to appearance as to assure anyone but an Indian we were not worth the squeezing; our clothing ragged, full of rents and stains, Harry's feet tied up in peices of blanket, and in fact, our general appearance would cause a special eye to be kept upon us, were we near our own people. When they found we were not possessed of money, they objected on the ground that their canoe (a birch bark one) was unfit for such a service, and in order to overrule their objections we displayed such articles as we had at command, as I have said, of filthy lucre we had none, but we finally struck a bargain by giving up a couple pair socks I had, all the remaining Tobacco of which I was possessed (no great quantity), a pair of Blankets, each contributing one, and poor Harrys only undershirt, which he peeled from off his back. These articles we laid aside, until their part of the Contract should be completed, then as they departed on their errand, we sat down to rest and await results.

These cunning savages failed not to impress upon us the amount of magnanimity they were exercising, spite of the tough bargain they drove, for, reasoned they: suppose we do not fetch the Horses, what then? —We should be compelled to leave them, and they would become theirs by night, and the saddles and blankets; Ugh—but we are the friends of the Bostons, and we go. Still fearing they might reconsider the matter, and that upon seeing the half starved brutes again, and the saddles, their Cupidity might cause them to leave us and possess themselves of the richer booty, I had to resort to stratagem, and lie to our red brothers. I informed them a large party of my white tillecums, of which I was one of the chiefs, would be here in two days, that by barking some of the big trees near the water, they would know the horses had been left for them to bring along, and if the animals were missed, a search would be made, and they would get into trouble. However, they did not swallow the bait as easily as I had hoped for. If, said one, the white men are so near, why are you so hungry? Intimating, they thought we lied, and that if what we represented was true, we should in all probability wait for them, or they might have imagined we were running away from them. But, a doubt existed, we might be right, and they concluded to adhere to the bargain made. This was soon made apparent to us who was anxiously watching, when we saw them crossing with one of the poor brutes, one Indian in the bow holding him short by the head, and at arms length, the other redskin sturdily paddling in the stern.

[space left for drawing of crossing of horses]

Landing him, they were not long in crossing the other, together with the gear. Having paid them as agreed, and having thrown in as a bonas a few needles, we parted company, they swiftly passing out of sight down the stream, and we, after packing, betaking ourselves to the hills above us, thankful for so much unlooked for good luck.

We were not exactly Livingston in the heart of Africa, but I fancy we felt somewhat as he would feel, upon the sight of other faces, and the sound of other voices than our own, and it gave us still grater zest, hungry though we were, for we were nearing the settlements.

I dare say you will think our lovely trip had been a short one, and scarce merited so much rhapsody of feelings as I claim at sight of a couple of Indians, but it must be borne in mind our trip had been an unusually severe one. Our supplies had given out, the country we had traveled was a very wilderness indeed; we were feeling acutely the pangs of hunger; the flour diet gave us a sensation of sickness when swallowed; we were footsore, and ragged, and these same redskins had relieved us, when in some difficulty, by restoring to us the Horses that were lost to us. These things are all reasons, which I conclude carry their weight; and made us feel that the parting with all of which were possessed (save one blanket each), was getting the service cheap, and as we were more than content, even so I ask you to be. Unfortunately it was too early for berries of any kind; so, like good, sound philosophers, we went without.

I may mention, these Indians informed us the white left some large canoes behind them at this place, 2 years before, but that they were carried away with the ice during the following winter. All this seems feasable enough; yet I strongly suspect the Indians in this section did not wait for such an event, but appropriated them.

We were anxious to reach a prairie said to be some 7 miles ahead, but halted a mile short of it, tied the animals, suspicious of Indians for the first time, and fearing they might be run off by them, and spite of a cold night, slept soundly.

June 10th.

73

We passed today an old delapidated hut, the former home of some trapper I fancy, and later on we came upon an Indian hovel, in which were an old squaw and child; they were evidently sleeping, when disturbed by our approach. I noticed a small clearing had been made of probably a couple of rods, a garden patch no doubt, but nothing was observable above ground. We were not slow in making signs for food, as she could not, or would not understand Chinook; but the old lady, whose features were undistinguishable for the layers of dirt planted there by the dust of years surely, looked upon us with such a spice of Old Nick in her composition, at the same time assuming a very demonstrative attitude, and hissing out what I fear was very bad and uncomplementary language; very sad certainly, at her age. We had no alternative but to search out the larder for ourselves; but our antequated friend was equal to the occasion; with a leap, hardly to be expected from one of her years, she stood guard over a heap of filthy rags and grass, from the midst of which issued an abominable stench of decaying fish or other matter, and a colony of flies of the blue bottle species, disturbed by so unusual a proceeding, rose from the heap with a buzzing sound, while the old fury, brandishing a hoe, set up such a series of yells and calls for some one unseen, aided by the shrill cries of the frightened child, that we beat a hasty retreat, fearing we might raise a hornets nest of Indians, and probably come to grief.

Good feed all along the mountain slopes, mostly bunch grass.

In the afternoon we had to raft a sheet of dead black water, which delayed us a couple of hours, as a quantity of drift timber had to be cut away in order to make a passage for the swimming of the animals. We were now fast coming to the lower levels, and found the country flooded so much that we were a great portion of the time wading our weary way along. Yet the land was even, and free from timber. But it is needless to say we were becoming very much exhausted for want of food, and the exposure consequent upon our amphibious mode of travel.

On the 11th June we made a bee line for a settlement ahead of us, and somewhat to our left. This we found to be an Indian Reserve, and a Catholic Mission; and we observed what appeared to be an unpretending church, built of logs, with a large cross at the entrance end, and as we drew near, we saw among the usual squalor of an Indian Village, one or two well dressed young bucks, and who spoke to us in scarcely intelligable English. But can it be credited; when we told them we were starving, not a mouthful of food of any kind would they place before us; we could not buy, we could only beg, and beg hard, but of no avail. We begged as famishing men find eloquence to suplicate; and surely our pinched faces confirmed our words, but neither our destress, our ragged appearance, nor the appearance of our starved steeds found one spark of pity in the hearts of these red devils, who, all save a few of the more curious, kept aloof from us. We asked for the priest, and an Indian was pointed out as acting in that capacity during the good fathers absence, for it appears he was absent. They told us in plain words to go from their Village quick, for no white men came from the direction we had come, and I fancy they put us down as hard cases, escaping justice; they even hinted as much, so we turned our back upon this inhospitable people, after learning from them (gratis) that Kamloops was 38 1/2 miles distant, but that we should strike a white man before we got there. As we plodded on, their ponies came round us, stared, snorted, and wheeled gracefully, galloping hither and thither, and not until then did we conceive the emaciated condition of our own animals. These Indians, living under spiritual guidance, could laugh at the condition of our animals as we turned from them, and in such a jeering manner as would have, I am certain, horrified the Priest, whoever he was, could he have heard them.

We made about 4 more miles, when feeling we could go no further, we camped for the night in a little dell, and lighting our first fire for many days, we comforted each other as best we could with the hope of reaching the white man spoken of on the morrow. (I had forgotten that these wretches had at least supplied us with a few matches, but our flour was gone, and we sank hungry and faint into our blankets, huddling together for warmth, for spite the warmth of the day, we shivered with the cold during the night.)

June 13th

–73

This morning early, while lying on our blankets, we heard the clatter of hoofs, and in a few minutes two young Indians, who were conspicuous at the Mission yesterday came up at a lope, and looking hard at us as they passed, rode on, the sound of the hoofs quickly dying in the distance. We afterwards ascertained they warned the settlers ahead of our close vicinity, and bid them be on the look out for us, as we were hard looking cases. Nay, it would appear this was ostensibly their errand. To resume, however. We set out bravely, with the settlements near us, we were cheerful, those of our own race were not far off, who would at least minister to our wants. Before midday, we espied a ranch in the distance, and soon after we were passing through a band of lazy cattle, and as we observed these signs of plenty, and the smoke curling from the chimney stacks, our sensations of hunger increased, and we hurried forward. Soon we were in the midst of a small knot of men; had shaken hands all round, and had been welcomed in true Anglo Saxen. To our enquiries for food, our host said Yes, we prepared to give you something to eat; a couple of Indians came along, and told us a pair of bad Bostons were coming, who looked like very hard cases, and that they were starving. We kind of wondered who, and what folks could be coming from that direction, as ours is the last ranch; but we guessed there was no cause for alarm, and so you will find the wife ready to help you to something to eat if you will follow me. And we were quickly indoors. The good wife welcomed us, and had we been lights of the land, instead of a pair of ragged and dirty tramps, so to speak, she could not have been more attentive, and desirous to please, as she helped us to the remains of a Sucking Pig, from which apparantly they had dined. And Oh! such Potatoes! great mealy fellows, which I remarked to her, were the first I had seen for 17 months. Then the sweet rich milk. But like sensible men, we ate sparingly, though it seemed hard to leave the table unsatisfied. I dare say it was best, the rich viends, after so long fasting would I fear have made us ill otherwise.

[space left for drawing of in sight of settlements]

Our host and hostess did not here bring their hospitality to a close, but a brief account of ourselves being given, they insisted upon our remaining a day or two to recruit, and offered us a bed. The latter we had to kindly refuse; we intimated to them, and truthfully, that we were not exactly alone, not being quite free from vermin produced probably from the somewhat unhealthy state of our bodies. We also found our poor animals were well cared for, and during the afternoon (it being Sunday), six or seven other men, put in an appearance, and with the Farmer and his hands we were quite a large party. These last-named furnished me with pipe and Tobacco, and all did their best to make the day a holliday to themselves, and a decidedly happy one for us. The men who had last joined us were making a road over or around a bluff (I forget which), somewhere in the vicinity.

The openhandedness of the early settlers, and the frontier people of the far west has become a proverb. It is therefore needless for me to extol them, save to add my mite to their praise by simply stating, to whomsoever is in need and deserving, it is seldom a refusal, or even a niggardly welcome is given. The Genuine American, the German, and the Britain vie with each other in their generosity to strangers; and, though I do not desire to give offense, I must say the Scandinavians do not as a rule show that hospitable trait of character. They are a very economical people, which in itself is quite as it should be, in order to succeed, for they generally begin farming poor, but long habits of economy have (so far as my experience leads me to judge) rendered them niggardly.

The Gentleman at whose house we were made so welcome, and at whose table our sore wants were supplied, and our animals cared for, was named "Kavenaugh." He told us he had that year about 45 acres under crop, had a large band of cattle, a good many milch cows, Horses, Pigs & Poultry, but that he found the wolves and Bear so troublesome, he had got rid of his sheep on their account. His place is delightfully situated on the banks of the Thompson, just at this place behaving itself as though in its passage to the sea nothing troubled its entire course, but that the great draw back was— no market. —Oats and Barley he could dispose of, but wheat he found no sale for. In fact, we saw his last years wheat in stack, not thrashed out; he had committed an error in sowing it, and another error in gathering it. Kamloops, the only mart, is nothing more than a recently sprung Village, far inland, and mainly owned by the Hudsons Bay Company, and having as yet no regular roads, the only means of conveyance is by pack train. A rough natural roadway does exist, certainly, and a stage runs from Cache creek on the Carriboo road, but it is not adapted for loaded teams.

My good host and his kind wife have two pretty children, a boy and a girl. And may god bless and prosper them.

On the following morning, learning our host was bound for Kamloops, we expressed a wish we were able to proceed in his company, when he crowned his generosity by giving each of us a mount on horses of his own, moreover promising to send our half starved brutes in, in a day or two.

I may never see that sweet faced mother again, but her memory I may not forget, for it will remain impressed, god bless her.

By evening we were in Kamloops, and at the end of our troubles. Here it was necessary to remain until the following Sunday, to take the stage before mentioned for Cache creek, at which place we should connect with Barnards Express stages to and from Carriboo to Yale. At Yale (the head of steam boat navigation) we were to proceed by steamer to New Westminster, my home.

My first care, upon reaching Kamloops, was to apply at the post office for the Party's mail; I found there a sack full of matter, which had accumulated for the past ten months, and the excuse was, as no means of conveyance could be found to transport it, and no authority had reached them as to its disposal from the Canadian government, to whom they had applied, they had kept it there, to await results I presume.

After some trouble, and a good deal of haggling, I made arrangements with one of our old packers "Xavier Lapine" to organize a party satisfactory to himself, to carry it, and 'ere I

left, I had the pleasure of seeing them depart. The price to be paid them was $370. and work with the party on their reaching them.

In due coarse, our animals having been driven in, I handed them over to Mr Tait, Charge de Affairs here for the Hudsons Bay Company, according to instructions received from Moberly. I also gave that gentleman a written account of the horse "Charley," and all this done, I prepared to enjoy myself for the balance of my stay.

Our boarding house was a well kept establishment, the proprietors being a Messrs McIntosh and McPhadden, and the charges were moderate.

Having authority to draw on the Hudsons Bay Company, we quickly had a little cash, and making all necessary purchases from "Mara and Wilson," we proceeded to the Thompson, and after clensing ourselves, we sent our rags floating down the stream, Blankets and all, and returned to our Hotel in a more presentable form.

The following Sabbath we took Stage, and in two days reached Cache creek, where we remained until Thursday, when we again took the stage to Yale, and on Friday evening reached that place, Yale being just eleven miles above Hope, the point from which we had started, just one year and eleven months previous.

And now, my reminiscence is done. I might go on to state I found an empty house, my goods intact but stored in a warehouse. My return to my empty home, and the replacing of everything therein as it used to be in the days that were gone. My sad thoughts as I lay stretched upon the bed my poor wife had breathed her last upon. My many visits to her grave, and my final sale of home and belongings, and my wandering away to seek another home, under another government. But to what end? I have fulfilled my promise, I have given you, dear Mother, a little insight of the ups and downs of life in a new country. Having yet before me the task of rewriting this "Two years reminiscences of my life" for the benefit of my own darlings, a labor certainly, but a labor of love, I shall conclude, trusting they in turn will preserve this little history as I feel sure you at home will do. I should not like my own little ones to experience the many troubles through life I have had to experience, and I should like them to have something to remind them of their father, after he has joined the vast army of the silent, when perhaps, a fathers voice, and fond mothers caress will be gone from them forever, and all that remains to them is "Memory of the past."

The End.

Your loving Son

RM Rylatt

[Space left for drawing of horses]

"Was he the Man"?   An Appendex—
To my Brother Harry—

The accompanying article, entitled "His Mystery"—was clipped from the weekly Oregonian of March 13th 1885—has been read by me with strange sensations. It is well headed

"His Mystery"—for it is surely an enigma to me, as to all others apparantly. Who was he? I too should like to know. I cannot divest myself of the certainty that the shrouded finger of mystery points me out my old chum "Harry Baird." I cannot tell you it is so; I cannot say, here is the last act in the life of one of the actors in my little drama. I can only send it to you as a mystery, and yet, every attributed peculiarity, the dead mans associations, wanderings, and vicinity all go to proove that the mysterious "H[enry?] Baird", and the "Harry Baird" of my little history are one and the same person.

Harry, upon our parting at Victoria B.C. was endeavouring to get on board a ship bound to Australia, and work his passage out. But Harry was no sailor; and it is more than likely he did not succeed, especially as he had promised to write to me from that country. He never wrote, nor did I ever hear from him again. And I am under the impression that, being for a time unsettled, with no fixed place of abode, he neglected to write in consequence, or concluded not to correspond with me until he could render a good account of himself, and finally, after so long a silence, concluded to remain obscure.

As a mystery, then, I give it to you, trusting you will attach it to the manuscript in your possession.

One thing does not coincide; his coming from California; but as so little was known of the man, even by those who were thrown most in his company, this can easily be attributed to an error.

Your loving brother

RM Rylatt

"His Mystery"— Who was he?—
from the Oregonian of March 13th 1885.

Of course somebody knows about the life of Henry[?] Baird,— its beginnings,— its rosy youth,— and so on. Some of us know a little of it, and of his death. He died up in the Kootnai country, a few miles north of the line between the United States and British Columbia, with a hole through his body, and his eyes staring up into the sandy bearded face of the ruffian who fired the bullet and hastened to cut poor Bairds clothes open to get at the $5000. dollars in his money belt.

I read, among the dispatches of the Oregonian some time in November, that a traveler for Eddy, Hammond & Co. of Missoula was missing; that he had money with him, and that the house would pay a reward. The name at that time did not make any impression upon me. In December, when a lot of us were whiling away the time in the Cascade mountains, I became acquainted with Mr Galbraith, on his way from Kootnai to Victoria, and he told me about the death of Baird. Then it occurred to me that I knew the man; and so I pressed my narrator for all he knew of the facts.

So much has been crowded into my busy days since then, that as I write now, I may not tell all that Galbraith told me, there in the cars, when time was plenty, and a good talker a godsend. But since we can know so little of the dead man anyhow, what I shall tell you will effect my purpose; which is to entertain the reader, and possibly draw further information from some one whose eye may fall upon my story.

When I first met Baird, he was clerk for Mr Ronan, Indian agent at the Flathead reservation, in Montana, but it seems these enterprising merchants of Missoula, Eddy, Bonner & Hammond, had found out the good qualities in the man, and had managed to get him into their service. Times were dull. The mining camps and saw mills were not drawing largely on the stock of the house, and it occurred to those thrifty traders that they could work off some of their stock, if they could get it accross the line into the region of the Canadian Pacific Railroad construction camps. So they fitted out Baird with a lot of kegs, well filled, and some other stock merchandise, and he left with a pack-train for the northern border.

On the way he spent one night at Galbraiths and seemed full of fore bodings; Said he did'nt like the business he had in hand; and tried his best to have these merchants take the stock off his hands at some price, so that he could turn his steps toward home. But he had nothing the Galbraiths wanted, and could not sell to them. They advised him to cache his liquors, and wait until spring, seeing that he disliked to take it to the line, nearer than which no liquors could be carried. He went forward, undecided as to what was best, but managed to sell out, and make collections amounting to $5000. with which he started back on the lonely trail through the heavy timber of that country. One man rode ahead, and another followed with the pack mules. It was early in the day, and they were straggling along some distance apart, Baird being in one of his unsociable moods. Just before coming to a turn in the trail, on a side hill, and when Baird was opposite the upturned roots of a large tree, there was a rifle shot, and he sat back in the saddle, stared rigidly for a second, then slid helplessly to the ground. The man ahead of him looked round, and took all this in at a glance. The same glance also showed him the murderer, as he stood behind the roots of the fallen tree, but instead of turning, he rode as fast as he could up around the hill, while the man in the rear turned back, and went as fast as he could in the other direction. Pulling out of the trail to the right, the man ahead came by a rapid detour to a point where he could look down through the timber and see his companion lying in the middle of the trail, with a tall man standing over him. The man had a sandy beard, and was dressed in a light brown suit of clothes, such as hunters, and miners, and all frontiersmen wear. Stooping over the trader, he felt his clothes, took out a knife, and cut through to the money belt, stripped it off and went away. The frightened man who watched this terrible peice of work went away too, and it was two or three days before the dead man was found. He was probably alive when he was robbed, though the bullet went through his spine. He was buried; and that was the last of Henry[?] Baird; a man whose life had been a mystery to all who knew him, and whose death had been as lonely as most of his days while alive.

When I met him, it was early in the summer of 1883. General Anderson, Chief Engineer of the Northern Pacific Railroad, with a commission to inspect the latest completed portion, was sidetracked by the Jacks river on the Flathead Indian reservation, four miles from the agency. The party included Major Ben Butterworth, late commissioner of Patents, Mr Perkins, Will and Tom Paton of New York, and myself. We were catching Trout, and eating them after Fred Ernest and his cooks had made them ready in the dining car of the special train. We were up about the Jacks and the agency for three or four days, off and on, awaiting orders concerning more railroad inspection, and Major Ronan, and his clerk, Baird, entertained us by getting old chief "Air-lie", and two or three hundred of his tribe to exhibit themselves in their native sports of horse racing and running. After a day of this sport, which had cost us a pretty good sum in prizes, and given us all the fun we cared for, in one day, we started from the plateau back to the train, dusty and hungry, with the Indians, old and young, men and women, cavorting and running ahead of us, and all around us.

Then Baird passed out of my mind until Mr Galbraith told about the murder, and I suddenly remembered my old friend. It has been hinted that he had family troubles over the division of an estate in the old country, though no one seems to know anything of the facts. He came to California in a ship, and was in the mines there. Then he came north, and lived for some time in Stevens County, Washington Territory, and finally drifted into Montana, where he had been some eight or ten years. He had been Miner, Teacher, Clerk, Trader and Packer, but always the same quite gentleman, and never talky about his past life. I have heard it said that an old Scotchman somewhere in Montana, by the name of McDonald, used sometimes to have long, confidential talks with Baird, when both were late over their cups, but what the silent man told his old friend, nobody knows.

He never wronged man or woman, nor seemed to care for money, was brave, but never quarrelsome; and died at last to be soon forgotten by men who were acquainted with him, yet knew him not.

Signed – *Howlett*

Index

Howse pass, 11; abandonment of, for alternate route, 56, 100; abandonment of provisions in, 58–59; cutting of trail into, 35–39; establishment of winter camp in, 39–41; exploration of winter conditions in, 45–46; journey of "Party S" to, 28–35; life in winter camp in, 42–52

Howlett, —, 233–36

Hudson's Bay Company, 24, 80, 112, 121, 122, 124–26, 127, 133, 137–39, 143, 147, 152–55, 158, 176, 179, 229, 230

Hudson's Bay trail, 23

hummingbirds, 218

hunting: depletion of buffalo by, 133, 142–43, 163–64, 165; destruction of game by, 172–73; feeding of sled dogs by, 146; futility of, at winter encampment, 44–45; preservation of game from, 121; by surveyors, 67, 68, 103, 146–47; territorial conflict over, 143–44; use of dogs in, by Indians, 32; wastefulness of Indian practice of, 165–66; wolves as threat to, 173

hyacinth, 16

I

Indians: amorous behavior of, 157–59; assistance from, with river navigation, 56, 57; character of, 55, 128–31, 133; conduct of dogs of, 140; cure by, for rattlesnake bites, 18–19; decline of power of, 131–32; destruction of game by, 172–73; disposal of dead by, 29, 124, 211–12; dressing of skins by, 127, 164; education of, 129; encroachment of civilization upon, 164–65; guarding of surveyors' provisions against, 136, 144, 157; as guides to survey party, 33, 43, 75, 91; as guides to wilderness wayfarers, 41, 42; handling of horses by, 222–23, 224, 235; hunting of buffalo by, 133, 142–43, 163–64, 165; imputation of super-

natural powers to, 148–51; lot of women among, 127–28; method of, for starting fires, 214; preservation of game by, 121; relations between Rylatt/Baird party and, 221–26; relations between survey team and, 31–32, 58, 74–75, 94, 120–21, 133, 136–37, 138–39, 156, 157, 158–59, 168–70; reporting of, by Rylatt/Baird party to white settlers, 226–27; reports on, to "Party S" winter camp, 47; subjugation of, 132–33; superstitions of, 28–29, 151–52; suppression of, by fur traders, 126, 139; trade of, with fur traders, 137–38, 139, 153, 154–55; trading for clothes with, 138–39, 159–60; travel of, through muskegs, 176; treatment of sickness by, 167–68; uprisings of, 131, 133; value of dogs to, 31, 32; wastefulness of hunting by, 165–66. *See also* under name of specific tribe

Iroquois, the, 130

J

Jackman, —, 49, 62

Jacks river, 235

Jane, John, 118, 176, 181, 187, 189, 192, 193, 195, 205, 206, 207, 211–12, 215, 217

Jasper house, 137, 142, 162, 170

Jennie (mule), 102

Johnny (Douglas Indian guide), 159–60

Johnson, —, 56

Joseph's Prairie, 65

justice, in mining communities, 25–26

K

Kamloops, British Columbia, 23, 47, 91; journey of Rylatt and Baird to, 187–229; layover of Rylatt/Baird party in, 229–30

Karraquenta (Indian half-breed guide), 173

Kavenaugh family, 227–29